Understanding Virtual Design Studios

Springer
London
Berlin
Heidelberg
New York
Barcelona
Hong Kong
Milan
Paris
Santa Clara
Singapore
Tokyo

Mary Lou Maher, Simeon J. Simoff and
Anna Cicognani

Understanding Virtual Design Studios

Springer

Mary Lou Maher, PhD
Simeon J. Simoff, PhD
Anna Cicognani, PhD
Key Centre of Design Computing and Cognition, University of Sydney, Sydney, NSW 2006, Australia

ISBN-13: 978-1-85233-154-2   e-ISBN-13: 978-1-4471-0729-3
DOI: 10.1007/ 978-1-4471-0729-3

British Library Cataloguing in Publication Data
Maher, Mary Lou
    Understanding virtual design studios
    1.Computer-aided design 2.Virtual computer systems
    I.Title II.Simoff, Simeon J. III.Cicognani, Anna
    620'.0042'0285

Library of Congress Cataloging-in-Publication Data
Understanding virtual design studios / Mary Lou Maher, Simeon J.
    Simoff, and Anna Cicognani (eds.).
        p.   cm.
    Includes bibliographical references.

    1. Virtual reality in architecture. 2. Communication in
    architectural design. 3. Work groups—Data processing. I. Maher,
    Mary Lou. II. Simoff, Simeon J., 1962- . III. Cicognani, Anna,
    1970-
    NA2728.U54 1999   99-31322
    720'.285—dc21

© Springer-Verlag London Limited 2000

Softcover reprint of the hardcover 1st edition 2000

34/3830-543210 Printed on acid-free paper SPIN 10658952

Preface

The idea of a Virtual Design Studio (VDS) has been around for many years. In the early days, establishing a way of transferring documents by file transfer was enough to establish a virtual design studio. Our expectations are greater now. Along with document transfer, we expect to be able to work with others at a distance as if they were in the same physical room. We have seen how email, video conferences, and shared whiteboards can provide environments in which we can do many of the things we are used to doing face to face. The internet has changed the way we communicate at a personal level and now affects the way we work professionally. Along with the new technology and the initial excitement, we have also experienced frustration when our expectations are beyond the capability for the technology to deliver. This frustration is due to the relative immaturity of software solutions to collaboration, and also due to the lack of software support for designing. We cannot just take a set of tools off the shelf and create a virtual design studio. We first need to understand what is possible in a virtual design studio, and then understand what the technology can provide. At a more fundamental level, we need to understand the differences between working in the physical presence of our collaborators and using technology to allow us to communicate at a distance.

This book looks at the range of considerations when establishing a virtual design studio, including the development of shared understanding through representation and communication. Along with these considerations, the book presents alternatives for network technology to address the various needs of collaborating designers. The needs range from the use and transfer of digital media to the feasibility of an online meeting with full video and audio communication. The book addresses these issues in three parts: the basics of a virtual design studio, communication and representation in a virtual design studio, and the comprehensive design studio environment.

In Part I, the basic concepts and technology of the virtual design studio are introduced. The first chapter sets the scenario and then comments on the actual practice of collaborating and designing using network technology. The second chapter presents the basics of network technology, specifically, how the internet works from a designer's point of view. The third chapter is a broad coverage of how we can create design documents entirely as digital media. These chapters cover the fundamentals for setting up a virtual design studio.

In Part II, the focus turns to communication and shared understanding. Chapter 4 presents the technology and strategies for using electronic communication. This is presented according to the type of communication, the tools available to achieve communication, and the implications of choosing one communication medium over another. Chapter 5 complements the communication chapter, where the information being communicated is expressed directly in words among people, to the communication of the design product through a shared computer representation. The issues in this chapter include the development of a shared organisation and a common vocabulary.

In Part III, different approaches to establishing a virtual design studio are presented. Chapter 6 gives an overview of the implications of a distributed design studio and considers in depth the loosely coupled solution. This distributed approach provides the most flexibility in the use of different technologies, but also requires a significant amount of management to ensure that communication really occurs. Chapter 7 considers the implementation of a central studio, located on a central server, where each participant "goes" in order to be in the virtual design studio. This approach facilitates communication and leaves document management to the individuals.

The book has a related Web site, which provides color versions of some of the illustrations of the book, on-line references to supporting software and other information related to virtual design studios. The URL of the Web site is http://www.arch.usyd.edu.au/kcdc/understanding_vds.

This book does not provide any answers to the problem of effective collaboration in a virtual design studio. Instead, the book tries to develop a better understanding of what is possible and how network technology can make the comprehensive virtual design studio possible.

Mary Lou Maher
Simeon J. Simoff
Anna Cicognani

Contents

Acknowledgements

The work on this book started in September 1996 after the completion of two virtual design studios initiated in 1995. We would like to thank all individuals and organisations that contributed in one form or another to the success of the research and establishment of the virtual design studios and the completion of this work:

- Milad Saad for his research on architectures for multi-user CAD, which plays an important role in virtual design studios.
- James Rutherford for his contribution to the establishment of the early virtual design studios and for designing the logo of the virtual design studio at the University of Sydney.
- John Mitchell for his ideas and great help as a consultant, client, assessor and designer in the virtual design studios.
- Student designers of the Australian and International Virtual Design Studios, and in Computer-Based Design classes, who bravely participated in this new form of design collaboration and who struggled with all the difficulties when traversing the pioneering path in the field.
- Doug Scoular and Andrew Winter, the system gurus, without whom the heterogeneous enabling technologies in the virtual design studio would have quickly come to a standstill.
- Mandee Tatum, VP Distance Learning and Education, Activeworlds.com, Inc. for the invaluable assistance in setting up a virtual design studio in Activeworlds environment.
- Fay Sudweeks for her critical assessment of the early drafts on internet technology and studio configurations.
- Rosie Kemp from Springer, who gently pushed the authors to complete their work.
- Anne Christian, the person behind the camera-ready version of the book.

Some of the results reported in the book are based on the research in computer-mediated design, done in parallel with the virtual design studios in the Key Centre of Design Computing and Cognition, University of Sydney. We would like to thank volunteer designers (John Mitchell, David Marchant, John Flower, Bruce Hill) who participated in the series of experiments in computer-mediated design, which extended our knowledge of this phenomenon and consistently improved the studio layout and technological support.

We would like to thank the Australian Research Council for the financial support of the research in computer-mediated collaborative design and virtual design studios. We also thank the various companies that have provided discounts (sometimes 100%) on their products. Specifically we thank Silicon Graphics for the loan of their workstations and the use of Inperson, Activeworlds.com Inc. for the use of the Activeworlds server software, TeamWave Software Ltd for TeamWave licenses, GraphiSoft for the use of ArchiCAD, University of British Columbia for the use of WebCT, and the BioGate Partners for the use of their BioGate Server installed in our Virtual Campus MOO. We thank Netscape Communications Corporation for the kind permission to use their logo and some of their icons in the illustrations of the book, QUALCOMM Incorporated for the permission to use elements of screen shots from their products in our illustrative materials, White Pine Software, Inc. for permission to use elements of their icons in our illustration.

Part One

Basic Concepts

One

The Concept of a Virtual Design Studio

Design is a complex, collaborative process. Rarely can a designer imagine, develop, and describe a solution to a design problem without interacting and collaborating with numerous other people such as the client, suppliers, other designers, manufacturers, etc. This interaction with others is not only necessary given the complexity of design, but actually shapes the design and influences the development of the final product. Design is inherently collaborative (illustrated in Fig. 1.1), except in those rare situations where the designer, client and builder are all the same person. The ability to effectively collaborate can result in a design that satisfies the needs of the many people that use the design. Lack of collaboration can result in miscommunication, delays in the design process and an inferior product.

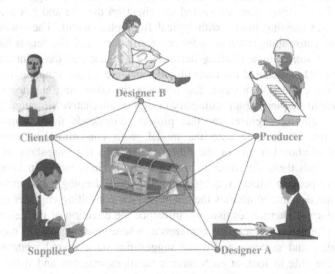

Fig. 1.1 *Design collaboration involves all participants in the development of a product.*

The virtual design studio provides an environment for collaboration that has no walls, an environment that facilitates sharing design information and supporting interaction regardless of place and time. The environment is not a tangible thing, in the sense of being a particular room in a building, or even a particular collection or package of communications software presented on a computer screen. The environment is dynamically created by the confluence of technology for communication and people involved in a specific design project and may change during the life of the design project.

In this chapter, we consider the scenario of a virtual design studio, i.e. what is it like to be a designer involved in a project that uses the concept of a virtual design studio? We then provide an overview of our experiences in setting up, and designing within, a virtual design studio. We consider how the designs were shared and communicated, as well as how the (student) designers used the various software tools. In response to a perceived lack of understanding of how designers collaborate in a virtual design studio, we set up an experimental study of computer-mediated collaborative design. This methodology and some of our observations are presented to set the stage for the remaining chapters. We do not examine any of the issues in detail here, we attempt to raise the level of awareness of what is possible versus what is actually happening.

1.1 Scenario

Let us consider a scenario that illustrates the concept of a virtual design studio. Anna is an architect in Sydney that is working on the concept design for an office building in Hong Kong. She has visited the client on the site and has prepared a preliminary 3D massing model with typical floor plan layout. The collection of requirements, constraints, relevant codes and regulations, and site details have been organised and stored in a briefing database. The database, the minutes of the meetings, the 3D model, and the floor plan layouts, are all illustrated and available as files on the project Web page. She contacts the consulting engineers for the project by email, requesting a preliminary design of alternative structural systems. John, the consulting engineer for this project, downloads the 3D model and sketches a few alternatives onto the model, with annotations to explain the implications of choosing one or the other. He takes a few snapshots of the 3D models and sends them via email as images to Anna. John works in London and was able to respond to Anna's request while Anna was sleeping. Anna makes some changes to the design and notifies the client and the consulting engineer of a brief meeting to discuss alternatives that will influence the direction of the design. They discuss the alternatives in a video conference, where the three parties can review the 3D models and sketches and make suggestions on a shared whiteboard, all while they are able to look at each other's facial expressions and listen to each other present their opinions and concerns. One issue in setting up the meeting is finding a time when all three will be awake. An important consideration in having a successful meeting is the knowledge of how the technology effects the sense of presence of the participants, and knowing where the advantages are.

The scenario described above is possible today. A designer can meet with consultants, the client and other designers without leaving her desk. During the meeting the individuals might chat socially, work on a specific agenda item or develop a design drawing to be shown to the group. The sketches, drawings, tables of data can be shared and marked up in a group meeting using a desktop computer (illustrated in Fig. 1.2). The latest version of the project, including minutes of meetings, drawings, notes, memos, etc. can be available by pointing to icons on the screen. This book describes how this is possible and establishes a framework for understanding the needs and implications in supporting the variety of human centred activities that make design collaboration possible.

Fig. 1.2 *A computer-mediated collaborative design session.*

1.2 Experiences

As a further elaboration of the concept of a virtual design studio, we describe two experiences in developing an environment and scenario for a virtual design studio; an international design studio and an Australian design studio. These experiences are described in more detail in (Maher, Simoff and Cicognani 1997b). Both experiences occurred in the university setting in which architecture students collaborated with each other. In the first, the international design studio, student collaboration occurred through the communication and sharing of design ideas. The students did not rely on each other for the development of specific aspects of their designs, each student developed their own project. The students from different universities had a similar design brief therefore encouraging the sharing of ideas. The universities participating in this studio included the Massachusetts Institute of Technology in the USA, the University of British Columbia in Canada, the National University of Singapore, ETH Zurich in Switzerland, and the University of Sydney in Australia.

The students in the international VDS started their projects in different weeks, due to the mismatch of semester dates. The students were physically present in their local studio at different times of day because of the different time zones. The design brief focussed on a common design problem but different design sites. The common design problem is the design of a living and working environment in a remote location that is connected to the rest of the world by electronic communication, that is, the electronic cottage. The site was selected individually for each physical studio space. The site for the Sydney students was in a national park located on Bantry Bay, near Sydney Harbour, accessible primarily by boat. The site was presented on the WWW as a selection of photos combined with a text-based description of the client's needs, shown in Fig. 1.3. The local students visited the site to get a "feel" for the place.

The premise of this project is that the desire to live in a pristine landscape, distanced from the urban chaos and rush, can be realised by obviating the need to work in the city. Instead, using today's communications and computing technology, the office is in the home, connected as required, not only to the city of Sydney, but indeed anywhere in the world.

The house as a shelter that integrates ideas for working and living has been a recurring theme among architects of the 20th century as they use the notion of 'house' -often for themselves, to explore their architectural theories. This project will be concerned with the design of a dwelling that also serves as a place of work for a specific individual. It is characterised as the 'electronic cottage'- a place that enjoys the benefit of two worlds: the natural wild landscape of a remote location and the quality of life that this can create; the connection to the world of design, industry and manufacturing through the electronic global communications networks.

Fig. 1.3 *Images and brief for electronic cottage design.*

The international studio was intended to encourage the student designers to share ideas through viewing the design concepts presented on the WWW, and through communication via email and video conferences. By eliminating competition, the students at different universities were being assessed independently, they were encouraged to share ideas through conversation and exposure to images, sketches, and drawings.

The second VDS, the Australian design studio, included the University of Sydney, the University of Tasmania, Launceston, and the University of Queensland. In contrast, these studio projects started in the same week, and the students were able to arrange a time when they were physically present in their physical studio place. In this VDS, the students individually developed alternative designs for the same site, and then one design was selected to be detailed, analysed, and documented collaboratively. Again, in contrast to the international VDS, the students in all participating universities had the same design brief, the same site (see Fig. 1.4), and the same client, architect Lawrence Nield.

The presentation of the brief for the Australian studio provided a selection of photographs of the site, a map showing the orientation of the site, and a Computer Aided Design (CAD) drawing that located other existing buildings. The project was the design of an Olympic exhibition building for the Sydney 2000 Olympic site. The students in the Australian VDS were involved in both synchronous and asynchronous communication. The asynchronous communication occurred through shared information on the WWW and shared data files. The synchronous communication was supported through video conferencing sessions. In this studio, the students needed to share drawings and design details. As the students progressed through the design, they needed to read and write to each other's drawing files and to develop the final concept as a group decision. This studio required more synchronous collaboration than the international studio.

The primary representation of design information used in the studios was images. Images were used to illustrate the precedent designs that the students thought were relevant to understanding their design, as well as images of their own designs (see Fig. 1.5). The precedent images were taken from other Web pages unrelated to the studios or were scanned from books or magazines. Images specifically developed for the design studio were used for the representation of sketches for the early stages of design development, for photographs of the site, and for plan, elevation, and perspective drawings when they were drawn by hand.

CAD drawings are an essential part of the representation and communication of design information in professional practice. In a VDS, CAD (see Fig. 1.6) becomes a vehicle for collaboration when the files and data can be shared and edited by a group of people. Shared, in this context, implies both that the files can be transferred from one physical studio to another, and that the information in the CAD files can be understood and manipulated by someone other that the person that created the file. In the Australian VDS, the students developed their own concept designs and then one was selected for further development.

Although the initial, individual designs were shared as images on the WWW, the development of the design selected for development required the use of CAD drawings that could be transferred and changed by the different participants. In order for the students to collaborate on the development of a design, they needed group access to the CAD drawings. In the international VDS, the students did not need to collaborate with each other to develop the design further. Therefore, they could choose to develop their designs using hand drawings or CAD drawings.

Text is an important way of communicating design information which often gets overlooked when documenting a design. The use of drawings for documentation dominates the communication of design descriptions and limits the use of text to simple annotations or labels of particular drawing symbols. We used text extensively in the presentation of the studio and brief to the students. Those students that used text to augment their images and drawings were able to communicate their ideas and intent associated with their design, where students that relied entirely on the images relied on the viewers' interpretation of the design.

The object of the project is to design a small exhibition building at Homebush Bay to accommodate an ongoing exhibition of the Olympic buildings and development. The building will meet the environmentally sustainable development (ESD) of the Olympic games. Students will work collaboratively with students from the University of Queensland and the University of Tasmania. Each student will develop their own concept design by 25 May. After an initial crit session, one concept design will be selected to be developed further. This design will be detailed by students from the three universities interactively. In other words, you will be part of an Australia wide design team. Thus, this is a very important exercise as it foreshadows what is likely to become a future mode of operation of building design teams.

Homebush Bay is the site of the major Olympic venues, including the main stadium, the main indoor arena, the swimming centre Velodrome, and other venues for over 20 sports, the 34 hectare show ground for the Royal Easter Show and extensive urban development. As well there will be a major transport infrastructure including an underground rail loop, a light rail, bus stations and parking for 11,000 cars. The purpose of the building is to show and explain this development and its buildings and infrastructure to the public as the design is finalised and implemented. It is assumed that the building will remain on its site.

Fig. 1.4 *Images and brief for the Olympic exhibition building.*

Fig. 1.5 *Sketch from the electronic cottage design.*

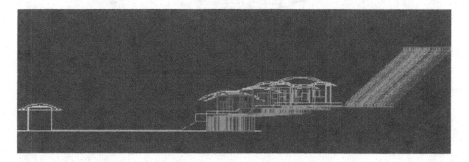

Fig. 1.6 *CAD drawing from the electronic cottage design.*

Video conferences have broadened the nature of computer-mediated human and inter-organisation communication patterns. During these sessions, the students imported their design proposals (design images, text, CAD drawings) into the shared whiteboard and then they discussed and modified them. Fig. 1.7 shows the contents of an intermediate page of a whiteboard document. Each student was asked to use a different colour for his input (the legend is saved on the first page).

The early video conference sessions were planning sessions in which the studio teachers talked about how the studio would be organised and what the brief would be. The later sessions were used entirely by the students to get to know each other and to discuss problems in getting information from one site to another. The final video conferencing sessions were used for work on particular portions of the design.

The students used email to communicate with each other and with the client, studio tutors, and studio teachers. To promote interpersonal communication, a hypermail tool was uaed to allow messages to be delivered to an electronic mailbox which can be read by the recipient as well as the other studio participants at any time. This allowed email messages to be archived centrally and be available on the

Web. The hypermail tool also provided a way of navigating through the messages according to date, subject, or the name of the person who sent the message.

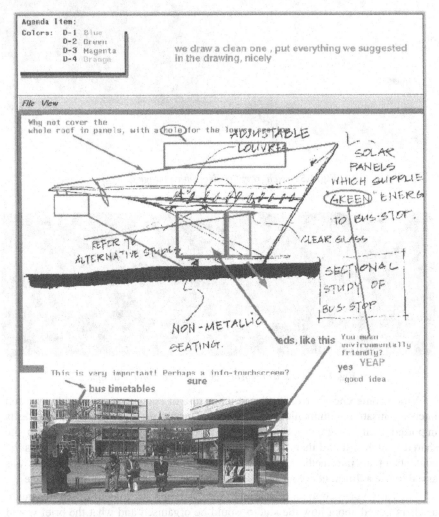

Fig. 1.7 *A whiteboard from the Australian virtual design studio.*

The virtual design studios organised in the academic environment show how the different technologies can support design collaboration. Many of the collaborative activities that would have normally taken place face to face in meetings or by plotting and sending paper documents from one person to the next, took place using electronic communication techniques.

In these studios, we were not able to compare the use of a networked environment for collaborative design and the face-to face collaboration. In the next section, we discuss some of the differences we observed in an experimental study.

1.3 Observations

Moving towards a virtual design studio has implications on the way decisions are made and designs are documented. The use of computing technology in design practice has shown that very little is understood about the phenomenon of collaboration within a distributed computer-networked environment, and there is a need for an appropriate computer representation for handling design documentation in an electronic format that enables effective collaboration among the professionals.

As part of our study of virtual design studios, we have developed an experimental methodology for computer mediated collaborative design (CMCD). The study is based on the method of protocol studies. The purpose of the study is to develop some observations on the difference between a designer working alone using a drawing program and two designers collaborating using synchronous computer-mediated communication (CMC) (Maher, Simoff and Cicognani 1997a).

We made an assumption when conducting the experiments that in order to collaborate, designers need to communicate both the form of the design and the semantics or function of the form. Communicating form alone would not be sufficient to developing a shared understanding when collaborating, while it may be sufficient when working alone as a memory cue. This assumption is the basis for our observations. We looked specifically at the nature of the information that was documented in the drawing program while working alone and the whiteboard during collaboration.

The experimental methodology requires that each designer participates in two design sessions. In each session, designers document their designs using the computer. In the first session, we established base data for each designer by asking him/her to design alone. In the second session, we asked two designers to design collaboratively.

During session 1, each designer is asked to work on Design Problem 1 (DP1), on their own, for approximately two hours. During session 2, a pair of designers is asked to collaboratively solve Design Problem 2 (DP2), again for approximately two hours. DP2 is a similar type of problem to DP1, but with a different brief. An observer recorded the session. The observer was allowed to reply to questions about the brief, if needed, during the experiment. In addition, the observer examined the needs of computer support in sessions 1 and 2. The observer was also responsible for helping to overcome technical problems that occurred during the experiment.

During each session data was collected by the observer taking notes on the general progress of the design process and by recording the windows of the design software as snapshots every 5 minutes. The detailed "visual" description of the design was based on window snapshots and final documented designs as represented in the files created by the designers. An example of a documented design is presented in Fig. 1.8.

Each designer's workplace included a Silicon Graphics Unix work-station and a Macintosh personal computer. We decided to use two computers rather than one so that the designers had a choice of technology that suited them personally and to alleviate the problem of lack of screen space. The video conferencing software (InPerson[1]) provided the video, audio, and shared whiteboard facilities. InPerson's whiteboard is organised as a notebook with multiple pages and different cursor icons for each participant. The multi-user work environment was Timbuktu[2] on the Macintosh. On the Macintosh, designers had multi-user access to a word processing program, a spreadsheet, a simple drawing program, a CAD system, 3D modeller, a simple database and a Web browser.

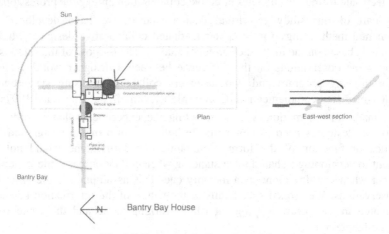

Fig. 1.8 *Example of a documented design.*

A coding scheme was developed to analyse the information on the drawing windows. We developed a two level coding scheme: one using a data-driven approach and the second a hypothesis- or expectation-driven approach. Using the data-driven approach, the elements of the documented designs were counted and categorised according to their text and geometry content. Using the expectation-driven approach, we classified the categorised elements as "semantics" or "structure".

We defined the semantics elements as those which documented the purpose of the design element and the structure elements to be those that documented the geometry of the design element.

We found that *designers tend to document very little information related to the purpose of their design, although there was slightly more during the non-collaborative sessions than during collaborative work.* This was unexpected as our assumption (stated above) was that collaboration required more explicit information about the purpose of the design forms. This observation may have been influenced by the duration of the design sessions and the use of 2D drawing tools and 3D CAD which do not directly support the documentation of semantics. The designers did not document the designs to a significant level - in fact, while coding the design documents, we had difficulty in understanding some elements of the

---

[1] Trademark Silicon Graphics
[2] Trademark Farallon

designs. These observations indicate that isolated, short duration, collaborative design tasks do not result in the documentation of design semantics. This conclusion has implications on the level of support needed in a collaborative design environment for documenting design semantics.

A significant amount of design semantics was communicated in conversation. Based on our observations of the designers while collaborating we found that *due to the intensive information exchange via video conferencing between the parties during a CMCD session, a valuable amount of the semantic information is left undocumented.* Designers described their design semantics verbally, through video and audio channels, and this information was not included in the final design document. It may be possible to capture the missing semantic information by recording the audio and video information designers exchanged during the session. In that case, we have to consider the audio and video information as part of the design documentation, a representation that is difficult to review and revisit.

We observed three different collaborative design styles:

- The designers worked closely the entire session in order to achieve a consensus on the design decision;
- The designers worked independently on two parts of the design checking with each other only at the interaction of the two parts;
- The designers established a leader who dictated the design decisions which were agreed to by the other designers.

These observations lead us to believe that different styles of collaboration need to be supported in a networked environment to support a virtual design studio.

The methodology of establishing two sessions for each designer to compare the effect of collaboration on design activity is a general methodology that can be applied to other studies. We found that by establishing base data for each designer, we could isolate the effect of collaboration on the resulting design documentation. Other applications of this methodology could be the study of the design process, the effect of negotiation, and the establishment of design styles.

1.4 Directions

Computer support for collaborative design is still in the early stages of development. The technology for sharing and communicating information across computer networks appears to be readily available and relatively easy to use. Most universities teach and encourage the use of CAD and, more recently, the use of the Internet for communication and shared information. Professional designers should be the real beneficiaries of this technology, where the development of the design models and documents is essential for communication of design ideas.

However, the reality of the situation is that the technology still needs to be developed further before there is a seamless and reliable integration of information and communication across a heterogeneous network of computer hardware and software. The added difficulty in using this technology in a design environment is the complexity of the way in which design information is communicated, with and without computer representation, and the incompatibility of the various software packages used in the building industry.

The idea of a virtual design studio raises numerous technical and social issues. The technical problems arise from technical difficulties in establishing a suitable environment for sharing information. These technical issues are present whether a fully virtual design studio is in place or not, but is exaggerated when distance collaboration is the only possible means of exchanging information. The social problems arise from a lack of understanding of the differences in working remotely and working face-to-face. Other considerations are the changes in social interaction when we do not have the familiar physical presence of human interaction.

The remaining chapters in this book are influenced by our experience in running virtual design studios and more formal experimental studies of computer-mediated collaborative design, as described above. Throughout the book we try to identify frameworks for understanding computer-mediated communication tools and techniques and we present models for representing and sharing design information. The selection and use of a particular communications technology or tools for recording digital design media will determine how successful the design project is. A more informed selection should result in a more successful collaborative effort.

References

Maher, M. L., Simoff, S. J. and Cicognani, A. (1997a) Observations from an experimental study of computer-mediated collaborative design *in* Maher, M. L., Gero J. S. and F. Sudweeks, (eds) *Formal Aspects of Collaborative CAD*, University of Sydney, pp.165-186.

Maher, M. L., Simoff, S. J. and Cicognani, A. (1997b) Potentials and limitations of virtual design studios, *Interactive Construction On-Line, Vol 1* http://www.thomson.com/default.html, http://arch.usyd.edu.au/~mary/VDSjournal

Two

Network Technology

Perhaps the most significant technology that has enabled the concept of a virtual design studio is network technology. A network is simply a connection between two computers that allows data to be transferred from one computer to another. The development of the Internet, a network of computers that uses a specific standard (TCP/IP) for transferring data, has extended the network to computers around the world. This subtle distinction between establishing a network of computers, to connecting to the internet, has implications on the way we perceive computers, information, and space. This is the most remarkable feature of the Internet technology - studio participants view the Internet as simply one unified space in which any computer can communicate with any other computer. All underlying components are hidden as illustrated in Fig. 2.1. All we need to know to initiate a working session is a partner's internet address.

Fig. 2.1 *The Internet as a unified space.*

In general, the reader does not need to know and understand all nuances and technicalities of computer network protocols to create and operate a virtual design studio. However, it is essential to form some basic mental image and comprehension of what stands behind the scene, taking into account that most of this picture is logical rather than physical. This chapter provides the necessary background for understanding current limitations of the underlying data communications and finding ways to cope with these limitations in virtual design studios. For a detailed description of the Internet technology, the reader is referred to the compact and well-structured monograph by Martin and Leben (1994).

2.1 TCP/IP Communication

We can view communications between studio participants at different levels. Ideally, all the levels below the communication of ideas and documents in the studio should be transparent, i.e. they should not be noticed by the participants. However, in computer-mediated environments lower levels of communication can influence the perception at higher levels.

We consider communication in computer networks in terms of sending messages from one node in the network to another. In order to understand each other, networked parties need to establish some common conventions. When it comes to computer networking and data communications these conventions are called protocols. Protocols provide the format of the messages and the rules for getting a message from one place to another - the routing algorithm, so that different nodes can communicate without losing information.

The TCP/IP standard includes the Internet Protocol (IP), the Transmission Control Protocol (TCP) and the User Datagram Protocol (UDP). In some senses, these protocols complement each other. The IP "encapsulates" TCP and UDP in much the same way that letters are enclosed within envelopes. In the same manner, the IP packet provides both destination and source addresses and other necessary information to get the data to the destination computer. Hence, routers (specialised computers for linking networks over long distances) and other machines between the two computers know where the message came from and where it is going to. In Fig. 2.2, we illustrate the idea of the TCP/IP delivery mechanism.

Each person involved in the design project sits at a specific computer connected to the internet. The origin and destination of information relies on the IP for addressing. In TCP/IP networks, every node (e.g. computer) has a unique IP address. IP addresses are 32 bit binary numbers divided into four 8 bit fields, for example, 193.140.136.2. The knowledge of what stands behind these numbers makes it easier to create rough estimates and expectations about the corresponding network as part of a virtual design studio. Martin and Leben (1994) provide a detailed description and explanation of the system of TCP/IP addressing.

TCP takes application data, cuts it into datagrams to fit in an IP packet and labels them in a particular order. These labels allow the receiver of the IP packet to identify missing packets and to arrange for them to be resent. The maximum size of an IP packet is 64K including the data and control information. In addition to the sequence number, TCP adds the so-called port number, which is the identifier for the program that has requested the data. For short queries and responses, which can fit into an IP packet, the TCP/IP standard offers the UDP protocol which does not require the TCP numbering and synchronisation at the receiving end.

Once the "letter" is ready it is "stamped" with the address of the source and destination computers. The full IP packet format is rather complex. Fig. 2.2 shows the main components. The other control fields are used by the routing and transfer algorithms. Once ready, the IP packet starts its independent way over the net. This is the reason why packets may arrive at the destination in a different order to the order sent. The TCP has the task of ensuring that every packet has arrived intact and restoring the original order. Sometimes, due to the absence of a single packet, there could be a considerable delay in the appearance of the application data at the recipient's end.

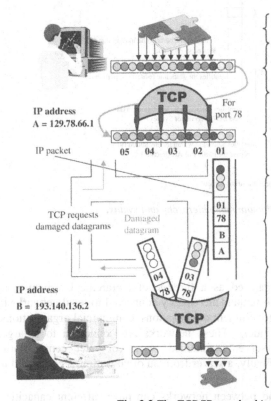

Designers collaborate through computer application programs

Data stream to be sent by one application to another application over the Internet

TCP divides the data stream into datagrams, numbers them and adds the port number of the specific program which requests these data

The IP transmits packed datagrams from one host to another, if necessary via different routes on the net.

TCP reconstructs the original data stream following the number sequence given at the source side. It requests damaged datagrams.

Receiving requested application data

Fig. 2.2 *The TCP/IP standard in action.*

Usually computers that are connected to the Internet are referred as hosts. Each host can be addressed directly by its unique IP address. However, to provide a more comfortable and meaningful way of identifying hosts there is a naming convention and a naming service. Each host has a unique name that consists of a string of alphanumeric characters. In a local network, the name space can be flat and each host can be addressed by a 1- to 8- character name which is easy to remember. In a large network, a hierarchical naming system is used, based on the conventions established for the Internet. These symbolic names are called domain names. Internet domain names refer to countries, groups of organisations, individual organisations and host computers within them.

The hierarchical structuring of domain names is reflected in their syntax as shown in Fig. 2.3. Domain names need to be translated to IP addresses before they can act as identifiers. This function is implemented through a service called the Domain Name System. In the case when the service does not operate properly, the knowledge of the IP address may help for connecting with another studio participant.

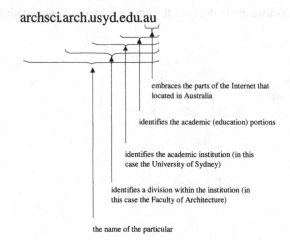

archsci.arch.usyd.edu.au

embraces the parts of the Internet that
located in Australia

identifies the academic (education) portions

identifies the academic institution (in this
case the University of Sydney)

identifies a division within the institution (in
this case the Faculty of Architecture)

the name of the particular

Fig. 2.3 *A domain name hierarchy and syntax.*

2.2 The Internet

Logically, the Internet[1] is organised as a three-level hierarchical structure, as
shown in Fig. 2.4. Individual computers are usually connected to local networks in
universities, research centres, government organisations, commercial organisations,
and now internet service providers. These networks are connected to a larger
regional network through a server maintained by a computer centre, large
university or large company. Finally, a server from an organisation is connected to
the Internet backbone.

The connections within and between networks can have different capacities,
indicating different speeds of transmission. Typically, a higher capacity is provided
for connections between regional networks and the Internet backbone. Fig. 2.4
illustrates the different capacities of the links with different shades. The speed of
the connection is a critical aspect of the connection to the internet for a virtual
design studio.

The speed of the connection between two points can only be as fast as the
slowest link. If the studio participants want to use video conference technology or
shared CAD, the partners should be large universities or organisations that have
high speed and broadband communication links to the backbone. If partners in a
virtual design studio have slow connections then it is more appropriate to use text-
based technologies with less bandwidth demand.

This hierarchical structure and even the capacity of the link remains invisible to
the user. What users perceive are the different network applications and services
that operate in a networked environment. Among the variety of these applications,

---

[1] In this book, we use the term "internet" with lower case "i" to refer generally to any (local)
TCP/IP network and with capital "I" to refer to the Global Internet.

the World Wide Web technology is the one that has the greatest influence in the implementation of the virtual design studios.

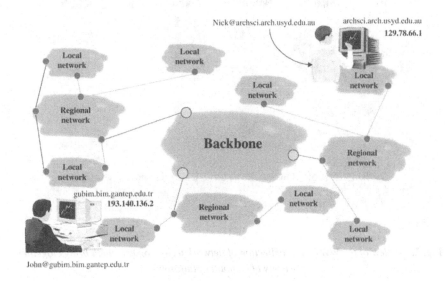

Fig. 2.4 *An internet logical structure.*

2.3 The World Wide Web

There are many definitions of the World Wide Web as many scholars attempt to specify what exactly stands behind the three "W's. In some sense, the World Wide Web is the software view of the Internet. The internet is defined by a set of standards or protocols for sending and receiving data in a network. On top of these protocols a web of information has, and continues, to develop and expand. The most obvious software environment of the WWW is the Web browser, through which information can be retrieved, viewed, sent, saved, and printed. The Web browser assumes standard formats for the representation of information in files. Any information on any computer in the world that is connected to the Internet and uses the standard representation and internet protocols is part of the WWW. The WWW implements a bottom-up approach by defining an architecture and lightweight protocol that runs on the variety of existing platforms. Through the application protocols, the WWW communicates with the other internet services. Fig. 2.5 shows the idea of information communication in the WWW.

The WWW is now defined as a set of files that follow certain standards. The standards for the files dictate how the information is stored and how different files are referenced. Where the TCP/IP standards defined the protocol for sending data across networks to different platforms, the WWW standards define basic formats for storing the data in files and allocating these files so that the Web browsers can display the data on any platform.

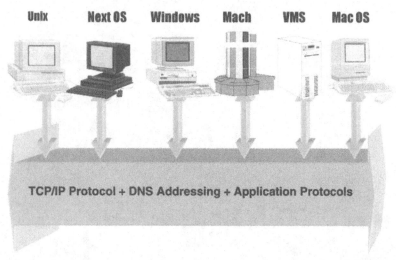

Fig. 2.5 *A view of the WWW as a collection of network technologies, which brings together a variety of computer platforms.*

The WWW standards can be roughly grouped into two categories: *standards for allocation and exchange* of data files and *standards for description of the content* of the data file. URI and HTML are the two most well known standards. The URI - Universal Resource Identifier-is the Web standard for *allocating* any resource on the Internet that is accessible from the World Wide Web - from a specific file on a specific server to an email account. Most people know it by its earlier name, URL - Universal Resource Locator[2], which we use here. They can recognise the simply formatted URL because it starts with "http://", in fact, we have started to take that for granted and begin the URL with the rest of the resource address. The URLs around are becoming as common as telephone and fax numbers - one can see URLs on business cards, advertisements, newspaper and magazine pages and other information sources. Fig. 2.6 illustrates the structure of a typical URL.

In this formatted string the portion to the left of the ":" specifies the protocol to access and interpret the resource. The right-hand side describes the address of the resource, which includes the server name, the path on the server file system that leads to the file and the filename. The path starts from the default directory of the Web server, which usually is a separate subdirectory on the local file system of the machine running that server. For example, the URL in Fig. 2.6 can be deciphered as "use 'http' protocol to access a file called 'index.html' which is located on the server 'www.arch.usyd.edu.au' in the server directory 'kcdc/vds96/elective/'".

---

[2] Universal Resource Locators - URLs, have been known by many names: WWW addresses, Universal Document Identifiers, Uniform Resource Names (URN).

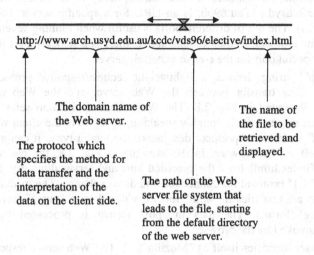

Fig. 2.6 *The structure of a typical URL.*

The URL standard allows a lot of flexibility in the description of resource location. For example, the *relative* URL "vds96/elective/index.html" can be used for reference instead of the *absolute* URL in Fig 2.6 from any Web document, which is in the "kcdc" directory on the "www.arch.usyd.edu.au" server.

The URL standard allows the omission of numerous "defaults". For example, Web servers usually allow a default file name, as shown in Fig. 2.7. The name "index.html" has become an almost standard default name, thus it can be omitted from the URL in Fig. 2.6. The idea of utilising the flexibility and "default" features of the URL is shown by the slider - using just the minimum necessary from the URL.

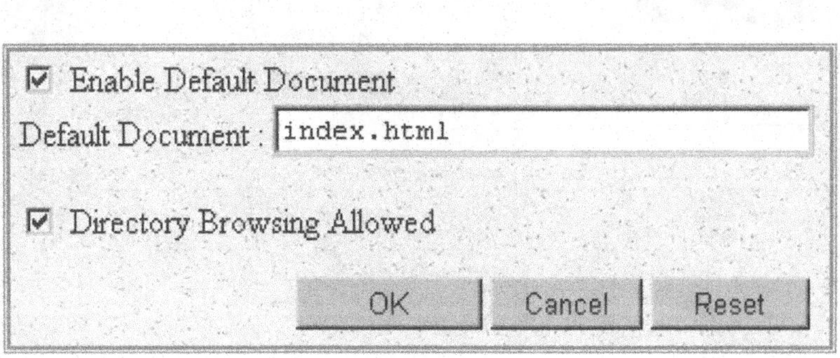

Fig. 2.7 *Setting up a default file name for a Web server (Microsoft Personal Web server).*

The "port number" is often another "default", omitted in most URLs. Formally, the port number is that part of an URL which appears after a colon (:), right after the server name. Each of the services on an Internet server checks on the particular "default" port number on that server[3]. Services can be set up to "listen" on any port. In such cases, the port number is specified explicitly in an URL. For example, http://www.arch.usyd.edu.au:8900, is an URL for a specific server that provides course materials. The use of different ports is useful when running several services under the same protocol. In the example above, there is a standard port for the web server and a special port for the course materials server.

The "http"[4] string denotes a lightweight request/response protocol, which regulates the data transfer between the Web server and the Web client. The paradigm is illustrated in Fig. 2.8. The Web client application sends a request message to the server, which, roughly speaking, states what the client wants to do (the "*method*" in terms of protocol designers), the media types it can accept, and identifies itself to the browser. In the example in Fig. 2.8, the client wants to retrieve file "index.html" from the specified host and server directory. It suggests using "HTTP 1.1" protocol for connection and data exchange. The media types that it can process are text files in "html" format, video data in "mpeg" format, image data in "jpeg" format. The data in "pdf" format is processed by external application, invoked by the browser.

The browser identifies itself as "Mozilla/4.5". The Web server response to the request consists of a similar header, which reports what is coming back: requested file or an error message, and the data itself. In this example, the server is able to use the "HTTP 1.1" protocol. It identifies itself and provides information about the requested file: date, media type (acceptable for the client) and length. The blank line after the header separates it from the actual data.

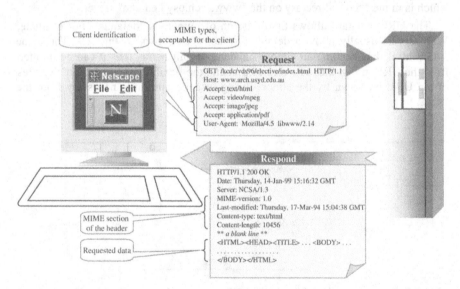

Fig. 2.8 *A Client/Server paradigm under the HTTP protocol.*

---

[3] 21 for FTP, 23 for Telnet, 70 for Gopher and 80 for HTTP.
[4] Hyper Text Transfer Protocol.

This example illustrates the main idea of how computers follow the client/server "etiquette". The key parts of the "etiquette" are (*i*) the descriptions of the *protocol* of exchange, including the *type of media*, and (*ii*) the text description of the *media* to be delivered, in terms of structure, content, and style.

Although it is the most popular on the Web, the "http" is not the only protocol. Names of some Internet client/server services (applications), like "ftp", "telnet", "gopher", are used directly as protocol labels. FTP is a protocol for moving a file from one host to another over the Internet. It follows the directory paradigm, specifying files using their filenames. TELNET is another application protocol, which opens a text-based terminal session on a remote host. When using a slow connection and text-based application, TELNET remains the most efficient and reliable tool. Fig. 2.9 shows how each of the protocols are associated with an application.

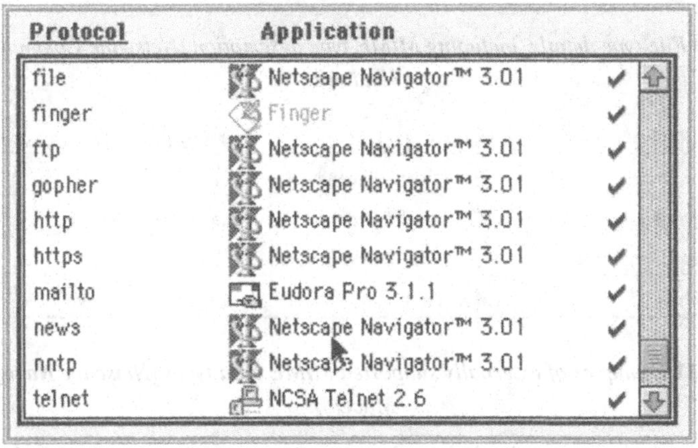

Protocol	Application
file	Netscape Navigator™ 3.01
finger	Finger
ftp	Netscape Navigator™ 3.01
gopher	Netscape Navigator™ 3.01
http	Netscape Navigator™ 3.01
https	Netscape Navigator™ 3.01
mailto	Eudora Pro 3.1.1
news	Netscape Navigator™ 3.01
nntp	Netscape Navigator™ 3.01
telnet	NCSA Telnet 2.6

Fig. 2.9 *Protocols and supporting applications (Microsoft Internet Explorer - MacOS).*

In addition to the protocol information, the Web browser and server use an extensible and open description of the kind of media (data, file) they exchange, known as "Internet Media Types", formerly referred to as MIME[5] Content-Types. The idea is shown in Fig. 2.10. A MIME description follows a two level classification hierarchy, expressed in a string of the following format: "type name/subtype name". In the example in Fig. 2.10, the type is "image" and the subtype is "jpeg". Some MIME types, like the "image/jpeg" in Fig. 2.10 are supported internally by the browser. The browser may not support others internally.

Examples of externally supported types are shown in Fig. 2.11. These file types are processed by an associated external application (as the example with the "pdf" file format in Fig. 2.8), or saved for later recall. As illustrated in Fig. 2.8, when a server transmits information back to the client, the MIME section of the header informs the client what kind of data follows and the client's interpretation then

---

[5] Multimedia Internet Mail Extensions.

depends on invoking the appropriate utility (whether internal function or external application), which corresponds to that data type. Virtual design studios usually operate with a large variety of data types. Roughly, the inclusion of a new data type is equivalent to specifying the "type/subtype" string and the utility associated with it. This simplicity of extension of the media spectrum is both an advantage and disadvantage - the Web is as far from standardisation now as it was in the beginning.

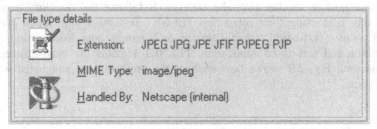

File type details

Extension: JPEG JPG JPE JFIF PJPEG PJP

MIME Type: image/jpeg

Handled By: Netscape (internal)

Fig. 2.10 *File type details, including MIME type description (Netscape Communicator - Windows).*

Mime Type	Application		Action	Extensions
application/mac-binhex40		Stuffit Expander™	Launch	hqx
application/x-stuffit		Stuffit Expander	Launch	sit
application/x-macbinary		Mac Binary II+	Launch	bin
application/x-zip		ZipIt	Launch	z,zip

Fig. 2.11 *Examples of externally supported MIME data types (Netscape Navigator - MacOS).*

The description of media is based on the notion of "markup". "Markup" is the information added to the content of a text file that describes elements of its content. What is known as "procedural markup" has been used widely for the description of the physical appearance of the text on a page in most electronic word processing and publishing systems. The idea of describing the purpose of the text in a file, rather than its physical appearance on the page, led to the concept of "generic markup". To separate the content from the style, generic markup identifies whole elements within the structure of a file, using codes to describe the role of each element. The set of markup rules, including the syntax for defining data elements and an overall framework for marking up the content of a file, constitute, a *markup language*. The markup flagship - the SGML[6]- provided the basis for the development of Web technologies. SGML specifies a strict markup scheme where every element in a file fits into a logical, predictable structure. According to the SGML standard, the markup for identifying the information and its meaning is defined as a pair of *tags* – an opening and closing tag - placed around every element of the content. Although a tag can be any string delimited by the symbols "<" and ">", tags in markup languages are usually English words or abbreviations,

---

[6] Standard Generalized Markup Language, ISO 8879:1986.

as illustrated in Fig. 2.12. The backslash symbol "/" distinguishes the closing tag from the opening one. In addition to the keyword, an opening tag can include some explicit parameters, providing additional control over the effect of the tag.

Creating a tagged file in a markup language involves adding text and inserting tags around the text. As shown in Fig. 2.12, these descriptive tags can be nested, defining the organisation of the content.

<topic><par>VDS: Handbooks and Help</par></topic>

Fig 2.12 *Markup involves adding start and end tags around portions of text.*

The principles of the SGML framework contributed to the development of Web technology in two ways:

1. The overall framework allows specifying any set of tags and rules (markup language) for describing the content of virtually any type of media;
2. By describing what the element of the media content is, but not how it will appear, a markup language, which complies with the SGML standard, is independent from any hardware and operating system. In other words, the parsing of the text is standardised, but the interpretation of content description is left to the browser software[7].

The HTML - the Hyper Text Markup Language, is the derivative[8] of the SGML standard that is currently used in Web browsers. The language provides the set of tags for presenting hypermedia content distributed over the Internet. Fig. 2.13 illustrates the way a text HTML file ends up as a multimedia page in the browser window.

This small example illustrates the elegance with which an HTML file incorporates both local and external resources through the URL. The basic components of the page reside in the same folder on the local server, thus all image references ("<img>") use relative URLs - only by file name. The "<a href>" tag specifies a link to another Internet resource from within a Web page. Hyperlinking has developed a whole new culture of information processing, where exploration and non-linear navigation integrates the traditional query/retrieval procedure with cognitive mechanisms of information discovery. HTML allows the specification of

---

[7] An analogy from photography illustrates the advantages of standardised media description. The international standard for film speeds and the bar codes for describing their values clearly specified the photographic media to be used. Complying with this standard, the manufacturers of films, cameras and processing equipment have made easy the use of different films on different cameras and the post-processing of different films on different equipment. For example, one selects a film labelled "ISO 200", puts it into the camera and closes the camera back. The camera computer reads the label from the bar code and interprets its value, setting up the combination of exposure and aperture values during the shot. After finishing the shots, the film is processed on a "C-41" compatible machine. The brand of the film and the manufacturer does not affect these operations.

[8] Earlier versions of HTML were based on some of the concepts of SGML. It is considered that full SGML-compliance has been achieved starting from HTML 3.0.

relatively complex and interactive multimedia structures in text files with a relatively simple language.

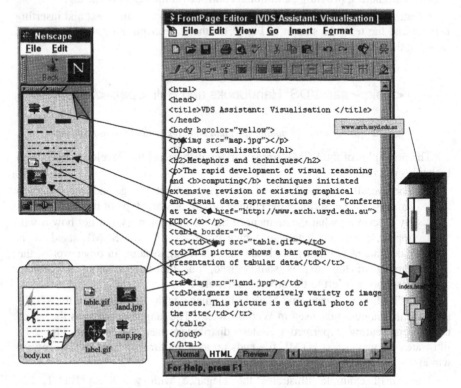

Fig. 2.13 *An example of HTML showing references to other files.*

HTML includes tags that describe the structure of the document, tags that are oriented more towards the appearance of the page layout, tags that specify hyperlinks and tags that provide input for interactive Web applications. Fig 2.14 illustrates the difference in the two ways of tagging a text. The tagging of the fragment in Fig 2.14a is oriented towards the page layout, which is not surprising taking into account that the file is a word processing file exported in HTML format. The tags used in this case define different parts of the text through explicit description of the font and its parameters (<FONT COLOUR="Maroon" SIZE=2>) and through the exact style for particular segments (<B> for displaying in bold style and <I> for displaying in italic).

The tagging of the same content in the file in Fig. 2.14b is oriented towards expressing the structure of the document. The header of the document is tagged by a markup for a header - level 3 (<H3>), rather than with a specific font style. There is no explicit specification of what size or style of fonts to use. Those parts of the text that were specified in italic and bold, are tagged now as "emphasised" (<EM>) and "strong" (<STRONG>), respectively. In this case, the presentation style is left to the browser. For example, the <EM>-tagged text is most likely to be displayed in italics on graphic browsers, but will appear in reverse video on character-based browsers.

```
<HTML>
<HEAD> <TITLE>Virtual Design Studio</TITLE></HEAD>
<BODY BGCOLOR="white">
<P>
<B><FONT COLOR="Maroon" SIZE=2>Virtual Design Studio</FONT></B>
<P>
<FONT FACE="Arial" SIZE=1> The concept of a <I>Virtual Design Studio</I>
(VDS) in this paper refers to a networked design studio. A conventional design
studio is a place in which designers work on drawing boards and/or CAD. The
VDS takes this notion and distributes it across space and time. In a
VDS:</FONT>
<P>
<FONT FACE="Arial" SIZE=1> - the design group is composed of people in
<B>various locations</B>; <BR>
- the design process and designers' communications are
<B>computer-mediated</B> and <B>computer-supported</B>; <BR>
- the information "inside" the studio is handled in <B>electronic form</B>;
<BR>
- the final design documentation is also in electronic form. </FONT>
</BODY></HTML>
```

a. Tagging oriented towards page layout

```
<HTML>
<HEAD><TITLE>Virtual Design Studio</TITLE></HEAD>
<BODY BGCOLOR="white">
<H3>Virtual Design Studio</H3>
<P>The concept of a <EM>Virtual Design Studio</EM> (VDS) in this
paper refers to a networked design studio. A conventional design studio
is a place in which designers work on drawing boards and/or CAD. The
VDS takes this notion and distributes it across space and time. In a
VDS:
<UL>
<LI>the design group is composed of people in <STRONG>various
locations</STRONG>;
<LI>the design process and designers' communications are
<STRONG>computer-mediated</STRONG> and
<STRONG>computer-supported</STRONG>;
<LI>the information "inside" the studio is handled in
<STRONG>electronic form</STRONG>;
<LI>the final design documentation is also in electronic form.
</UL>
</BODY></HTML>
```

b. Tagging oriented towards document stucture

Fig. 2.14 *Same content, different tagging, different interpretation by different browsers.*

Fig 2.15 shows the difference in the page layouts produced from the HTML files in Fig 2.14 by the same graphical browser[9].

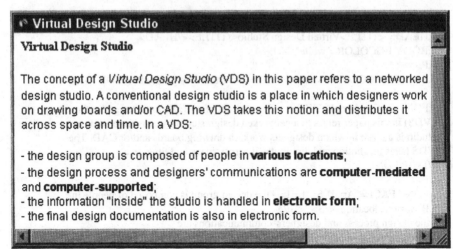

a. Browser's interpretation of the tagged text in Fig 2.14a

b. Browser's interpretation of the tagged text in Fig. 2.14b

Fig.2.15 *Same content, different page display which leads to different perception.*

When both "<I>" and "<EM>" tags are interpreted in italic by this browser, the "<B>" and "<STRONG>" tags' interpretation differ in colour. Following the SGML standard, HTML does not define how an application, such as a browser or an authoring tool, should behave. Consequently, a page developed in a

---

[9] AOL Press 2.0, which is also an authoring tool.

WYSIWYG[10] editor may look different from how it was intended to look when displayed by different browsers. In general, WYSIWYG authoring requires the solution of problems that do not exist when editing HTML code. This is one of the arguments in favour of participants in a VDS knowing HTML. We will discuss the different formats recognised in HTML in Chapter 3. Here, we refer to an aspect of Web reality that has to be taken into consideration.

The HTML is being developed constantly. On the other hand, browsers' world changes almost every day. The result of the competition of ideas and programming art is that most browsers have bugs in their implementations. Usually, by the time the bugs in the current version are fixed, the HTML standard changes and a new version of the browser - with new bugs - appears on the battlefield. Apart from the other inconveniences, this quickening in the software developing cycle can often lead to display, presentation or printing problems. Designers in a VDS have to take these considerations into account when developing Web based design documents[11].

Even the most sophisticated HTML tags and style sheets do not go beyond the flat two-dimensional page format. On the other hand, architectural and engineering projects require intensive three-dimensional simulations, interaction and animation, in a way that designers can explore design ideas and alternatives beyond the text- and image-based representations.

In some sense, VRML[12] can be considered as the current 3D complement to HTML. Although not a markup language, VRML is a simple, platform-independent language for publishing dynamic 3D Web pages. The coalescence of VRML with HTML pages and applets can produce very effective Web deliveries. Combining both 3D and 2D information often results in messages that are much better than either 3D or 2D alone. VRML adds that missing part to the Web technology that integrates the 3D and 2D information worlds - the worlds of geometry, text descriptions, images and other multimedia components, into a coherent model.

The world in VRML is modelled as a directed acyclic graph[13] - a hierarchical scene graph in VRML terms - whose nodes represent objects and their properties. Such a structure can handle both simple and complex objects, and large worlds which consist of groups of objects. The language specifies more than 50 different node types, including a variety of grouping nodes.

A VRML graph computing combines relational data structures with message interactions in an object-oriented system. Nodes store their data in various types of fields - from a single number to an array of 3D rotations. Nodes in the scene graph communicate through a message-passing mechanism. Each node type specifies the names and types of messages (*events*) that instances of that type may generate or receive, and "ROUTE" statements specify event paths between event generators and receivers. Nodes of *sensor* type combined with other nodes via "ROUTE" statements are the basis for all user interaction. They generate events, as the viewer

---

[10] **What You See Is What You Get.**

[11] Details of this development are discussed in Chapter 5.

[12] Virtual Reality Modelling Language.

[13] In such a graph, nodes may contain other nodes and may be contained in more than one node, but a node must not contain itself.

moves through the world or when the user interacts with some input device. For example, the real time component is introduced in a scene graph via the *TimeSensor*. Additional (not built-in) behaviours of objects are defined in *script* nodes, which can be inserted between event generators (typically sensor nodes) and event receivers. Scripts can be in any supported scripting language[14]. For example, combining a node in a scene graph, a TimeSensor and some animation scripts can generate moving objects.

As a result, VRML defines most of the semantics necessary for representing 3D worlds - geometry, material properties, texture mapping, animations and hierarchical transformations, light sources, viewpoints. When it comes to sharing 3D geometry, VRML plays a similar role to that of DXF and DWF in sharing 2D CAD drawings. Designed to fit existing standards of the Internet and WWW, VRML files may contain references to image and other multimedia files in the standard formats of digital media, accepted on the Internet. Fig. 2.16 shows how a simple geometric object like a cube can be enriched by mapping texture on it from an external file.

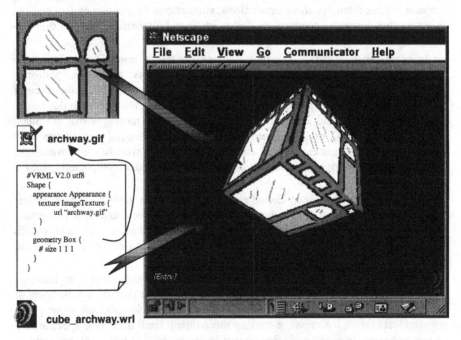

```
#VRML V2.0 utf8
Shape {
    appearance Appearance {
        texture ImageTexture {
            url "archway.gif"
        }
    }
    geometry Box {
        # size 1 1 1
    }
}
```

Fig. 2.16 *Adding texture from an external file to a simple geometric primitive.*

Switching between 2D and 3D information representation requires the integration of VRML and HTML. Although the Internet standards allow two-way integration, at this stage, browsers support embedding a VRML file inside an

---

[14] The current version of VRML specification defines bindings for the Java and JavaScript languages.

HTML file. Through the <OBJECT>[15] HTML tag any type of digital media file can be embedded in the Web page, assuming that there exists the appropriate plug-in or application able to display it. Popular HTML browsers do not support VRML files, thus, it is necessary to equip VDS nodes with VRML support[16].

The prototyping mechanism for encapsulating and reusing a scene graph is a key feature when using VRML in virtual design studios. Geometry, object properties, and related behaviours can be encapsulated, allowing the definition of a new node type in terms of a combination of existing node types.

Fig 2.17 shows individual objects represented as separate VRML files[17]. The cube in Fig 2.17a is similar to the one in Fig 2.16, except it uses a different image file for the texture. Figs. 2.17b and 2.17c visualise more complicated forms, which are based on external VRML files with primitives. The reader can see that the archway in Fig. 2.17c includes the cube from Fig. 2.17a.

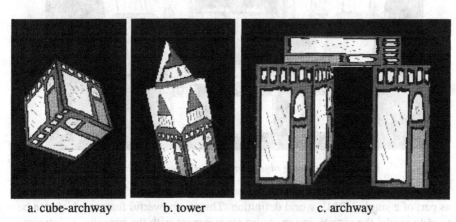

a. cube-archway   b. tower   c. archway

d. floor

Fig. 2.17 *Visualisation of objects described in VRML.*

---

[15] The <OBJECT> tag aims to replace the proprietary <EMBED> and <IMG> tags.
[16] For detailed information on VRML with references to various sources see the online version of Carey, R. and Bell, G. (1997). The Annotated VRML97 Reference Manual at http://www.best.com/~rikk/Book/Book.html.
[17] Examples in Figs 2.23-2.26 are based on the copyright-free VRML examples provided by Silvere Martin-Michiellot and Daniel Schneider at http://tecfa.unige.ch/guides/vrml/examples/worlds/.

These pictures illustrate the benefit for the virtual design studios from the development and reuse of VRML design libraries. Fig. 2.18 shows a world built from the objects described in Fig. 2.17. Although the world in Fig. 2.18 looks primitive, the idea is a powerful one. Constructing 3D models and presenting them in a standard format that is independent of the application that was used to generate the model and that can be displayed on any hardware platform, facilitates the collaboration and integration needed in a virtual design studio.

Fig. 2.18 *Combining objects in one world described in VRML.*

Using VRML, objects and worlds stored anywhere on the Web can be included as part of a single VRML world definition. This is a powerful feature which can be used to model the virtual design studio environment with the potential to integrate 3D virtual world VDS environments and 2D desktop VDS environments.

The introduction of HTML for creating information that can be seen by anyone has resulted in numerous Web sites populated with a vast amount of handcrafted hypermedia. Browsers are usually so forgiving for incorrect HTML that the Web contains quite a lot of loosely written HTML files. For sharing information HTML is fine, but the lack of data structuring and more strict document definition makes it difficult for reliable automation of Web information processing. Some of these issues have been addressed in the newer versions of the standard[18].

However, the idea of enriching documents in a way that enables computer programs to do something more than displaying them opened the path to the *descriptive* markup implemented in the potential successor of HTML - the XML[19] standard. The idea is simple: completely separate the document from its presentation. In other words, the tags around the elements of text do not need to specify how to format that element, or what to do when people click on it. They only have to describe what the element is by defining the role of each element of text in a formal model.

---

[18] The current version is HTML 4.0.
[19] EXtensible Markup Language.

The following examples explain, without going into the details of XML, the presentation and document design aspects that this concept brings to the virtual design studios. Web-based bulletin boards are a common communication tool used in VDS for asynchronous communications. Suppose that some VDS participants are on a business trip and have little palm-top machines with them, others are working on big monitors, a third group is on the site and has only cell phones with teeny screens. If the bulletin board messages are marked up in XML, then a different set of display rules can be specified for the big monitors, the palm-top screens, and cell phones respectively. Furthermore - another set of rules can be used to produce top-quality hardcopies from any of these platforms.

Suppose that the VDS manager wants to set up a bulletin board which uses the core of Web technology for publishing messages. Suppose that for the next run of the virtual design studio the VDS manager wants to add some intelligence to such a bulletin board, which will not only assist the archiving, search and retrieval procedures, but also the analysis and research in studio communications. Rather than cleaning the HTML tags and manually parsing the content of the file to identify different fields, the VDS manager would like to have a clear message. The structure which describes the semantics of different parts of the message this can then be used by the other programs. Thus, the VDS manager creates something identical to the tag structure shown in Fig. 2.19a.

```
<sticker>                                   <!element sticker (head, body)>
<head>                                      <!element head (to, from, subject)>
<to>All teams</to>                          <!element to (#PCDATA)>
<from>VDS Manager</from>                    <!element from (#PCDATA)>
<date>25-08-1998</date>                     <!element date (#PCDATA)>
<subject>HTML Assistant</subject>           <!element subject (#PCDATA)>
</head>                                      <!element body (#PCDATA)>
<body>
Note the Web Page Assistant on the Virtual
Design Studio page (under 'Web On-line
Tools'). It's advantage is that you can learn
the core tags.
</body>
</sticker>
```

a. tag structure   b. document type definition

Fig. 2.19 *Tag structure and DTD that specifies a format for a bulletin board message.*

XML offers a means to specify tags. Tags specification is based on the SGML notion of document type definition (DTD). Fig 2.19b shows the DTD for the structure in Fig 2.19a. Without getting into the details of DTD syntax, the recursive description in Fig 2.19b reads as: The "sticker" consists of "head" and "body". The "head" includes "to", "from", "date" and a "subject". They all contain just text. The "body" contains just text.

The DTD description can be saved in a file. Therefore, it is not necessary to make a new description set for every new message on the bulletin board - it is enough to include the following reference to the DTD file in the beginning of a message file (assuming that the DTD file is called "sticker.dtd" and resides in the same directory, where the messages are saved).

```
<!doctype sticker SYSTEM "sticker.dtd">
```

Furthermore, in a virtual design studio, all DTDs can be kept on a single site and referred to via the complete URL. In addition, preliminary development of design DTDs can improve the consistency in the final design documentation. XML technology also offers the opportunity to develop a set of design DTDs which can specify a design markup language. In general, using one DTD that describes a lot of documents is similar to the use of a database schema for these documents.

The order and hierarchy in XML tag description also means support for smart editing and authoring tools, which do not allow authors to create an XML file whose structure does not match the selected DTD. This does not make designing good documents or good presentations easier than in HTML, but it does mean that the problems are clearly separated.

Though the WWW began as a set of simple protocols and formats, at the moment, it accommodates various sophisticated hypermedia technologies and information retrieval concepts. Not all of these "extensions" to the core of Web technology are an accepted standard. Moreover, some of them are platform dependent. Such extensions should be used in virtual design studios only with agreement from all participants.

Another problem with the current concept and structure of the WWW which directly affects virtual design studios are the URLs that point to documents that no longer exist. These occur when designers update, rename or delete their works from the studio Web. Such collisions can occur both during the design project and after the delivery of the final design document, when some of its elements reside in different parts of the virtual design studio. The system has no way of registering links to one's document and it is up to the author to notify his readers of the changes. Theoretically, the Xanadu (see Xanadu FAQ, 1998) approach overcame this problem since it did not allow deletion of documents from the system, but it is still far from completed practical implementation.

2.4 Implications

Readers will perhaps be surprised that in a period of only three years there have been developments that radically change the way that people think about computers and communications. There are two important effects of networks on designers: the first is the way designers communicate with each other and access information, and the second is how we design and use our physical environment.

The way that we communicate with each other and access information is changing radically as more and more people use computers for email and the WWW. We find that our understanding of how information is stored and transferred becomes important to our ability to function in this new world, as is shown by the popularity of "Being Digital" (Negroponte 1995). In this book, Negroponte defines terms such as bits, baud, and RAM in a way that ordinary (that is, not computer specialists) can understand. Negroponte goes beyond these definitions to provide a vision of a world in which physical space is only one way of existing. The important aspect of this book, however, is the recognition that people now accept the computer as an integral part of their lives. We now hear conversations in grocery stores and street corners about how much RAM someone's computer has and whether they should get a faster modem. This indicates that computers are no longer useful only to the specialist, they have become as common as televisions and telephones.

The way that we design our physical environment will also be affected by the "information age". The effect of the internet is the reconsideration of how we live and work in a digital world. Our urban development and perception of where we live may change, as predicted in "City of Bits" (Mitchell 1995). We are being drawn into a world in which our location in physical space is increasingly less important than what we are doing or have to say. The effect of this on our cities is a reconsideration of how our buildings and infrastructure are organised. As designers, we need to respond not only to the way technology changes how we design, i.e. in virtual design studios, we also need to respond to how technology will change what we design.

This chapter has focussed on the basic networking concepts, protocols and standards that enable a virtual design studio. The technology of the network is fundamental to providing the infrastructure needed to move information from one location to another. Without this infrastructure, we would still be moving atoms instead of bits (Negroponte 1995), a slow and expensive process in comparison. The next chapter looks at the concept of digital design media - a critical component of a successful virtual design studio.

References

Martin, J. and Leben, J. (1994) *TCP/IP Networking: Architecture, Administration and Programming,* Englewood Cliffs, NJ, Prentice Hall.
Mitchell, W. J. (1995) *City of Bits,* Cambridge, MA, MIT Press.
Negroponte, N. (1995) *Being Digital,* Media Technologies Inc.
Xanadu FAQ, 1998, http://www.aus.xanadu.com/xanadu/faq.html.

Three

Digital Design Media

Digital design media is the basis on which design information can be shared across a network. The title of this chapter is borrowed from a book, (Mitchell 1995), in which a more comprehensive treatment of the representation of designs as digital data and the ensuing implications are given. There are many ways to categorise the representation of design descriptions, digital media being one view. Here, we focus on four different types of digital media: images, CAD models, text, and hypermedia. Realising that other media, such as sound, movies, and virtual reality, are relevant to the representation of a design description, we have selected these three as the most commonly used digital media in current virtual design studios. A consideration of the conceptual organisation of the representation of designs is given in Chapter 5, whereas here we look at how different media allow the designer to express and manipulate different ideas.

3.1 Images

The use of images to represent design concepts and geometry is common in both virtual and traditional design studios. In a virtual design studio, an image is stored in a file and is represented in bitmapped format. We distinguish between the representation of an image and the technology used to display information on a computer. There is a difference between editing a text document, reading email messages, browsing Web pages, viewing animations or "fly-through" photo-realistic 3D models of designed spaces. However, these are all based on the same visualisation principle – all information is displayed on the computer screen or printer/plotter in a digital or bitmapped format. Although all information is displayed in a bitmap, not all information is stored in bitmapped format. Instead, as a matrix of pixels, computer graphics can be stored as a list of geometric primitives, which results in a set of numerical coordinates and mathematical formulas that specify the position and the shape of each primitive in the list. The underlying representation of design information has implications on how the information can be edited.

We use the term *digital image* to refer to information that is stored as a bitmap, and to *image processor* as the class of programs that manipulates such images. The advantage of digital images in a VDS lies in a basic premise of the VDS; a digital image can be transferred from one computer to another, regardless of the hardware or software platform that created it. Digital images can be created by taking a drawing or sketch on paper and scanning the image into a file. This process implies that anything that we can put on paper can be stored and manipulated as a digital image. Computer generated sources of digital images include: rendered 3D models, digital photographs, digital video, etc. The increasing availability and use of digital image processing means that anything can become part of the information available in the virtual design studio.

Bitmap images are specified by the description of the pixels that constitute them. Each pixel in the digital image has an *address* so the image processor can change and display its characteristics. The quality of a digital image depends on characteristics related to how the array of pixels is stored: *resolution, colour* and *intensity* of each pixel, and *compression* of the matrix data.

The image resolution is the number of pixels (or dots) that fit a unit length. It is measured by the number of *dots per inch* (dpi). The higher the resolution the better the quality. Higher resolution images contain more pixels than an image of the same dimensions with lower resolution. For example, compare visually the images of the same size, presented in Fig. 3.1 a and c, whose resolutions are 72 and 36 dpi respectively, where the higher resolution image is a better quality image. On the other hand, the images in Fig. 3.1 a and b are of the same resolution, and, although different in size, they are perceived visually as images of the same quality.

The maximum resolution of an image depends on its source, i.e. paper or computer generated file, and its output device, i.e. paper or screen. Resolution only makes sense for digital images. An image on paper effectively has infinite resolution, and an image in a computer file is limited, ultimately, to the resolution of the source image. The best resolution of an image for presentation depends on whether the presentation is done on paper or screen. Generally the presentation of an image on the screen requires a lower resolution than the presentation on paper. This has to do with the way we see light and colour on the screen and how light is reflected on paper. Using a low resolution for digital images that need to be printed results in *pixelation* - large pixels that produce very coarse-looking output. Using a high resolution (i.e. pixels smaller that what an output device can reproduce) increases the file size unnecessarily and may increase the time required to print or distribute the image. What is high and low depends on the source image and the resolution capacity of the printer or display device.

Regardless of the print size specified for an image, the size of an image on-screen is determined by the pixel dimensions of the image and the monitor size and setting. Current screen technology typically supports resolutions of 72 and 96 dpi. Consequently, when the resolution of an image is higher than the screen resolution, the image appears larger on-line than its specified dimensions. For example, when you display a 2-x-2 inch image with a resolution of 192 dpi on a 96 dpi screen, it appears in a 2-x-2 inch area of the screen.

In virtual design studios, image information is shared across hardware and software platforms. Studio participants need to have an idea about the screen resolution available to each participant. It is common sense to restrict the maximum image size in pixels allowed in online documents by the monitor with the lowest resolution. For example, if most participants in the studio are equipped with notebook computers with active screen areas of 800 x 600 pixels, then this could be the limit of the image size.

a. Image size: 256 x 256 pixels; Resolution: 72 dpi   b. Image size: 128 x 128 pixels;
                                                          Resolution: 72 dpi

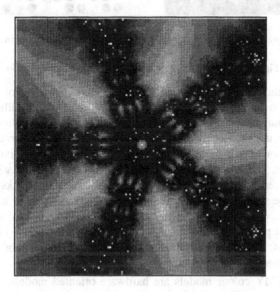

c. Image size: 256 x 256 pixels; Resolution: 36 dpi

Fig. 3.1 *Computer generated jewelry design - variations of size and resolution.*

In the virtual design studio, the efficient and adequate use of different media for digital images requires extensive knowledge of colour theory and models, and practical knowledge and skills in operating with them.

A colour image is made possible by associating colour information with each pixel. The composition of a pixel varies depending on the output device, as illustrated by the example in Fig. 3.2 (as different shades of grey). On the screen, whether it is a colour monitor, LCD, active matrix display or data projector, each pixel is shown as a *single colour* (Fig. 3.2a), formed by the visual mixing of red, green, and blue light components, known as the *RGB colour model*, shown in Fig. 3.3a. The RGB model is an additive model with an origin, which coincides with the position of the "black" colour dot. The bits for each pixel, using this model, indicate the amount of red, green and blue colour associated with the dot.

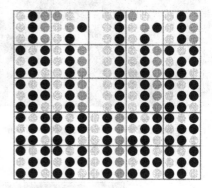

a. Screen representation of 25 pixels   b. Printer representation of 25 pixels

Fig. 3.2 *Representation of pixels on different output media.*

On paper, each pixel is formed from lots of much smaller coloured dots that blend together to give the impression of a single colour, roughly illustrated in Fig. 3.2b. Taking into account that the paper usually provides a white background, printing devices use the CMY difference colour model, complementary to the RGB model, as shown in Fig 3.3a. In this case, the bits for each pixel indicate the amount of cyan, yellow and magenta, which, if subtracted from white leave red, green and blue respectively. In practice, due to impurities in the inks, the reflection of light from the surface of the ink and incomplete coverage of the white paper, the mixture of the cyan, magenta and yellow does not produce a good black. Therefore, most printers use a four-ink schema, adding a separate black ink to the printing process. This schema implements the CMYK colour model, which uses four halftone screens - one for each ink.

RGB and CMY colour models are hardware oriented models. Artists usually operate with concepts like tint, shade and tone, rather than the mixture of colours. The HSB model operates with the concepts of hue, saturation and brightness which are closely related to the human perception of colour. In this model, hue is the colour as described by the wavelength of light reflected from or transmitted through an object, for instance, the differentiation between green and cyan.

Saturation, also called chroma, refers to the strength or purity of the colour, for instance the differentiation between blue and purple. Brightness (also called lightness, intensity or value and represented with the respective letter in the abbreviation, instead of "B") stands for the relative lightness or darkness of the colour, for instance, the differentiation between dark green and light green.

The HSB system can be illustrated as a circular or hexagonal cone or double cone as shown in Fig. 3.3b. Hue is displayed as a location on the circle of the cone and is expressed as a degree between 0° and 360°. The central axis of the cone is the grey scale progression. Saturation is the distance from the central axis of the cone, measuring the amount of grey in proportion to the hue in percentage. Brightness is measured as a percentage from 0% (black) to 100% (white).

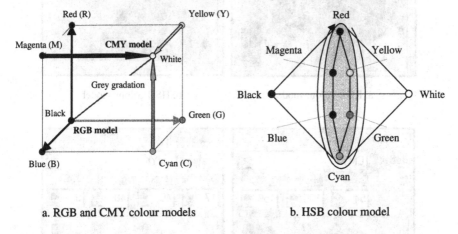

a. RGB and CMY colour models   b. HSB colour model

Fig. 3.3 *Common colour models used in image processors*

The collages in Fig. 3.4 illustrate the idea of conversion and the use of visualisation schemes which correspond to different colour models. The conversion between HSB, RGB and CMY[1] models is straightforward. The addition of the black component to CMYK makes the conversion to and from this system much more sophisticated. The amount of black to be added into various colour representations depends on the visual response to colours, the kind of paper being printed and even the content of the images. Algorithms for conversion to CMYK vary considerably from one image processor to another. Each program addresses the issues of matching the screen colours to the colours as they appear in print through its own set of colour correction facilities.

The number of possible colours that can be displayed is determined by the number of bits per pixel, more bits means more available colours and more accurate colour representation in the digital image. This characteristic is referred to as *pixel depth*, also called bit resolution or colour depth. More bits also means more flexibility for image processing.

---

[1] HSB, RGB are often referred to as "colour space coordinate systems", whereas CMY is referred to as a "process colour system".

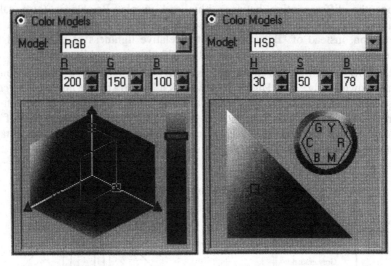

a. RGB colour model   b. HSB colour model

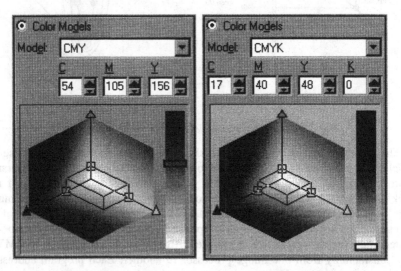

c. CMY colour model   d. CMYK colour model

Fig. 3.4 *Interactive visualisation of the same colour represented in different models. The illustration is based on elements from the colour selection display of CorelDRAW image processing system.*

Changing the size of a bitmap image refers to changing the pixel dimensions (and therefore file size) of an image. Increasing the size of an image means increasing the number of pixels. In this case, the image processor creates new pixel information interpolating the colour values of surrounding pixels. The result of such an operation is an increase of image coarseness as shown in Fig. 3.5. This is the reason why once an image has been scanned or created at a given resolution, increasing the resolution in an image processor does not improve the image quality.

Decreasing the size of the image is connected with loss of information from the original image. Depending on the scale of decrease, the resultant image is blurry and creates the impression that the source was "not in focus". This effect is illustrated in Fig. 3.6. Another rule of thumb is to avoid decreasing the resolution and then increasing it again - the result will be considerable deterioration in the quality of the image. In other words, a bitmap image does not posses the ability of a vector image representation to preserve quality in resizing (see Fig. 3.7).

The issues of image size in the context quality become critical when there is transition between different media. For instance, designers in the virtual design studio develop and share their representation in electronic form, thus compromising on the image quality in the work drafts in the name of speed in sharing them. The above mentioned issue in resizing the bitmap format can restrict the quality of printed versions of documented designs.

Image processing operations map each pixel in the original image to an appropriate place in the new image. The operations performed by image processors can be grouped into two major categories – "geometry" operations: manipulation of pixels' addresses; and "colour" operations: operations over colour/intensity values of the image. Geometry operations do not change colour parameters, but may or may not change the number of pixels in the image. Rotation is an example of a geometry operation that may add pixels to the image. When a square is rotated by 45 degrees the length of its diagonal becomes the new size of the image side, which means that the image processor adds additional pixels (background) to fill the empty parts of the image. Some rotations, like the "flip" operations, preserve the number of pixels of the original image. Colour operations, for example, adjustment of the brightness and the contrast, do not affect the number of pixels.

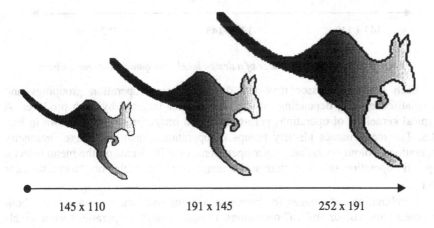

145 x 110   191 x 145   252 x 191

Fig. 3.5 *Increasing a bitmap image of a design label - the image becomes coarse (the initial image is 145 x 110 pixels).*

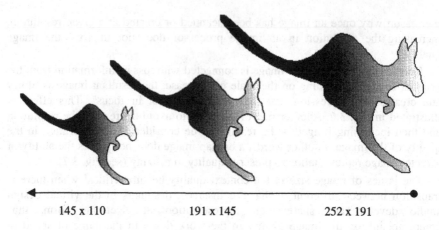

145 x 110   191 x 145   252 x 191

Fig 3.6. *Decreasing a bitmap image of a design label - the image looses its sharpness (the initial image is 252 x 191 pixels).*

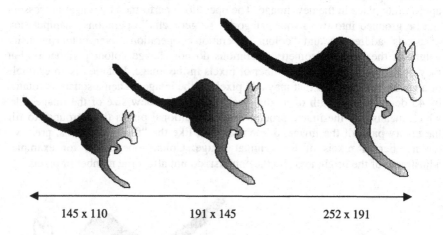

145 x 110   191 x 145   252 x 191

Fig. 3.7 *Scaling a vector image of a design label - the quality does not change.*

Each image processor may use different terms, operation groupings and specialised effects, depending on the type of user targeted by each producer. A typical kernel set of operations performed by an image processor is shown in Fig. 3.8. The menu names identify groups of operations, such as "image" geometry operations, colour operations, layer operations, etc. The items on the menu select a specific operation that will change the image, such as "blur" or "increase color depth".

Combinations of images (or layers in a composite image) can involve both geometry and colour "micro" operations. In some complex operations some pixels may not be mapped. In these operations, the value of the pixels in terms of address and colour values are estimated by interpolating algorithms. Examples of such algorithms are the procedures used to resize a bitmap image.

Image	Colors	Layers	Selections
Flip			Ctrl+I
Mirror			Ctrl+M
Rotate...			Ctrl+R
Add Borders...			
Crop to Selection			Shift+R
Canvas Size...			
Resize...			Shift+S
Arithmetic...			
Deformations			▶
Effects			▶
Filter Browser...			
Blur			▶
Edge			▶
Noise			▶
Sharpen			▶
Other			▶
User Defined Filters...			

Colors	Layers	Selections	Masks	Capture
Adjust				▶
Colorize...				Shift+L
Grey Scale				
Histogram Functions				▶
Negative Image				
Posterize...				Shift+Z
Solarize...				
Channel Splitting				▶
Channel Combining				▶
Edit Palette...				Shift+P
Load Palette...				Shift+O
Save Palette...				
Set Palette Transparency...				Shift+Ctrl+V
View Palette Transparency				Shift+V
Count Colors Used				
Decrease Color Depth				▶
Increase Color Depth				▶

a. "geometry" operations   b. "colour" operations

Fig. 3.8. *A typical set of image processor operations[2].*

From a user's point of view composite operations and effects do not differ from simple ones. Image processors use a variety of metaphors to describe individual operations or a set of them, for example, the arithmetic metaphor. In this metaphor, image operations are described in terms of mathematical operations.

Fig.3. 9 illustrates a typical specification for the "addition" of two images. This and similar "image arithmetic" operations take usually two source images as arguments and produced a third image of the same type as the two source images. The two source images are specified by labels, in this example these are their filenames. In this case each image is a different view of a 3D model of the bus stop design. The result is a superposition of the pixel values. Fig. 3.10 illustrates the result of the operation selected in Fig. 3.9. The original two images are shown in Fig. 3.10a and b. The result of the addition operator is the image in Fig. 3.10c.

Arithmetic metaphor is a particular case of the more general and ambitious image expression evaluation. In a way, similar to arithmetic operations, there can be defined functions and expressions in symbolic form, where each argument represents an image. Procedures that stand behind the image expressions approach extend the capabilities of image processors beyond image editing and combining, to creation of artificial images, which is essential element in virtual design studios.

---

[2] Menus are from Paint Shop Pro 5 by Jasc Software Inc.

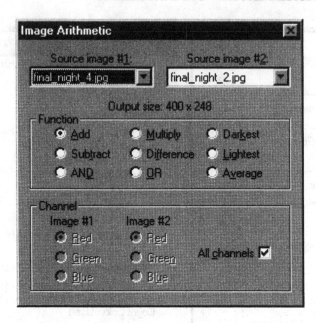

Fig. 3.9 *Image arithmetic - it looks simpler than a calculator tool (Paint Shop Pro).*

Image processors usually provide also additional optional effects. The architecture of an advanced processor like Adobe Photoshop allows the incorporation of a virtually unlimited number of such effects (or filters) in the form of plug-ins to the system. The family of such effects spans from simple "blur" or "sharpen" effects to sophisticated art effects like "watercolour", "dry brush", "plastics" and so on. Fig. 3.11 illustrates the changes that such "single-click" effects can make to the image. Fig. 3.11 b and c show the results after performing "sketch" and "texture" effects to the original image in Fig. 3.11 a.

Compression is important for displaying and sending images across networks. Since compression involves a loss of information, an image may be archived in its original uncompressed format, but distributed or made available on the Web in a compressed format. The amount of memory needed to store image data can grow quickly. When it comes to storage for images the proverb that a picture is worth a thousand words causes some doubts and disbelief among computer specialists. For example, a 10 inch by 10 inch image with a resolution of 72 dpi and 8 bits per pixel colour requires 1.48Mbytes. The disadvantage to large image files is the delay in displaying the image on the screen, as well as the delay in downloading an image from another server.

The most common compression formats are those recognised by the Web: JPEG and GIF. The JPEG compaction scheme allows typical compression of 10:1, although, in some highly correlated images compression rate can achieve 100:1. For colour rich images (with much more than 256 colours), JPEG format preserves better quality for online images. For images, like scanned drawings, sketches and diagrams, where there is no need of more than 256 colours, GIF format is preferable.

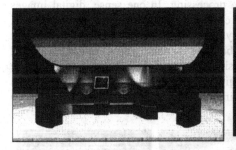

a. Source image 1   b. Source image 2

c. Resultant image

Fig. 3.10 *Image arithmetic: the product of image "addition"*

The GIF format has two considerable advantages – it allows a transparent background colour and can easily combine and display more than one image in one file. Transparency allows the visual integration of the image with the background. Compact animations, when used appropriately, can replace a considerable amount of verbal explanations. All compression techniques lose some information and, depending on the image, this loss may not be visible. For archival purposes digital images should be stored in their original uncompressed format. This format can be either the proprietary image format, used by the image processor where the image was created or an uncompressed format, which the image processors in the virtual design studio can understand.

Digital image processing has become an essential skill for the use of the computer to communicate design information. In the 80's, the focus in architectural design was on the production of CAD drawings, in the 90's, designers are coming to terms with digital image processing. In one sense, digital images provide another media for expressing creative ideas, where, in another sense, digital images, e.g. digital photography, provide a way to share and transfer information that previously could only be done as photographs, or fax. A digital image can reflect an existing scene or design. However, the benefit of digital image processing in design is the ability to "digitally" modify an existing scene or design or to create a scene in the same way a painting is created.

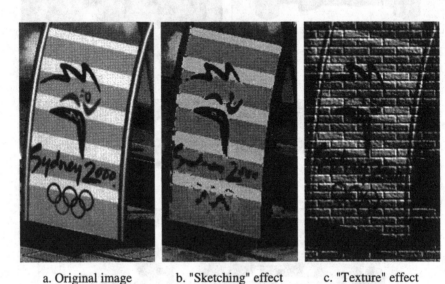

a. Original image   b. "Sketching" effect   c. "Texture" effect

Fig. 3.11 *Digital image modification (Adobe Gallery Effects).*

3.2 CAD and 3D Models

CAD, an acronym with many different expansions, has come to refer to a class of programs that assist in modelling and documenting the geometry of a design. CAD drawings differ from a digital image because they explicitly represent the vertices, lines, wire frames, solids, and/or surfaces of the object(s) so they can be edited and assigned properties.

CAD technology started as drafting programs for developing design documentation. They operated primarily in a two-dimensional environment, imitating the way design documentation is produced on a drafting table using paper and pencil. More recently, CAD technology has diverged from a simple imitation of drawing on paper to allow the advantages of working with a computer representation of geometry. Typically, CAD drawings are created from a predefined set of parameterised basic primitives such as line and curve segments, arcs and circles, and text. The advantage of a parametric definition is the variety of ways in which a primitive can be defined. This variety is illustrated in Fig. 3.12 for an arc primitive represented by three parameters.

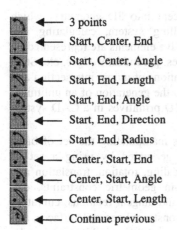

← 3 points
← Start, Center, End
← Start, Center, Angle
← Start, End, Length
← Start, End, Angle
← Start, End, Direction
← Start, End, Radius
← Center, Start, End
← Center, Start, Angle
← Center, Start, Length
← Continue previous

Legend

• **Angle** - specifies the angle included in an arc.
• **Center** - specifies the centre of an arc segment.
• **Direction** - specifies the direction of the tangent line in the start point of an arc.
• **End** - specifies the end point of an arc.
• **Length** - specifies the length of the chord between the start and the end points.
• **Radius** - specifies the radius of an arc.
• **Start** - specifies the start point of an arc.

Fig. 3.12 *An arc as a parameterised geometric primitive of CAD.*

Parametric representation provides unlimited scaling capabilities. This becomes an important issue in virtual design studios, where computer screens have smaller dimensions than the paper sheets used to plot design drawings. This means that CAD technology allows the use of the data for drawings at different scales. An architectural plan designed at urban scale can be developed at a detailed level with related plans, elevation, and sections using the same basic primitives. The drawing is developed in full scale and the choice of scale limits is related to the level on which particular details are investigated. This flexibility of a CAD geometric model means that it can be applied in any design domain connected with geometric modelling. Examples, from mechanical, architectural and electronic circuit design domains are shown in Fig. 3.13.

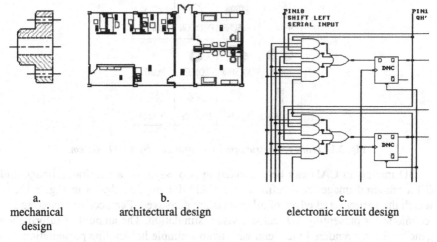

a.
mechanical
design

b.
architectural design

c.
electronic circuit design

Fig. 3.13 *An arc as a parameterised geometric primitive of CAD.*

Further development extended the CAD concept into 3D geometry, which involves the use of a surface or solid modelling system, calculating and representing 3D shapes. In this case the basic primitive elements are represented by solid shapes such as spheres, ellipsoids, torus', cubes, pyramids, wedges, etc. Such sets of primitives combined with the Boolean operations of union, intersection and subtraction over basic solid shape primitives allows the generation of an unlimited number of shapes. A typical set of basic 2D and 3D primitives in a CAD system are shown in Fig. 3.14.

CAD systems include powerful capabilities for manipulating the set of basic graphic primitives. Additional elements can be generated by using a set of implemented geometric transformations such as scaling, rotation, translation and stretching. CAD systems also incorporate built-in geometric constraints, e.g. relations of intersection and bisection, orthogonal and tangent relations, curvature and convexity. These allow the designer to easily construct lines and surfaces, and to combine them into realistic objects. All primitives and their combinations can be resized, trimmed and divided into equal parts, without loss of accuracy.

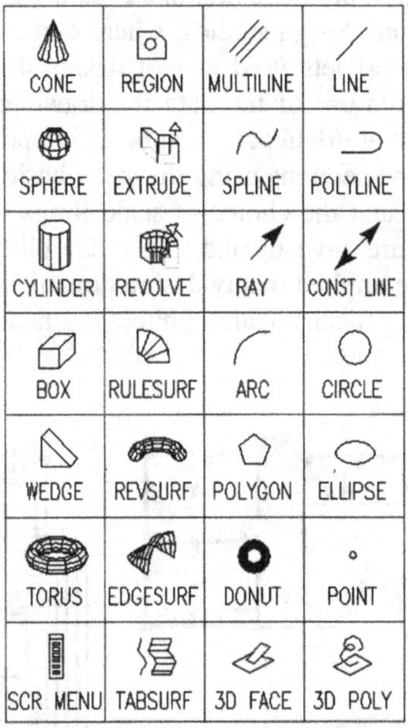

CONE	REGION	MULTILINE	LINE
SPHERE	EXTRUDE	SPLINE	POLYLINE
CYLINDER	REVOLVE	RAY	CONST LINE
BOX	RULESURF	ARC	CIRCLE
WEDGE	REVSURF	POLYGON	ELLIPSE
TORUS	EDGESURF	DONUT	POINT
SCR MENU	TABSURF	3D FACE	3D POLY

Fig. 3.14 *Main geometric primitives provided by a CAD system.*

3D models in CAD can be presented in two ways: (*i*) a wireframe image and (*ii*) a rendered image. A wireframe is a CAD drawing, as shown in Fig. 3.15, in which the vertices and edges of all objects are displayed. Perspective rendering is a technique for presenting 3D realistic visual simulation. The amount of information generated for a rendered view can vary from a simple hidden line presentation to a photorealistic presentation that takes into account light sources and material properties.

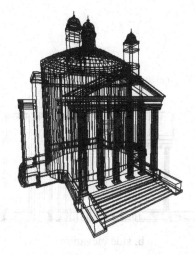 

a. 3D wireframe model   b. Rendered 3D model

Fig. 3.15 *3D CAD techniques.*

Rendered presentations of CAD models complement physical models, allowing possibilities such as seeing a photorealistic view of an interior space or a series of spaces. Each perspective is constructed from a particular viewpoint. Traditional rendering is a labor-intensive activity, thus usually it is limited to one or two perspectives, in contrast, once a 3D model is represented in the CAD system any number of perspectives can be generated, including the plan and elevations shown in Fig. 3.16.

In mechanical, electrical and electronics engineering, CAD systems are complementary part to computer-integrated manufacturing (CAM), where digital representation is used to transfer designs from collection of ideas into a final working product. Integrated CAD/CAM systems generate a process plan for the developed design, which then is executed by computer-controlled flexible manufacturing lines.

In architecture design CAD systems remained for a relatively long period of time a drafting tool for design documenting. With the introduction of 3D virtual environments (worlds), which mimic the spatial arrangements of the physical world, the role of CAD systems changed to tools for producing "buiding blocks" for these worlds. Computer-integrated implementation of design ideas is no longer a privilege of engineers – architectural designers can use CAD systems to develop 3D models of objects for designing and populating the space in virtual worlds. The 3D model of the dome in Fig. 3.15 becomes a product, the building itself, when placed in a virtual world. Consequently, the CAD system is becoming a valuable design tool for the developers of virtual design studios that use virtual worlds as underlying technology. The "manufacturing" in this case is the generation of the code, which describes the 3D object and needs to be incorporated in the repository of objects used by the virtual world. CAD systems usually create a single representation, although there might be several versions for a given design. This code then is interpreted and displayed by the rendering engine of the virtual world.

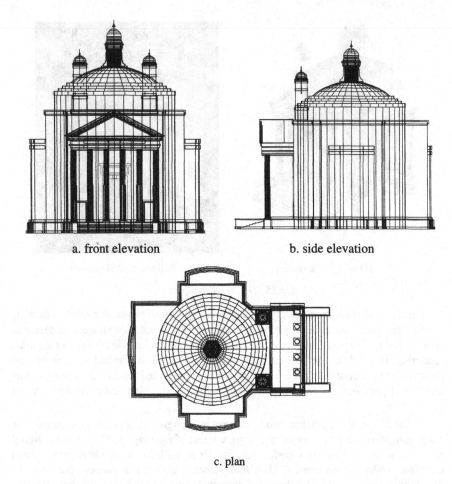

a. front elevation   b. side elevation

c. plan

Fig. 3.16 *2D CAD drawings derived from the wireframe model in Fig. 3.15.*

Fig 3.17 illustrates the various uses of a 3D model for generating different representations of the design of the electronic cottage in our virtual design studio. Each presentation emphasises particular aspects of the developed design. The generation of various views supports visual reasoning about different aspects of design developments. It is a paradox, but not everyone does favours geometric precision and accuracy of CAD drawings. In the virtual design studios, some designers tend to appreciate working with CAD systems during conceptual design, referring to quick "maturing" and reflexion of design concepts. Others find that CAD drawing does not have such stimulating effect on creativity – precise geometry tends to fix the design into particular form at an earlier stage. One way to avoid this influence is the "fuzzification" of the lines in CAD drawings, which decreases the sharp geometry and presence of CAD lines, as shown in Fig. 3.17a. Fig. 3.17c shows one of the drawbacks of CAD drawings as digital design representation – the emphasis on the form with very little attention to the semantics of design solutions.

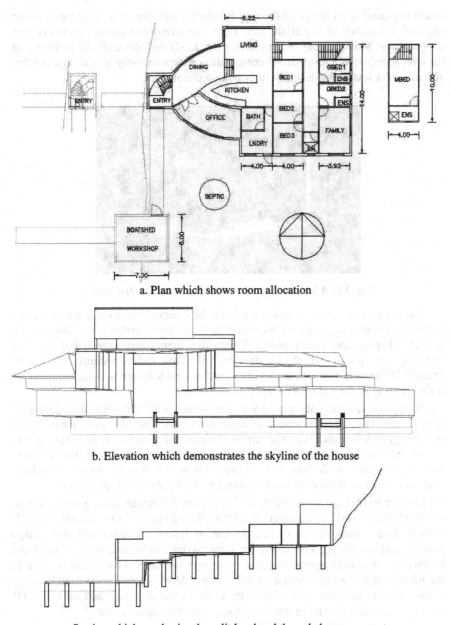

a. Plan which shows room allocation

b. Elevation which demonstrates the skyline of the house

c. Section which emphasize the split level and the pole house concept.

Fig. 3.17 *2D CAD representations of a house designed in a virtual design studio.*

Rendering, by taking into account the physical characteristics of the objects in the design, can produce a photorealistic visualisation of the 3D model. The physical characteristics include material properties, textures, colours, illumination and shadow data. An example of such a 3D model is shown in Fig. 3.18, in which the model is placed in an image of the site. Rendering simulates various aspects of the physical behaviour of materials with light, including reflectivity, radiosity and transparency. Moving from an expectation that CAD includes only 2D geometry of the envisioned design towards 3D composition serves not only as a design aid, but also as a data source for design visualisation technologies.

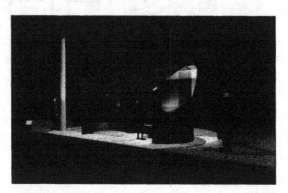

Fig. 3.18 *A bus stop from the Australian virtual design studio.*

The realism of visual simulation allows the comparative evaluation of design alternatives based not only on technical and functional criteria, but also on the aesthetic impact and user's needs. Where the clients and expected users of a building were previously shown drawings of plans and elevations, the use of realistic 3D models provides the ability to understand a design without requiring an understanding of the notation of technical drawings.

3D models are the data source for creating the walk-throughs, thus designers have the ability to explore design solutions both from "outside" and "inside". This technology is filling niches in a spectrum of fields connected with designing spaces - from architecture, through the design of game and educational environments to movie production. In design, such a facility allows the designer to go beyond the stage of documented ideas to simulate the use of their design configurations.

In order to manage complexity, CAD data can be organised as a set of layers. Although this idea of layers originated from 2D drawings, it can be applied to 3D models. In a virtual design studio, the use of layers facilitates different design professionals in sharing and editing the same model. Architects, and structural and mechanical engineers operate on their corresponding layer. Layers can be used in the traditional sense that layers are used in paper drawings, or can be used to group certain objects together. This flexibility is up to the designer, and allows CAD models to be useful for more than the production of documentation.

Object-oriented CAD systems provide the basis for linking the geometry of CAD elements with associated database fields, which specify some non-geometrical information, for instance, finishes, materials, estimates of energy consumption and expenses. This additional information is used for generating 3D "virtual reality" models from the CAD drawings. The non-geometric data can change the appearance of the component depending on whether the design is being viewed as a 2D plan or elevation or a rendered model. The extension of this association of non-geometric data for CAD objects has implications for all stages of a design, from a more complete documentation of conceptual design to include the designer's intentions, to a more complete representation of the final product for facilities management.

3.3 Text

One of the first widespread applications of computers for the majority of people outside the computer science community was word processing. We use the term "text" here to include the representation of information about a design that is primarily words, rather than primarily graphics with words as labels. Text, as a representation of design ideas, complements images and CAD by providing a representation that facilitates the creation and modification of formatted documents and annotations. Although text may appear on images and CAD drawings, the underlying representation may be a bitmap of the text rather than its corresponding *ASCII characters*. The ASCII[3] character (more precisely the character and its corresponding ASCII code) is the basic building block of text representations. An ASCII character representation allows a person to manipulate the words and numbers, format, font, and style of the document. An image of the text cannot be edited as a word, only as a graphic.

Text can be organised and stored in various formats, depending on the application used to create and process the text. Fig. 3.19 illustrates the organisation of texts. Essentially, *words*, as collections of characters and/or numbers, are the effective primitives in text processing. Further, they are grouped, referred and presented according to the application metaphor.

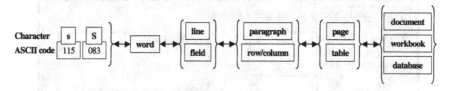

Fig. 3.19 *Text primitives and hierarchy of their organisation.*

The most well known type of text document is a word file. The simplest text editors manipulate raw ASCII files. They do not add properties to the text. Word processors are used to create and edit manuscripts in which the text has properties such as font, size, style, colour, etc., as illustrated in Fig. 3.20. In addition to characters and words, word processors operate with *lines, paragraphs* and *pages*. These are the primitives in which words are organised in the word processing model. Each of these primitives has its own model. For example, a text line can be defined as a sequence of words with spaces between them which ends with the end-of-line symbol. However, even such a simple concept as a text line has considerable diversity among different word processing applications. For example,

---

[3] ASCII stands for American Standard Code for Information Interchange.

for better formatting, some models include the concept of "soft" spaces, which can be added or taken out only by the word processor if formatting requires. Other models include unlimited line lengths. Such a variety can cause compatibility problems among the inexperienced participants in the virtual design studio.

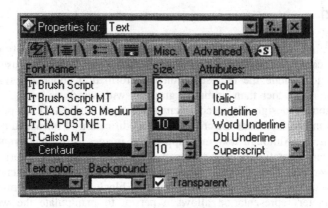

Fig. 3.20 *Some typical text properties (Lotus Word Pro).*

Further up in the hierarchy are the models of a paragraph and page. A paragraph is defined as a sequence of lines with common properties and a page is a sequence of paragraphs. Paragraph features include alignment, indentation, and spacing (see Fig. 3.21).

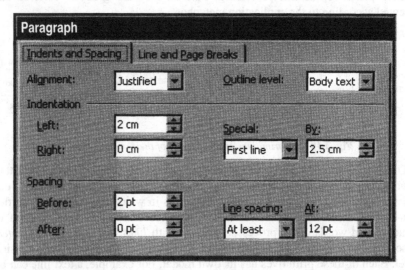

Fig. 3.21 *Properties of the paragraph model (Microsoft Word).*

The model of a page, however, differs across text applications. Word processors are usually oriented towards a hard copy output, thus a page includes a main body, headers, footers and footnotes, as illustrated in Figs 3.22 - 3.25. In contrast, the Web page model is oriented towards the screen and, in general, does not include these attributes. Although word processors can include images, the focus is typically on the format of words. Where images are included, the word processor may provide the facilities to resize the image and control the way the text flows around the image.

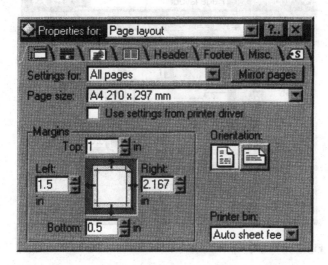

Fig. 3.22 *Page properties connected with the paper format (Lotus Word Pro).*

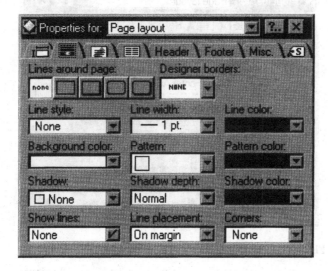

Fig. 3.23 *Page properties related to the page appearance (Lotus Word Pro).*

Similar to image processors, different word processors, although they follow similar document models, differ considerably in the file formats, which they use. Editing files created using a word processor usually requires the same application that created the file, or the transfer of the document into a standard for exchanging text. A commonly used standard is RTF[4], however it has numerous problems in preserving the original format.

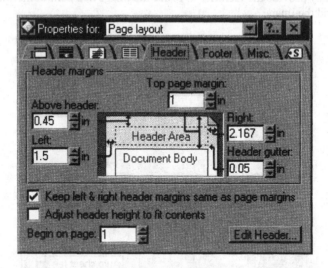

Fig. 3.24 *Page properties related to the header (Lotus Word Pro).*

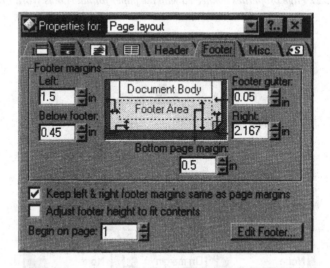

Fig. 3.25 *Page properties related to the header (Lotus Word Pro).*

Other text applications include spreadsheets, databases, and WWW page design applications. Spreadsheets are used to organise text, including words and numbers, into rows and columns, i.e. in a tabular format. Conceptually, the basic building block is the *cell* (see Fig. 3.26). Each cell has unique address for referring to its

---

[4] RTF stands for Rich Text Format.

content. The content is clearly categorised: numerical or non-numerical. Mathematical operations and functions are available for manipulating the numbers and generating various statistics. Spreadsheet processors have the capability to reorder the rows and columns, sort the content of the rows and columns given criteria such as alphabetical order or magnitude of the numbers. Several spreadsheets can be combined in a single workbook.

In a virtual design studio, a spreadsheet format provides active media for tabular data. For example, the brief analysis table in spreadsheet format, as shown in Fig. 3.26, compactly represents the design results. Column G, labelled as "Difference", calculates for each room and for the whole house the difference between the area required in the brief and the designed area.

	G6		=	=F6-D6			
	A	**B**	**C**	**D**	**E**	**F**	**G**
1			**Brief**		**Designed**		**Difference**
2	Room/Area	No	Area (m²)	Total	Area (m²)	Total	Totals
3	Reception/Foyer	1	8	8	10	10	2
4	Living	1	24	24	28	28	4
5	Dining	1	16	16	17	17	1
6	Study/Office	1	14	14	18	18	4
7	Master bedroom	1	16	16	16	16	0
8	Ensuite	1	8	8	8	8	0
9	Guest bedroom	2	8	16	8	16	0
10	Ensuite	2	4	8	4	8	0
11	Bedrooms	3	12	36	12	36	0
12	Bathroom	1	10	10	10	10	0
13	Shower	1	3	3	3	3	0
14	Kitchen	1	15	15	18	18	3
15	Family	1	10	10	14	14	4
16	Laundry	1	8	8	8	8	0
17	Garbage	1	2	2	xxxx	xxxx	#VALUE!
18	Workshop	1	8	8	8	8	0
19	Boatshed (2 dingies)	1	40	40	40	40	0
20	Plant Room	1	8	8	xxxx	xxxx	#VALUE!
21							
22	Total Room Area			250		258	8
23	Discounted Circulation (30%)			75		77	2
24	Functional Area(m2)			325		335	10

Brief analysis

Fig. 3.26 *Brief analysis in spreadsheet format.*

Note the error message in cells G17 and G20, which illustrates the categorisation of cell content: cells F17 and F20 have non-numerical content.

The table paradigm is also used also in database management systems - another form of handling text information. Databases are created using applications that specialise in the efficient storage, retrieval, and reporting of large amounts of data. Conceptually, the *table* is the basic primitive in a database. Fig. 3.27 illustrates the brief analysis table specification in a database management system. A spreadsheet is considered a simple (single-table) database with its capabilities to sort and present data.

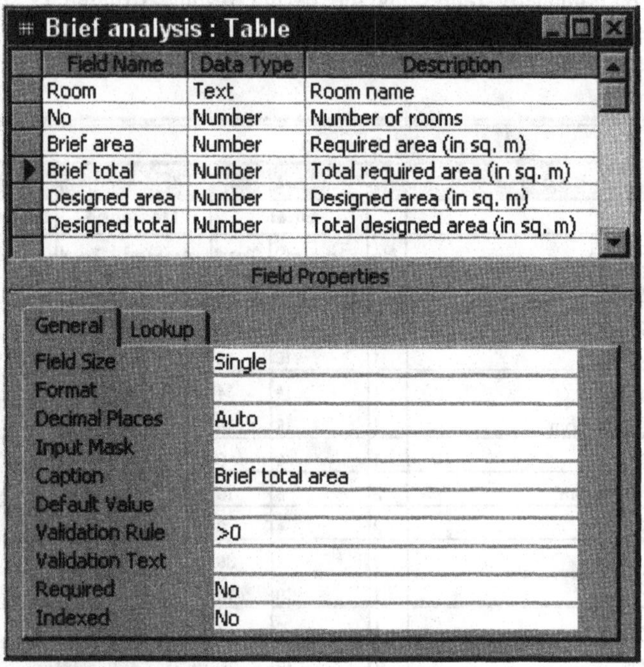

Fig. 3.27 *Brief analysis table as database definition.*

However, database tables are rarely used in this way. Usually each table represents a description of an entity from the design project. Tables are linked and organised according to some hierarchy or relations that are established between the entities. Fig. 3.28 shows the relations within a database formalisation of a design brief. In this sense, databases provide a way to represent concise information organised into tables.

Database management systems may have the capability to store and retrieve multimedia data, but the more common use is to store and retrieve words and numbers. In a design studio environment databases can be used to store the briefing data, the design description data, and the catalogue data for design products. Once formalised in table form, design information can be queried in order to retrieve relevant portions. For example, the information that we have about the difference between brief requirements and actual design, shown as part of the table in Fig.

3.28, can be retrieved by the query formulation shown in Fig. 3.29. The result of query execution is shown in Fig. 3.30.

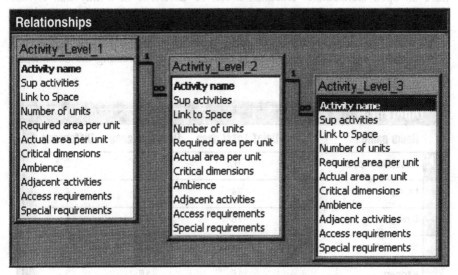

Fig. 3.28 *Relations within a database model of design brief.*

Field	Room	Brief total	Designed total	Difference: [Designed total]-[Brief total]
Table	Brief analysis	Brief analysis	Brief analysis	
Sort				
Show:	☑	☑	☑	☑
Criteria				<>0
or:				

Query formulation I Query name: **Difference**

Fig. 3.29 *Database query formulation.*

Usually databases are not used to store paragraphs of text in natural language.

Text processors have a full text retrieval function - the capability to search for combinations of key words or phrases across the entire document, spreadsheet or database. However, although dealing with text, the word, spreadsheet and database processors remain specialised applications, which means that documents, tables or databases can only be displayed and edited when open either by the application that has created the file or by a compatible application.

As part of the move toward integrated information management, considerable efforts have been taken towards development and implementation of standards for exchanging information. One of the most successful ideas is the design of *markup languages* for text description. The basic idea is to separate the content of a text document from the document structure and presentation style. Then markup information is everything in a text file that is not content. Usually this information is presented in the form of tags. Markup approach became popular after the introduction of SGML[5] a standard, which defines an overall model for the marking up of documents and provides the syntax for tag definition. Markup languages have an open architecture. Documents can be described in a way that is not dependent on any hardware, operating system or application software, which complies with the standard. Markup tags are ASCII text indicators that surround texts, textual descriptions of images, scripts or other accepted text descriptions of digital media objects. This approach is currently used in creating the documents that are stored as Web pages.

Room name	Brief total area	Designed area	Difference
Reception/Foyer	8	10	2
Living	24	28	4
Dining	16	17	1
Study/Office	14	18	4
Kitchen	15	18	3
Family	10	14	4
Total Room Area	250	258	8
Discounted Circulation (30%)	75	77	2
Functional Area(m2)	325	335	10

Record: ◄◄ ◄ [1] ► ►► ►* of 9

Fig. 3.30 *Result of query execution.*

3.4 Hypermedia

Hypermedia is a more general term for hypertext, implying that different types of media can be included in the document. This is of importance in a virtual design studio, not only due to the platform independent way of storing document formats, but because all the different design media can be included in one type of document. We focus on Web document formats because they provide a set of protocols for representing hypermedia that can be viewed on any computer hardware or software platform that recognises the standard protocol. The standards for representing hypertext on the Web include a markup language, called HTML (Hyper Text Markup Language), and a network application protocol, called HTTP (Hyper Text

---

[5] Standard Generalized Markup Language introduced in 1986 as an international standard (ISO 8879).

Transfer Protocol). The types of text on Web pages include paragraphs, lists, and tables as in word processing documents. The types of media are not restricted. As more media types are invented, standards for their representation are incorporated into the internet protocols and newer versions of HTML. Examples of media currently supported are: images, animated images, movies, sound, and virtual reality.

One aspect of hypertext and hypermedia that is not present in any of the other design media types presented in this chapter is the concept of links. Text and (multi)media become hypertext and hypermedia when a link can be created between a text, image, or other unit of media, and another document. This is done in a manner consistent with other properties of media in hypermedia, by associating tags with the media. This concept of hypermedia, that of linking information together in ways other than linear progression, distinguishes this media type from all others. Now we have the capacity to create interactive, user directed information systems in which the user determines the path through the information.

Although there are many similarities in creating a text document and a Web (or hypermedia) document, there are several principle differences:

- *Structuring*. Rather than a flat stream of characters, the text is divided by tags into discrete objects of information, placed in strict hierarchical context. Fig. 3.31 illustrates the concept of tagged text. All symbols which are part of a tag, except the standard tag delimiters "<" and ">", are coloured. The text objects are surrounded by an opening tag, e.g. "<a HREF=""> for a hypertext link and a closing tag, e. g. "</a>";

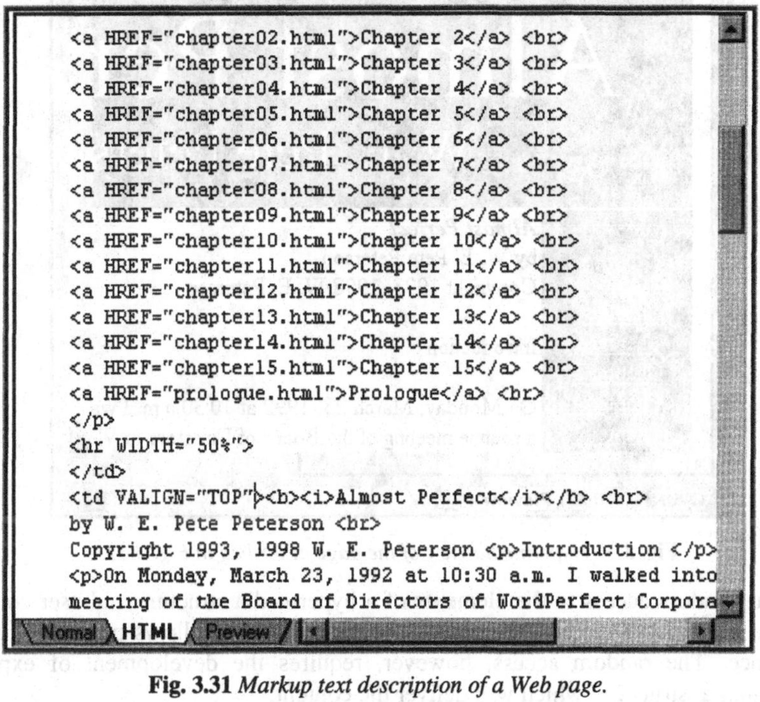

```
<a HREF="chapter02.html">Chapter 2</a> <br>
<a HREF="chapter03.html">Chapter 3</a> <br>
<a HREF="chapter04.html">Chapter 4</a> <br>
<a HREF="chapter05.html">Chapter 5</a> <br>
<a HREF="chapter06.html">Chapter 6</a> <br>
<a HREF="chapter07.html">Chapter 7</a> <br>
<a HREF="chapter08.html">Chapter 8</a> <br>
<a HREF="chapter09.html">Chapter 9</a> <br>
<a HREF="chapter10.html">Chapter 10</a> <br>
<a HREF="chapter11.html">Chapter 11</a> <br>
<a HREF="chapter12.html">Chapter 12</a> <br>
<a HREF="chapter13.html">Chapter 13</a> <br>
<a HREF="chapter14.html">Chapter 14</a> <br>
<a HREF="chapter15.html">Chapter 15</a> <br>
<a HREF="prologue.html">Prologue</a> <br>
</p>
<hr WIDTH="50%">
</td>
<td VALIGN="TOP"><b><i>Almost Perfect</i></b> <br>
by W. E. Pete Peterson <br>
Copyright 1993, 1998 W. E. Peterson <p>Introduction </p>
<p>On Monday, March 23, 1992 at 10:30 a.m. I walked into
meeting of the Board of Directors of WordPerfect Corpora
```

Normal HTML Preview

Fig. 3.31 *Markup text description of a Web page.*

- *Multiple presentations.* Text code, which complies with a markup standard, means that coded information can be represented and visualised in a variety of ways. Figs. 3.32 and 3.33 present different views on the same information. Fig. 3.32 shows the content, formatted according to the layout described by the tags. Fig. 3.33 presents only links to and from a page, visualising the logical page structure without the actual content of the pages. This view uses the information about page titles;

- *Compatibility.* The text data in a word processor file can only be seen and edited when opened in the same, or a compatible, word processor application. The text on a Web page can be seen by any Web browser and edited by any Web page design application since the format is standardised. The advantage to Web pages for transferring text information in a virtual design studio is the ease of sharing and modifying design documents;

Hyperlinks. The text in a word processor is the same as the text in a book or magazine. The reader will generally start at the beginning and proceed according to the progression of page numbers. Usually such documents have an intended order and are expected to be printed. The text on a Web page has hyperlinks, that is, certain words or collections of words are linked to other pages. The effect of this is that the text on Web pages is not linear, the reader need not start at the beginning and read in a linear progression.

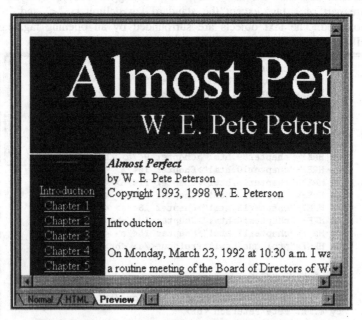

Fig. 3.32 *Hypermedia view of the page described in Fig. 3.31.*

The random access to the elements of a hypermedia structure and user control contrasts the paper media, where the information design follows particular linear sequence. The random access, however, requires the development of explicit navigational structure, which will deliver the content.

In the virtual design studio, the use of hypertext and hypermedia is not just for converting or translating word processor documents in an HTML format. Conversion takes the word processor document and transforms it to an equivalent document. The only difference is the underlying file format.

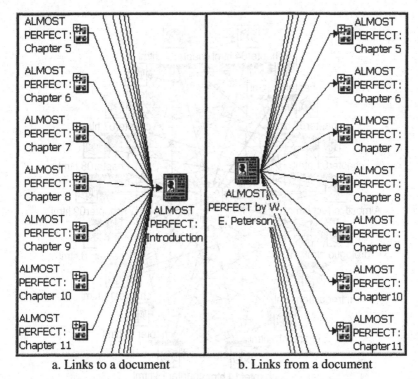

a. Links to a document   b. Links from a document

Fig. 3.33 *Selected views of the links to and from a Web page.*

By contrast, sharing information through a Web page delivery involves rethinking the information design and switching from the style of hard copy and word processing documents, where the logical structure is perceived visually by the reader, to documents, where logical structure is explicitly encoded with the appropriate use of hyperlinks. The idea of information presentation and progression needs to be reconsidered when using hypermedia, since users often get "lost" in hypermedia.

Information design is a key component of the virtual design studio – it is part of the studio design, for information sharing and documentation. The development of navigational structure means framing the content of the document. Hence, hypermedia design can be characterised as a ballance or compromise between predefined structures and in-context access to related material. The compromise results in a set of rules for organising a high-level structure, like a linear or hierarchically indexed one, which includes in-context hyperlinks within its elements. Developing a design that corresponds to the goals and content is in some sense a discovery of that unique match.

For example, the Web version of Pete Peterson's book "Almost Perfect" (1998) is an example of a hypertext, which preserves the random access style of a printed book. Each chapter (web page - html file) has links to all the other parts of the book. A visualisation of this structure is shown in Fig. 3.34.

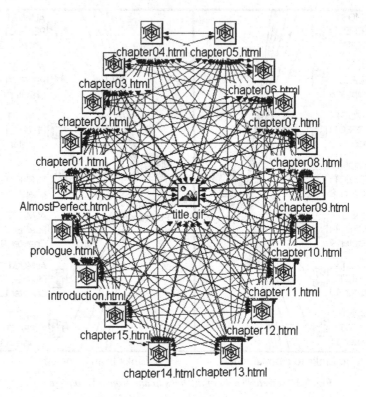

Fig 3.34 *A Random access hypertext structure.*

3.5 Summary

This chapter has focussed on the representation and technology of the digital design media that enable a virtual design studio. This technology is finally coming of age and is more common on desktop/personal computers in designers' offices. The effect of widespread use of digital design media is the ability to share and modify more easily design information as computer files. Without this technology we would still stay within the limitations of the typewriter, drawing boards and physical models when collaborating on design projects. The next chapter looks at another key component that enables virtual design studios – digital communication technologies.

References

Mitchell, W. J. (1995) *City of Bits,* Cambridge, MA, MIT Press.
Pete Peterson, 1998, Almost Perfect, http://www.fitnesoft.com/AlmostPerfect
Xanadu FAQ, 1998, http://www.aus.xanadu.com/xanadu/faq.htm

Part Two

Communication and Representation

Four

Communication in a Virtual Environment

In a VDS, communication becomes a central aspect of the design activity. Although we usually think of communication as a conversation or a memo, communication can be more broadly defined to include the explicit statement of ideas for yourself or another person to comprehend. An extreme view is that designing is communication. Designers communicate their ideas when they sketch, model, and draw during the various design phases. In a VDS, communication is primarily computer-mediated and this may have implications on the kinds of designs produced as well as the ability to progress and direct the design.

In a physical studio, communication is taken for granted. A person can discuss a particular issue by talking directly to someone in the same room. When communication and design representation are computer-mediated, this ease of informal discussion is affected by a set of communication tools. In some ways, communication is facilitated by computer-mediation. For example, the widespread availability of email has made it easier and more common to keep colleagues informed of activities, events and decisions etc. In other ways, communication is different and possibly inhibited by computer-mediation. For example, it is harder to get and keep someone's attention if you cannot walk to their drawing board and physically interrupt their work to convey an important message. However, there are distinct differences between a computer-mediated discussion and a face-to-face discussion, one of which is that (social) hierarchies tend to be less important and participation rates tend to be higher.

Communication tasks fall into two categories in a design project: managing the design process, such as scheduling meetings; and discussing and documenting design decisions, such as clarification of the brief or negotiation of different design alternatives. For both purposes - managing and designing - specific tools are used in order to maximise the use of resources, like computer power, or time spent on a specific task. Understanding the different types of tools for communication can assist in choosing the appropriate tool for each task. Computer-mediated communication can be understood in terms of the access to the information. For example, communication can be:

- An exchange of information in real time, such as a conversation or file transfer;
- Access to information at any time, where designers can store and retrieve data at any time, independently of location and other users connected.

The quality of the communication among users depends largely on the availability and suitability of communication tools. The selection of communication tools to use in a VDS can influence the ease and accessibility to the design information and the design team. It is important for the success of a VDS to select appropriate communication tools, to reduce the effort on learning how to use them, and to improve the efficiency of the whole environment. In this chapter, we look at the various types of communication tools and the implications of their use in a VDS.

4.1 Computer Mediated Communication

Computer Mediated Communication (CMC) is an area of study that investigates the communicative exchange between users in computer-based environments. CMC has become a wide field of research in the last decade, dealing primarily with Internet-based communication resources. Studies cover a wide range of topics, from collaborative aspects [among many, see (Sanderson 1996); (Sudweeks and Allbritton 1996)] to therapeutic and self-identity issues of online communities (Turkle 1995). Some of the most important findings of CMC studies are that online communities invite personality changes, collaboration, and the development of a shared, special language.

The aspect of CMC that considers the development of a community is relevant to a VDS because the ability to effectively collaborate depends on the development of a community. An important aspect of a virtual community is a sense of common interest or purpose. In "The Virtual Community", Howard Rheingold defines virtual communities as "social aggregations that emerge from the Net when enough people carry on...public discussions long enough, with sufficient human feeling, to form webs of personal relationships in cyberspace" (Rheingold 1995).

Design as a social activity is a view of designing that takes into account the social nature and content of the interaction among the people involved in the project. For example, the observation that CMC invites personality changes may explain how a member of a design team is shy and reserved in a face-to-face meeting but is outspoken in a CMC exchange. Recent research in CMC that helps identify the considerations for effective communication in a VDS includes:

- Cooperation and collaboration;
- Differences and similarities between face-to-face and computer-mediated interaction (Condon 1993);
- Register change and development (Cherny and Weise 1996);
- Agreement, consensus, and group activities (Jessop and Valacich 1993); (Lebie, Rhoades and McGrath 1996).

Collaboration and cooperation are important issues for a virtual design studio. Collaboration implies that the members of the design team share a common goal. Cooperation, although a similar phenomenon, implies only that the design team work together. Experience shows that computer-mediated communication does not inhibit collaboration or cooperation, in fact, CMC encourages collaboration by providing support for communication across long distances. Choosing the most effective tools for the people and the project can limit the frustration of using inappropriate technologies and have the benefit of increasing the amount of communication so that collaboration is facilitated. This requires an analysis of the skills of the people involved, the hardware and software available, and the kind of information that will be shared.

The differences and similarities between face-to-face and computer-mediated communication provide insight into the effective use of CMC tools. For example, whether a meeting is face-to-face or computer-mediated, there is an initial socialising phase. Allowing time and providing information about individuals so this socialisation can occur can make a computer-mediated meeting more effective. A difference between the two types of communication is the lack of body language and gestures in CMC. This lack is sometimes compensated for by the use of special characters to communicate facial expressions or the use of capital letters to get attention (commonly thought of as yelling in CMC). Assuming that design is a social activity, it is important to recognise the differences and similarities so they can be accommodated and the social activity can proceed in the new environment.

Register change and development occurs through an extended use of CMC. As virtual design studios become more common and the use of CMC for designing becomes an established mode of collaboration, we would expect to see some changes in the language used to communicate design ideas. Now we rely on spoken language, sketches, and documentation to convey design ideas. In most cases, we rely on the presence of the designer to explain the design even when models, drawings, and sketches are available. The use of CMC may introduce a new set of symbols, words, and icons to communicate design ideas.

Research in agreement, consensus and group activities has led to the development of tools to facilitate collaboration. These tools can mimic the face-to-face negotiation techniques by providing online access to arguments for and against a particular decision with facilities for voting or just presenting views in a decision making meeting. This area of research looks at the basic issues in groups working together and how CMC can facilitate decision making. This aspect of CMC may simply be used passively as the tools are introduced to the design environment, or more actively in using the results of the research to influence the way that design teams make decisions.

4.2 Communication Tools

Communication tools in the context of a VDS comprise the software and hardware that makes communication possible across distances using networked computers. Although communication tools have been used with the intent to facilitate communication across distances, they also provide a means to share data in files of different format. Communication tools in a VDS provide the means for sharing information across a wide spectrum of activities. For example, these tools are used to:

- Contact other members of the design team;
- Pursue ideas on the development of the design;
- Exchange and access archived information;
- Present ideas to others connected to the design brief (e.g. the client);

- Keep records of the development of the design (e.g. by a design journal).

In general, only when a task is enhanced and facilitated by the use of a communication tool, can that tool be considered successful in the environment. Appropriate feedback and observations on the use of tools are helpful to encourage users to develop appropriate skills, and to modify the environment according to the users' needs.

The access and exchange of information over computer networks can be executed in two ways:
1. synchronously, and
2. asynchronously.

A synchronous exchange of information requires that users are present at the same time, on the same "channel" of communication (for example, videoconference, chat channel, or shared sketching board). In an asynchronous environment, users do not need to rely on the presence of others to access the information they need (for example, databases, web pages, bulletin board). Both kinds of communication are important for a VDS. Designers need to have real time feedback and to access data archived in a common database.

The following table highlights some of the communication tools used in a virtual design studio. The type of software is the generic term used to refer to a class of software. The type of information refers to the type of data transferred on the network.

4.2.1 Asynchronous Tools: Email, List Servers, Bulletin Boards

Asynchronous tools allow flexibility in the access of information and sending messages. Users can choose when to access the messages and files and can respond when they have time. There are various software packages that provide similar functions. The choice of which software to use depends on factors such as hardware and network configurations as well as the various features provided. Here we give a general description of asynchronous communication tools that we have used in a VDS and which we found to be successful in enhancing the ability to share design information.

Table 4.1. *Communication software*

Type of software	Type of information	Type of communication
Email	text, data files	asynchronous
List serves	text, data files	asynchronous
Bulletin boards	text, data files	asynchronous
Talk, chat	text	synchronous
Broadcast	video, audio	synchronous
Video Conference	video, audio, images, text	synchronous

Fig. 4.1 illustrates the idea of computer-mediated asynchronous communication. The user sends, stores, retrieves, and reads files and messages. Although the user is ultimately communicating with another person, the interfaces

provide utilities for communicating with network locations, files and directories, invoking various formats, plug-ins and applications. In essence, the user is interacting with the software to put information in a certain location on the network. As we will see later, this is conceptually different to synchronous communication, where the user is communicating more directly with another person.

Fig. 4.1 *A scenario of computer-mediated asynchronous communication in VDS.*

In asynchronous communication, the action at the different studio sites usually takes place at different time. For example, in Fig. 4.1, a message sent on Tuesday can be read on Friday, and a project group in one of the nodes can have an informal discussion on Saturday night, while leaving computers to download required documents and put another document on the server. If this was Saturday night on the West Coast of the United States, then a designer in the Australian part of the virtual design studio is most likely to retrieve that document on Monday morning. The synchronisation in this communication mode is very loose - communicated information is processed on demand. Consequently, the time and bandwidth requirements are relatively low. Thus, during the time between sending/saving and reading/retrieving, the information has to be stored in some location(s) on the net. The location usually has to be specified during the set-up of the virtual design studio.

Email

Email allows users to send and receive messages in an electronic mailbox. Users send messages by typing text in an email composer window, as they would type a letter, putting it in an envelope (specify the email address of the recipient) and sending it. An email message can have several components: a text message similar to a letter or memo; file attachments such as image files, word processor files, CAD files, or animation files; and quotes from previous messages. Email has become a common form of communication, typically used for sending short, informal messages, URLs and attached files. In a VDS, it is important to understand all the capabilities of email so that its use can extend beyond short messages to include a means for sharing files and sending more extensive information directly to a person's mailbox

Fig. 4.2 shows a typical composition window for preparing a new email message. The top part of the window allows the user to specify:

- Who the mail goes to;
- Who it is from;
- The subject of the message;
- The people who will receive copies (Bcc is a blind copy where the recipient does not see the person copied);
- The files that are attached to the message.

The bottom part of the window contains the message itself. This is where the user types the text to be sent and may include quotes from other messages. Once the message is finished it can be sent immediately or put in a queue. In a virtual design studio, the second mode is preferable for "batch" processing of large volumes of outgoing messages and attached files.

Advanced email clients also allow users to embed multimedia applications in their messages. Many of these clients are transforming email into a more extended and comprehensive tool that can be accessed by any other application running on the same computer. Recent highly integrated office suites, like Microsoft Office, Lotus SmartSuite and Corel Office provide email functionality accessible from each of the office applications, supporting asynchronous communications without leaving the application environment.

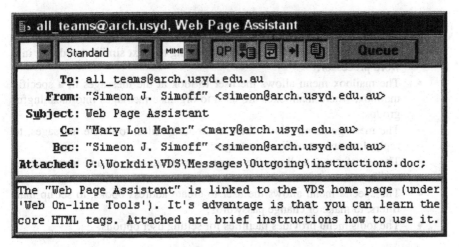

Fig. 4.2 *Composition window for an email message (Copyright QUALCOMM Inc.).*

To be able to send and read email worldwide a person needs to have an *account* on a system connected to the Internet. The account could be opened on the employee (university, commercial organisation, architecture design studio or building company) host, on an internet service provider host and/or on a website, which provides free email accounts. Opening an account means getting a mailbox (a directory on the host system) and an email address. Then email can be read and sent with specialised email client software like Eudora[1], built-in email clients in web communication suites (e.g. Netscape or Internet Explorer), or through a web interface provided at the sites of free email providers[2]. Participants in a virtual design studio can set up their office email account to redirect received messages to a web-accessible free email account while travelling. Email can also be retrieved using a specific host, which is not the original user mailbox address, via a Web browser, extending the access to one's own mailbox to virtually any platform connected to the Internet.

Email programs have many features to assist the user in managing their email correspondence. Some of these features are:

- Automatically checking for incoming mail at specified intervals;
- Notifying the user when a new message has arrived;
- Notifying the user when a sent message has been received and when it has been read;
- Filtering messages according their size, sender, or subject;
- Storing messages in different mailboxes.

According to the email software used, various options are available when reading and composing new messages. Fig. 4.3 shows the interface of one of the most common email programs, Eudora. The menu items reflect the type of things you can do with the program.

---

[1] http://www.eudora.com.
[2] e.g. http://www.hotmail.com, http://mail.yahoo.com, http://www.mymail.com.

- The file menu allows the user to open and close other text files, to send and check email, to print email files, and to quit the program;
- The edit menu provides facilities for editing the text similar to editing in a word processor;
- The mailbox menu allows the user to look at the messages in a specific mailbox, where mailboxes are used to organise messages into meaningful groups;
- The message menu allows the user to attach files, to delete messages, to reply, forward, or redirect messages;
- The transfer menu allows the user to move messages to and from various mailboxes;
- The special menu allows the user to create address books, to set up mail filters, to make or change passwords;
- The tools menu provides facilities for setting user options.

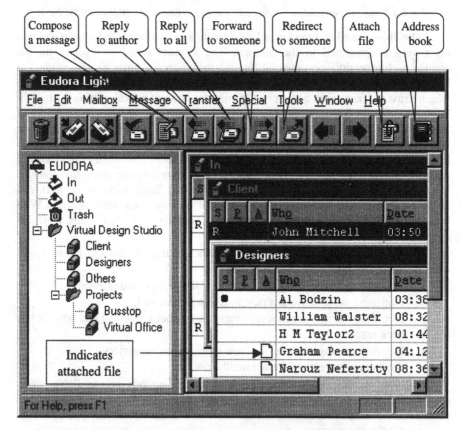

Fig. 4.3 *The interface of the Eudora Pro email client (Copyright QUALCOMM Inc.).*

Email clients provide remarkable flexibility for message communication. However, for handling discussions and decision making the email alone may not be able to provide sufficient support in a virtual design studio. In such cases, dedicated tools like list servers and bulletin boards come into consideration.

The recent popular use of email has resulted in a large amount of correspondence that previously may have been done by phone call or casual conversation (or, in some cases, the communication may not have happened at all). With the increasing use of email for communication, the management capabilities of email programs are essential for effective email correspondence.

Compared to fax transmissions and to postal mail systems, email has the advantage of reaching the recipient quickly and effectively. Not being related to a specific geographic location of the recipient, an email message can be sent from anywhere, and read from any computer connected to the Internet.

In a VDS, the exchange of computer files is a useful feature of email. For example, a design report can be sent among VDS members for its revision and approval; drawings can be easily exchanged to be completed by the different members of the design team; discussions can be carried forward by several participants at once. Whereas previously a file was moved from one computer to another using a file transfer program, now people tend to use email to send files from one part of the network to another as well as to inform a specific person of the content of the file.

As a point-to-point kind of messaging, email provides reasonable privacy and confidentiality. Specific encryption options allow users to exchange any kind of information with restrictions, in case messages are intercepted. This aspect may become especially important when the information exchanged is classified.

List Servers

We refer to software that facilitates the development, maintenance, and use of a list of email addresses of people with a common interest as list servers. This type of software works in a manner similar to sending an email message. LISTSERV[3] is a commonly used example of this type of software. Software similar to LISTSERV is "Majordomo"[4]. LISTSERV is an email distribution software, for electronic mailing lists, that contains a list of users subscribed to that list. Each time a message is sent to the list server, it is forwarded to all the members of the list. Members have the capacity to automatically subscribe and unsubscribe, by simply sending a message to the automated administrator. Sometimes, the messages sent to the list are first checked by a moderator and then forwarded to all the other members.

An advantage of using this distribution software is that communication reaches users interested in the same issues rapidly and effectively by putting the message directly in their emailboxes. Moreover, the list is automatically updated when users join or abandon the list. For users familiar with email-like tools, list servers can be used easily.

---

[3] http://www.listserv.net/listserv.stm.
[4] http://www.majordomo.net.

One of the potential disadvantages of this tool is that all the users on the list get all the messages. If the list server is not moderated, there is a possibility that it will be used incorrectly, with unwanted, long, or repetitive messages (also called "spamming").

In a VDS, a list server would be useful in setting up a virtual organisation or VDS team. The list might distribute discussions of "know-how" and "state-of-the-art" design solutions, which project participants would like to protect. On the other hand, the issues discussed on the list may be too narrow and not interesting to the general audience. In this case, it is preferable to run the list in the so-called *closed* mode. Fig. 4.4 illustrates the subscription procedure to a "closed" project-oriented list in a VDS, based on the Majordomo list server. Messages 1 and 4 on the "left-hand" subscriber side constitute the usual email "dialog" in a LISTSERV subscription scenario.

The major difference for closed lists is the manual approval of subscription (the "right-hand" side in Fig. 4.4) required for each individual subscription. Initially, each member of the team would be added to the project list of email addresses in the list server. As the members of the team changed, the members could subscribe or unsubscribe to the list server. Regular correspondence about the project, changes made to the brief or documentation, and information on meetings could be sent to all interested people in a manner similar to sending one email message.

Another feature, which list servers support, is organisation memory. Through archiving the messages a list server presents discussion tracks, although it keeps it in a *linear* fashion. The archiving, however, provides a handy new feature - generating digests from the messages received by the list server for a specified time interval. For example, a designer who is away or on a slow connection or just does not have a steady Internet connection, can log in with the email client once a week. Retrieving all messages sent to the list in a digest format means that s/he will get the studio issues in one single message, without mixing them with other email messages in the mailbox.

Bulletin Boards

A bulletin board allows participants to post and read messages written by others, through a board-like messaging system. Initially, bulletin boards were used by special interest groups to carry on discussions on various topics of common interest, whereas now bulletin boards are also used in professional settings. As a community building tool, bulletin board users discuss their interests, learn each other's personalities, make friends, and make enemies. New users, coming into the community for the first time, learn the community's rules, priorities, and dynamics, as would someone who moves into a new neighbourhood in real life. If the administrator does not alter the content of the bulletin board then the board offers a complimentary tracking of community development.

The procedure for contributing to a bulletin board is similar to email, where a user sends messages to an email address which corresponds to the address of the bulletin board. A specific program processes the messages, sorting them by various selected keys, and displays them in the format requested by a reader.

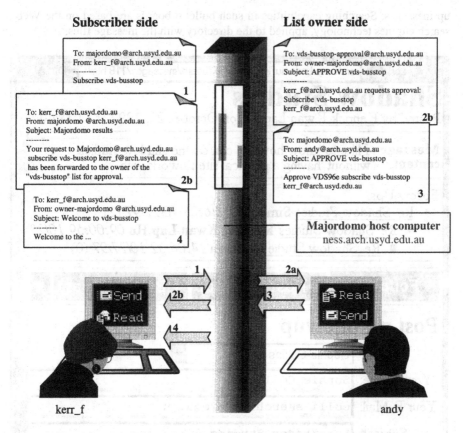

Fig. 4.4 *"Closed" lists require "approval of subscription" by the list owner.*

The major difference between a bulletin board and a list server is that the message sent to a list server is sent directly to each user's emailbox whereas a message sent to a bulletin board is viewed by the users when they go to a specific place on the internet. Thus, a person does not need to have an email account to be able to participate in the "life" on the bulletin board. The advantage of the bulletin board is that messages do not get mixed up with all the other email messages that a person receives and therefore the messages can be seen as a coherent group representing an asynchronous discussion. At a glance, readers can keep track of discussions and access old messages that are kept on the bulletin board.

The minimum functionality of a bulletin board includes posting messages, displaying the list of posted messages, reading messages and posting follow-ups to particular messages. Fig. 4.5 shows a bulletin board interface implemented as a Web page[5]. Each message is stored as an HTML file (note the end of the URL fragment in Fig. 4.5), thus it can include URLs, images and links to other Web pages. The file also incorporates the form description necessary for posting follow-

---

[5] The bulletin board program is based on Matt Wright's WWWBoard script
http://www.worldwidemart.com/scripts/wwwboard.shtml.

up messages. Searching capabilities in such bulletin boards are based on the Web search engines technology, applied to the directory with the message files.

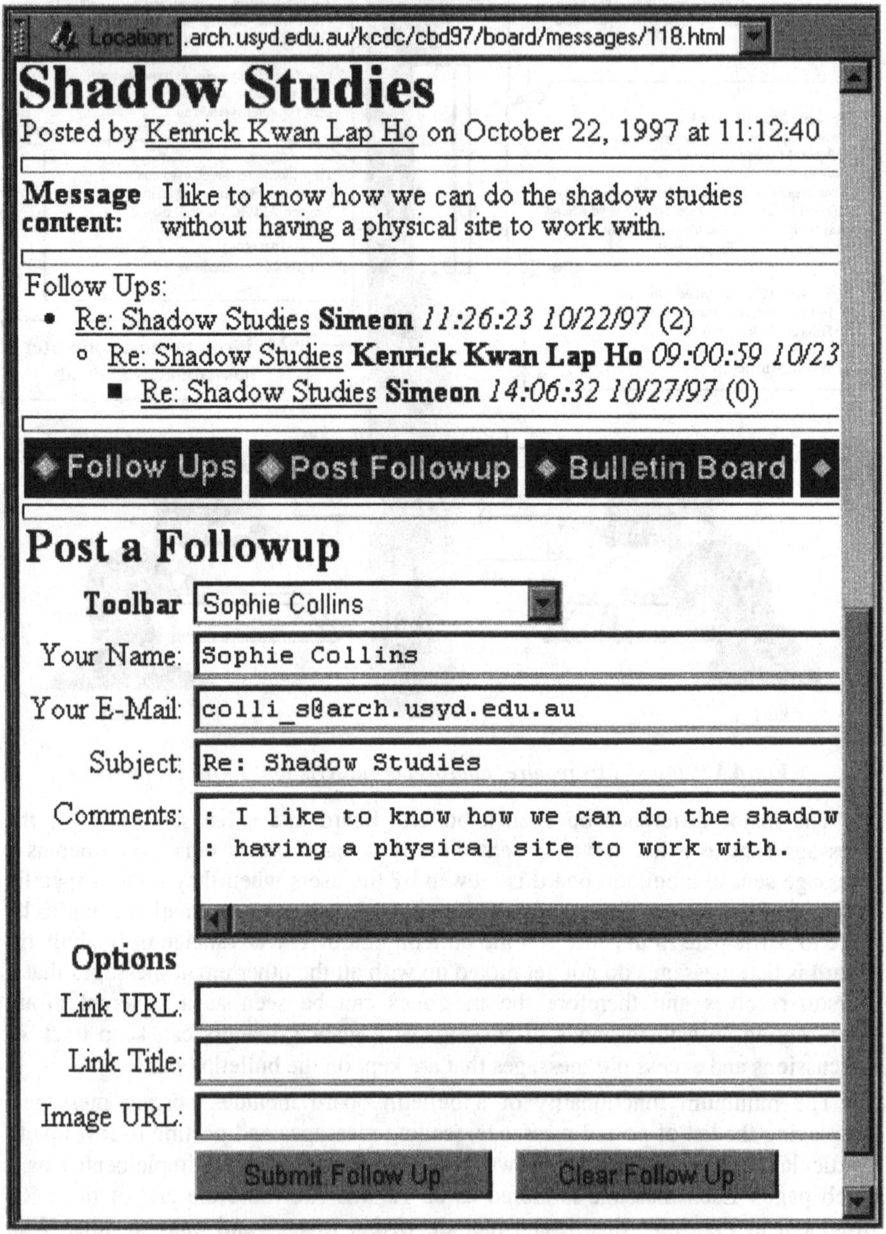

Fig. 4.5 *An example of a bulletin board system, which utilises the core of Web technology.*

Hypermail[6] is a tool which combines mailing list and bulletin board functionality. Email messages sent to the bulletin board email address are sent to individuals on a list and then converted to HTML and placed on a Web page with threaded discussion capabilities.

A bulletin board is basically a database of threaded messages that can be accessed by those with access rights. Fig. 4.6 shows an example of such a bulletin board - the WebCT bulletin board tool. Usually, such tools are part of "full-bodied" courseware or groupware client/server suites. This means that to have access to such a bulletin board tool one needs to have the appropriate access rights to the server. This, and similar tools, offer powerful message handling functionality, shown in the left frame in Fig. 4.6, based on the log in and history information about the user. Thus, the board can limit the display only to the unread messages, or to a particular thread. Messages can be searched, sorted by particular criteria and even compiled in a form similar to the digest format in list servers.

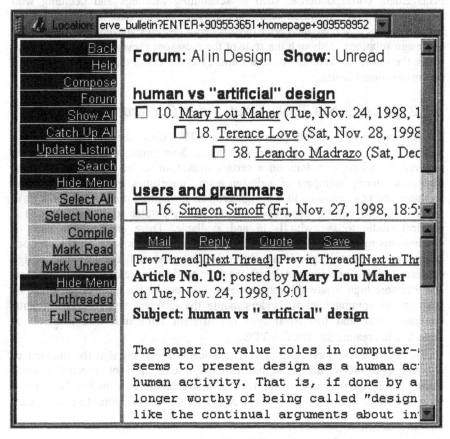

Fig. 4.6 *An example of a bulletin board system with rich functionality.*

---

[6] http://lune.server.csc.liv.ac.uk/.

Many packages for collaborative work include bulletin board systems as a tool. WebCT[7], FirstClass[8], and Lotus Learning Space are examples of courseware which include software for managing bulletin board systems. FirstClass also offers the possibility to exchange files and have "drop zones" where users can leave their files for others to retrieve. Bulletin board functionality is slightly changed in the eRoom[9] project space, where a relatively simple message board tool is combined with a voting tool. Proxicom Forum[10] and Caucus[11] are examples of sophisticated stand alone bulletin board systems. In the latter one, a discussion thread can be forced to an end by locking the board on that topic.

In a VDS, a bulletin board can be used to record the information and correspondence related to a specific project. For a firm that has several projects at a time, a different bulletin board could be used to capture the information exchanged for each project.

In our experience, students in a VDS tended to use the bulletin board for management correspondence, such as scheduling meetings and deciding who would be working on which tasks or clarifying design issues. Protected team bulletin boards also contained brief threads about design solutions and discussions on design solutions. Although the style of the messages remained similar to email, where the sentences were short and informal, the content of the messages focussed on organisational issues.

4.2.2 Synchronous Tools: Chat, Video Conference, Broadcast

Synchronous tools are indispensable in a VDS, since they allow immediate feedback from members of the design team. Sometimes, prompt feedback is required for taking decisions on a certain matter, or to have an open informal discussion among members of a design team. Sometimes, on line collaboration produces the key solutions in a design project. By using synchronous tools, it is possible to see who is connected and available, similar to looking around a physical studio to see who is in and available. There are various types of synchronous tools, each assuming a certain amount of bandwidth in the network connection and each providing different channels and features for design communication. Choosing a tool with the most realistic sense of physical presence, and therefore high bandwidth requirements, may not be the most efficient use of this type of communication. Understanding the different types of synchronous communication and the advantages of different communication channels is important to creating an effective VDS.

Fig. 4.7 illustrates synchronous communication, showing that the interaction, although computer-mediated, is between individuals and not directed towards storing a message on the network. This scenario demonstrates the two basic types of synchronous communication - via dedicated server and point-to-point mode.

---

[7] http://www.webct.com/webct.

[8] http://www.firstclass.com.

[9] http://www.wridge.com/.

[10] http://www.proxicom.com/products/forum.

[11] http://www.screenporch.com.

The action takes place at the same time, although partners could be in different time zones.

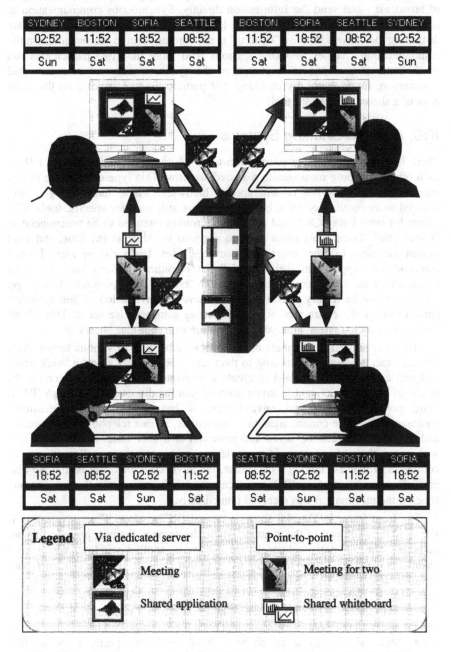

Fig. 4.7 *A scenario of computer-mediated synchronous communication in a VDS.*

In synchronous communication, users do not need to refer to a central database to exchange information: they connect point-to-point or point-to-many - in a form of broadcast - and send the information directly. Synchronous communication is generally not mediated, unless someone is in charge of interrupting users who are disturbing the conversation by "booting" them, forcing them to disconnect from the communication channel. Working sessions with more than two participants run much better if someone is in charge of the synchronisation of communicated information, for example, by checking that participants are working on the same page of a shared whiteboard tool.

IRC, ICQ and Chatting Systems

There is a collection of communication tools which allow individuals to talk to each other by typing messages to a shared window. This type of software is low bandwidth and does not require special hardware. These tools are generally referred to as *chatting systems*, but acronyms are still used for specific tools. IRC stands for Inter Relay Chat, and ICQ is an acronym intended to be pronounced as "I seek you". These tools allow users to see who is online at any time, and send instant messages to other users, and exchange files. Users can be alerted when someone who appears in their "buddy" list is online, making sure that their messages are delivered successfully. Although "talking" by typing tales time to get used to, it can be a very effective way to have a conversation. When typing, a person can see the entire sentence before letting someone else see it. This allows the opportunity to review what you "say" before everyone else "hears" it.

IRC is organised in channels of discussion, according to various topics. New channels can be created, according to the users' needs. Users select a "nickname" and join a pre-existing channel or create a new one. It is possible to control the access to each channel, and to invite users to join the discussion. Although IRC is more popular as a social environment, it has potential for professional communication. The communication is immediate, as in a telephone conversation, and the discussion can be saved and reviewed at a later time. A "conversation" with more than one person is possible, as in a conference call, without the confusion of who is "talking". Of course, the advantages of being online are also part of communicating in IRC, users can send information via the internet and check if the information was received immediately.

The front frame in Fig. 4.8 shows a typical IRC window. The conversation is shown in the main part of the window, where the name of the user precedes his/her message. The alternative channels are shown in another window, where each channel is identified by the topic discussed in that channel. IRC uses the metaphor of radio, where different channels run different conversations and the messages in each channel are broadcast to all connected users. Unlike chatting in a virtual world environment, when IRC is not running on a user's computer, the messages and the users do not exist in the sense that once the messages are broadcast they are gone. More similar to a telephone call, there is no permanency to IRC environments, they are only relevant when a person is connected to a particular broadcast.

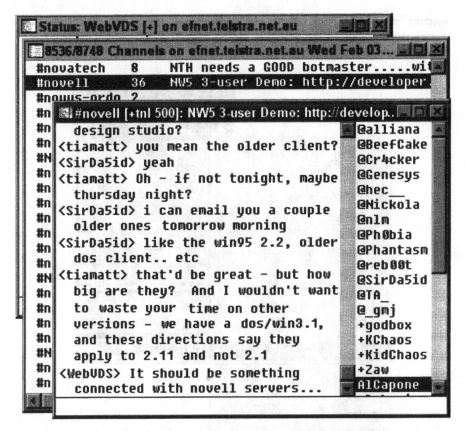

Fig. 4.8 *Major work windows of an IRC client.*

ICQ[12] is an example of a point-to-point communication tool, which refers to a main dispatching server that contains all the names of ICQ users. Unlike IRC, ICQ can initiate contact with a user that may not have a chat window open. In this sense, ICQ is like calling someone to have a conversation rather than joining a conversation in a particular chat window. ICQ also allows multiple chat windows, postings to multiple users, and file exchanges.

Fig. 4.9 illustrates the windows in an ICQ system. The user has a pull down menu that allows him to communicate asynchronously, using his local email client or sending files or web addresses, or to communicate synchronously, allowing him to be available to others running ICQ. Each user maintains a list of people he communicates with. The windows on the right side of Fig. 4.9 show whether the people in the list are online or offline, away from their computer, or temporarily unavailable. Other chatting systems, such as Java-based online chatting windows embedded in Web pages, or paging systems can be used[13]. External communication

---

[12] http://www.mirabilis.com
[13] For example: http://www.worldvillage.com/wv/cha/html/javachat.htm, or http://pager.yahoo.com/pager

systems are useful for integrated environments, which do not have that communication facility, for example, adding an embedded private chat window to 3D environment with public chat facilities.

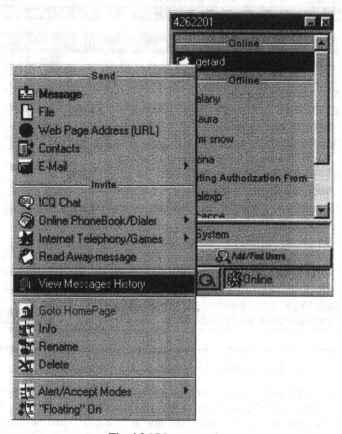

Fig. 4.9 *ICQ menu options.*

Other tools not specifically designed to be chatting systems can include a synchronous chatting interface. For example, video conference software, like CU-See Me, has a chatting facility that allows multiple users to type messages to each other. The unreliability of audio or video sources is compensated for by the capacity to communicate with other users in different communication channels.

Video Conference

Video conference tools allow video and audio contact between users: they can see each other with a good approximation of real time video stream while talking. This stream occupies a large bandwidth and often users need to be on a fast network to achieve acceptable connections. Video conference software running via the Internet suffers from the lack of adequate bandwidth. Although video seems to be a valuable addition to a design session, it is often used only at the beginning of the session, and then abandoned because of a focus on the design model. However, when the tool is used as the basic source of contact between the parties, for example in a negotiation process where the parties need to have immediate feedback on some issues, video must be reliable and of good quality.

Fig. 4.10 shows a snapshot of a video conference session. The left side of the window contains the video image of the users in the video conference. The right side of the window shows a shared drawing board. Not all video conference software includes a shared drawing board. We illustrate Inperson[14], below, because we find that for design meetings a shared drawing board is essential. The menus of the video conference software are indicative of the functions available.

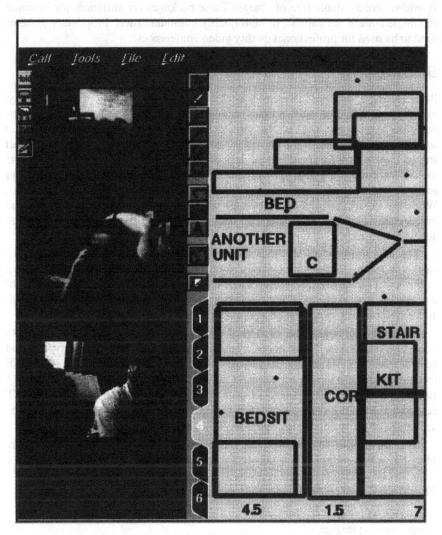

Fig. 4.10 *A snapshot from InPerson videoconference software.*

---

[14] Trademark Silicon Graphics.

The "Call" menu allows a user to initiate a call, join an existing session, or to invite someone to join the session. The tools menu allows the user to select from an array of tools, which control the call, audio, video and network properties. The file menu allows the user to save the session as a file, to import another file etc. Files that can be imported include image files, 3D models, and VRML files. These capabilities assist in a design meeting by allowing the users to collaboratively view and comment on design representations in various formats.

There are free video conference packages available on the Web. Some have counterparts that are commercial and cost money, others do not. CU-See-Me[15], which runs on Mac OS and Windows, and Microsoft NetMeeting[16], which runs on Windows, are available free of charge. These packages are sufficient for informal meetings, but are not capable of high quality communication. Proprietary systems need to be used for professional quality video conferences.

Broadcast

Broadcasting a session is in many ways different from a video conference. Firstly, broadcasting is a one way action: an audience will get the broadcast on their computer screen, but will not be able to interact with the content. However, in some broadcasting software packages, like MBONE[17], it is possible to select shared tools which do not affect the broadcast itself, but simply allow participants to talk or draw on a shared whiteboard. Secondly, broadcasting has different software and network requirements for who receives and who sends the broadcast. While the broadcaster needs a powerful machine, a good and stable network and appropriate software, the "audience" only needs a small software application to access the broadcast.

Fig. 4.11 shows a test MBONE session. The whiteboard, with its drawing tools, can be shared by all the participants. Only one user is broadcasting video, as shown in the small video window. Other windows are updated with the current status of the session, the names of the participants, and other network information. Text, audio, and chatting windows are also available.

Broadcast technology has been used for a variety of purposes, many similar to television broadcasts. News items, training sessions, and lectures are typical and current uses of broadcast technology. For an educational VDS, MBONE technology could be used, for example, to broadcast lectures to a wide number of students, geographically located in near or distant areas. Alternatively, MBONE could be used to deliver a presentation to a group of people on a network, with the advantage of using only a small portion of bandwidth belonging to the audience.

The broadcaster supports the full weight of the video and audio transmission. MBONE was developed in a university environment for use within universities. Commercial quality broadcast software is now available, for example PlaceWare[18]. PlaceWare is used professionally for training and seminars.

---

[15] http://www.wpine.com.

[16] http://www.microsoft.com/netmeeting.

[17] http://www.mbone.com.

[18] http://www.placeware.com.

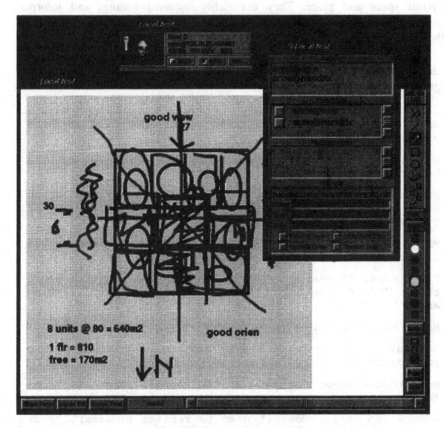

Fig. 4.11 *Snaphot from MBONE.*

4.3 Virtual Worlds

The concept of a virtual world (VW) is relevant to the VDS because the same software environments that support VWs provide support for the participants in a VDS. VWs and virtual communities originated because people found they related to others regardless of whether they shared a geographic community.

VWs are supported by software that allows multiple user connections (usually accessible via the Internet), and manages databases. Users connect to these worlds using their software clients to engage in various activities: chatting, building, playing games, and holding business meetings. VWs are places where users go and talk to others, in real time, or where they perform other activities that do not require real time interaction, such as building things, personalising the space, publishing a community newsletter.

We refer to a VW as an inherently collaborative computer environment that provides facilities for navigation around virtual places and actions by the participants, as well as communication. Generally, VWs use a metaphor of physical space and place. They use richly-described settings and informal communication styles to create the illusion of "being there", in the company of other people.

VWs are used for social, educational, and professional reasons. An example of a discussion in the Virtual Campus at the University of Sydney[19] is shown in Figure 4.12.

```
Mary says, "What did you think about the City of Bits
vision? (anyone?)"

sam says, "it appears futuristic and yet is what is
happening now"

anmore says, "i enjoyed it , but in particular the notion
of a bozxo filter, the discussion with Virillio and the
general language level-casual"

Maria say, "the language is really base too me too much Sci
fi wording not really appropriate"

Fyock says, "I really liked it too, it made me think about
things I do on the computer and net but don't really think
about""

Maria say, "But thinking is so important!!"

Des says, "can computer truely replace paper and face to
face contact?!"

Mary thinks maybe the computer can augment paper and face-
face contact

anmore [to Des,]: does it need to replace necessarily, or
run simultaneously?
```

Fig. 4.12 *Conversation in a text-based virtual world.*

The widespread use of communications software has created new kinds of communities. The effect of this is a reconsideration of how we work together, in contrast to the effect it has had on how we relate to each other informally in VWs. The concept of a VDS can be built upon the experience and successes of VWs. The communications software described here generally provides environments in which sharing is maximised and security is minimised. How these environments will translate into the design profession is yet to be seen. The potential is clearly positive, reducing travel and the cost of sharing information and access to expertise.

The use of VWs as collaborative environments is quite recent compared to the other popular tools. VWs are now mixed types of environments that support both kinds of the communication seen above. As asynchronous tools, VWs can be used to store documents, create and access archives, and drop files for everyone's use.

---

[19] http://www.arch.usyd.edu.au:7778.

As synchronous tools, they allow users to talk to each other in real time, participate in meetings and discussions, follow presentations, and interact with other objects in the environment (for example, slide projectors, or blackboards). The biggest strength of VWs is their support of both synchronous and asynchronous activities.

Users can build the environment for their personal use, own a personal space to put objects - for example, personal documents - and hold private meetings. Ultimately, the sense of community created within VWs by virtue of their constructive aspect has positive effects on familiarity and collaboration among its citizens.

VWs can largely be characterised in two categories: graphical and text-based. We present both types here, and emphasise the use of text-based VWs because they can be the basis for both types.

Graphical VWs rely mostly on the representation of the environment, how the environment can be accessed, and they dedicate a certain effort to designing an interface that facilitates interactions between users and environment. An example of a graphical VW is shown in Fig. 4.13. The 3D world mimics the physical world in such a strong way that the user immediately sees what is available in the VW. The menus and other icons provide functionality beyond seeing and moving around the VW.

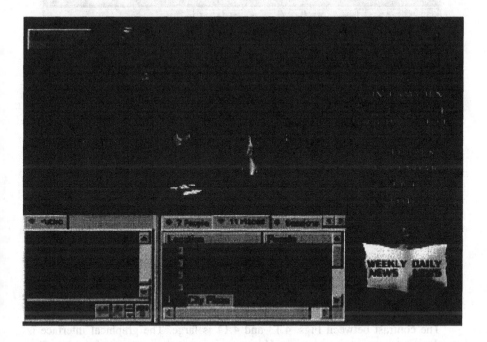

Fig. 4.13 *Interface to blaxxun Colony City.*

VWs based on graphical representations are widely used to support VDSs. The visualisation of the VW, usually with 3D means and objects, seems to be important for the useability of that VW. In this case, the reproduction of physical properties within the VW becomes the design focus. When planning the design of a VW, it has to be taken into consideration that some graphical aspects might concern users. For example, "seeing" a map of the VW, or the objects around, might be of primary importance to some users. Understanding users' and tasks' needs before planning a graphical VW could be time and effort saving.

Text-based VWs are usually represented by narrative descriptions, even if the use of icons and pictograms is diffused. The representation of text-based VWs is not the focus of the world design, neither is the modality of interaction between users and environment, and users among themselves. In text-based VWs, the interface problem is secondary to the quality of re/actions among the elements of the world. Re/actions are generally defined following a metaphor of reference for the whole environment.

At a first glance, text-based virtual environments seem to be extremely limited, and restricted to a typed/read linguistic interface only. Fig. 4.14 shows a text description of the Main Hall in the Virtual Campus as an example of a text-based virtual world.

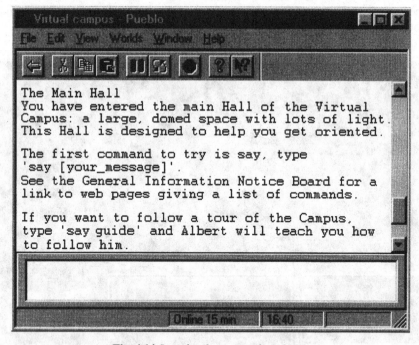

Fig. 4.14 *Snapshot from a text-based VW.*

The contrast between Figs. 4.13 and 4.14 is large. The graphical interface is much more appealing to a novice. However, it is not the richness of the interface that makes the environment more interesting. Even though we observe electronic communication increasingly, including sound, graphics, animation, and video, VWs show a complexity in the construction, use, and relationships among users, which has little to do with new standards and protocols for exchanging data. The language foundation is independent of the interface. The linguistic structure of text-based VWs can be the basis for the VW and a graphical interface can be built on top. For example, integration with web based interfaces[20] facilitates the use of the text-based software.

Choosing a metaphor for the VW is essential to establish and maintain a coherence of the environment. For example, in a university type of environment we expect to have a similar set of activities and places to a "real" university: lectures, courses, learning materials, offices, faculties and libraries. Users understand the use of spaces in the VW by virtue of their names (for example, conference room, library, meeting room).

VWs can be used in a VDS as meeting places and as repositories of information related to that VDS. Designers leave their documents, drawings, notes, and slides in their personal rooms. They can decide to share them with others, or to keep them private.

VWs are becoming important tools for creating collaborative environments. Designers approach them as places, where they interact with others on a design task. Certain flexibility in the design of the environment is also essential for adapting to new requirements, for example, the need to share a specific tool or the creation of new design instruments.

Designers are supported in a VW when they:

* Meet, brainstorm, discuss a specific issue;
* Sketch;
* Exchange, archive, and retrieve information;
* Design new tools that support activities in that same or similar VW.

4.3.1 Communication in a Text-Based VW

Communication in a text-based VW can be either synchronous or asynchronous. The asynchronous communication is achieved by mail very similar to email, or by leaving messages on notepads and blackboards in a specific office or meeting room. Synchronous communication is one of the main attractions of a VW, since it provides a place inhabited by other people who can react immediately to what is said and done in the VW. Synchronous communication in a text-based VW is more rich and complicated than communicating with IRC. IRC allows only direct communication: we type some words, and the other people in the room with us see those words on their screen. When people are in the same physical place, they communicate as much with tone of voice, body language and facial expressions as with the words they utter. We are so good at interpreting these cues that we often do it unconsciously, and their loss is noticeable: it is hard to tell when someone is joking when you cannot hear their tone of voice. Communication commands in text-based VWs attempt to make up for the loss of these secondary forms of communication.

---

[20] for example, the BioGate system, http://bioinfo.weizmann.ac.il/BioMOO/BioGate.

The most basic communication command in a text-based VW is "say." The user types "say" followed by whatever he wants to say, and everyone in the room then "hears" what he has said. For example, if a character named "Gottfried" types:

```
say how do I get to Mary's office?

everyone else in the room will see on their screen:

Gottfried says, "how do I get to Mary's office?"
```

Using the "say" command is not much different from talking on IRC.

Another basic communication command in a text-based VW is "emote," which allows users to represent non-verbal communication. The user types the command followed by a phrase or sentence; and everyone in the room sees the character's name followed by that phrase. For example, if Gottfried types:

```
emote looks serious.

        everyone else in the room will see:

Gottfried looks serious.
```

The emote command allows users' reactions to each other's words and actions to appear much more natural. Basically, all communication in a room is broadcast to all people in the room. There are some commands to overcome this broadcasting default. The "whisper" command allows a person to whisper to another person so that only the person being whispered to can see the message. The "page" command allows a person to specify a message for another person delivered, regardless of their location in the VW. The "to" command allows a message in a room to be directed specifically to one person, allowing the speaker to respond directly. With these commands, talking with someone in a text-based VW becomes a richer activity.

4.3.2 Navigation in Text-Based VW

Text-based VWs not only create an environment in which one is communicating with people physically present; it also creates the sense of being in a physical place. In text-based VWs, as in the graphical VWs, users are situated in a whole virtual environment. Text-based VWs are made up of many rooms, through which users can move. Rooms are the fundamental building block of most text-based VWs. A user is presented with the room description whenever she enters a room.

In addition to the description, the user sees where he can go to from this room and who and what are in the room. Users can move from one room to another by typing the name of the exit. For example, from the Main Hall of the Virtual

Campus[21], it is possible to go to the classrooms by typing the word "classrooms". This is the most direct form of navigation and it mimics the way we move around physical space, that is, we walk through doors between rooms, halls, and circulation spaces. After typing the command, a new room description would appear on one's computer screen, describing the classrooms. One benefit of this kind of navigation for VWs is that people may run into each other as they wander through the rooms, just as in a physical building.

A second method of moving from room to room in a text-based VW is teleportation. This method is made possible by the spatial nature of the VW. Teleportation is widely believed to be physically impossible, but the laws of physics place no such restrictions on virtual teleportation. Teleporting from one room to another in a VW means "jumping" directly from place to place, without passing through all the intervening rooms. There are two standard ways of doing this. Firstly, by specifying the name of the room one wishes to teleport to, by entering a command such as "@go to The Hall". This command will take the user from his/her current location, and move him/her to the room called "The Hall". After typing the command, the description of the hall will appear on the user's screen. The other way to teleport is to "join" another user currently in the VW, by entering a command such as "@join Waldorf". This command will move the user to the room Waldorf is in, wherever that may be. Special ways of controlling teleportation can stop users from joining others, for example during a private meeting, or accessing rooms which are not public.

4.3.3 Actions in a Text-Based VW

Users do not just interact with each other in a virtual environment; they can also manipulate and change the environment itself. There is a wide variety of things that one may "do" in a text-based VW. These things are the results of entity manipulation, by the VW designers. One may smoke cigarettes (and not get cancer!), record a lecture on a virtual tape recorder, or write a message on a message pad. It is important to distinguish actions from non-verbal communication using the "emote" command, which we discussed above. Using the "emote" command simply causes a message to be displayed on other users' screens. If Wilma types "emote picks an apple and eats it", others will see the sentence "Wilma picks an apple and eats it", but there is no apple (not even a virtual one) which she eats. However, there might be a consequence of her eating an apple, for example, she might get more "strength", which gives her the ability to move faster in the VW.

Actions involve the manipulation of objects existing in the virtual environment. If Fred creates a virtual drawing table, complete with facilities for drawing straight lines and translating from one format to another, then Wilma will be able to take the drawing table and move it to her office. She may look at it and see a description of it (just as she sees a description of the room when she enters it), and make use of whatever functions Fred gave the drawing board. Activities performed in VWs can be similar to activities performed in real life. The kind of activity is usually related

---

[21] http://www.arch.usyd.edu.au:7778.

to the metaphors used to represent virtual objects. For example, one can sit on chairs but not on a blackboard.

The creation of objects, or entities, which become part of a user's property is another important aspect of VWs. New entities can be created starting from existing ones, by "cloning" them. To start with, the new object will inherit all the features of the "parent" object. Then, it can be modified according to users' needs.

Users may create objects that remain in the virtual environment, whether or not the objects' owners are present in the VW. For example, a user can create a personal office and place notes or books for others to access when s/he is not there. Skilled programmers can create quite sophisticated objects, such as a robot-like object that can answer questions and make conversation, or a projector with a slide carousel that can be displayed to everyone in the same room.

4.4 Use of Communication Tools in a VDS

Communication tools can be used for any aspect of a VDS. In this section, we present how the various tools have been used in our experience with educational studios and propose how they can be used in a professional setting. The decisions regarding which aspects of a studio to support with communication tools depends on the specific goals of the educational VDS and the needs of the participants in a professional VDS.

The VDS environment is enriched and refined by the participants' interactions. One difference between a physical and virtual design studio is the possibility to modify the environment quickly and effectively, according to the needs of the situation. For example, if client and designer are meeting privately, they need a set of specific tools that can be accessed privately by only these two participants. If a meeting is scheduled for multiple participants, participants may bring the tools into the meeting room- e.g. a shared whiteboard where they have previously taken notes - that they are going to use for that meeting.

Communication tools can be adapted in accordance to the information shared: text, graphics, sound or mixed media. In a VDS, participants help to define what is needed for better interactions. In some VDSs, it might not be necessary to introduce a wide range of different media, rather it might be an advantage to focus on only a few, reaching a high level of skills on a small number of tools. In this way, participants can cope more easily with inevitable technical difficulties.

The purpose of communication tools within a VDS is to make the exchange of information more effective, by speed, access, and useability. Whenever the exchange becomes difficult, or particularly slow, communication tools should be re-evaluated for the tasks for which they are needed, and eventually modified.

In Table 4.2, we show the variety of functions of communication tools in an educational VDS. Both teachers and students use communication tools to interact with the learning environment, for exchanging, archiving and retrieving information. In professional VDSs, communication tools can be used by the designer, client, producer, and supplier as shown in Table 4.3[22].

---

[22]see also Fig. 1, Chapter 1.

Table 4.2. *Use of communication tools in an educational VDS.*

From	Teacher	Student
To		
Teacher	To organise the course material and activities	To give lectures, tutorials, deliver information, crit sessions
Student	To ask for help, get course information	To exchange information regarding the course, meet, brainstorm, discuss

Table 4.3. *Use of communication tools in a professional VDS.*

From	Designer	Client	Producer
To			
Designer	To discuss the design, follow the various stages of the design process	To establish the brief, discuss issues related to the design presentations	To establish and manage the construction process, to send documentation
Supplier	To select materials to be used in the construction	To discuss and agree on selected materials	To manage construction materials

4.4.1 Effective Use of Communication Tools in a VDS

Very often, participants approach a VDS with little knowledge of the communication tools and procedures on how to make contact with other VDS participants. Training and briefing is necessary to cover topics regarding communication issues soon after the studio project starts, in order to allow all participants to reach a certain level of skill and knowledge. At the beginning of the studio, participants may experience a level of frustration that needs to be understood, and dealt with as soon as it appears. Through use and experience, rather than extensive training, VDS participants are able to use all the available tools with reasonable confidence.

The most common problems encountered in VDSs regarding the use of communication tools are:

- Difficulty in understanding the use of the tool;
- Limited accessibility (e.g. only from certain platforms);
- Difficulty in finding or delivering the information required;
- Technical problems while using the tool;
- Scarce support on the tool features.

Ways of addressing these problems are:

- Adequate support with online manuals, with pertinent examples of tasks that need to be performed within the VDS;
- Adequate support and contact with technical staff and other participants;
- The possibility to choose between various tools if one fails to be technically efficient;

- Specific training and updating on tools;
- Adequate maintenance of the VDS environment.

Participants should also be invited to re-think their way of communicating ideas. For example, learn how to sketch effectively using a computer-based shared whiteboard or to scan sketches into the computer-based drawing system.

4.4.2 Alternative Communication Channels

Allowing participants flexibility in the use of communication tools is important for the success of a VDS. Here, we consider some alternatives with respect to different communication channels. When choosing a particular tool for communication, the extremes are to assume that all channels are needed for effective communication, or to assume that one communication channel can serve all needs. When considering the alternatives it is important to know how the different communication channels facilitate different communication needs. Some of the communication channels and their alternatives for computer mediation are presented below.

Talking = communicating in natural language with other users. This can be achieved by talking directly in a microphone, typing on a keyboard, typing on a shared whiteboard and sending text messages in the form of email or web pages. Talking into a microphone assumes the use of a tool such as video conferencing or an internet telephone. This kind of communication is spontaneous and can facilitate discussions in which ideas are quickly presented. Typing on a keyboard still assumes a talking-like communication since natural language is used, but it provides a very different kind of communication exchange. Typing allows the person to review and edit the information being exchanged in a way that is not possible when talking using an audio connection. Typing also allows communication exchanges to be reviewed after the fact, where audio communication is generally lost. In general, talk using an audio tool tends to be more spontaneous and typing tends to be more thoughtful.

Collaborative sketching/drawing = drawing on the same "paper" following a design brief. A drawing can be exchanged between participants in the form of a file, or the same drawing can be jointly edited using software that allows multiple access by users. Drawing tools are embedded in this shared software, which simulates a CAD system or a similar sketching board. Computer-mediated sketching can be both extremely useful and very frustrating. Sketching is useful because it allows the communication of concepts that are difficult to articulate with words. Sketching can be frustrating because the sophistication of the tool being used can hinder the process with complexity or impoverish the communication process due to a lack of facilities, such as a scale or grid. Many of the sketching tools associated with video conferences or shared drawing board tools are much simpler than CAD systems, and have proven to be frustrating when designers need to express size and scale. Using a CAD system as a shared drawing tool is possible technically but, again, may not be the right tool due to the complexity of the user interface and the time needed to share the software in real time. In general, a synchronous communication exchange should use a sketching tool on top of a

CAD drawing and asynchronous communication should use CAD drawings as the shared documentation.

Seeing others = seeing an image that represents participants. This is possible with video conference software in which the image is live, that is, the person is in a video screen that refreshes at speeds that provide full motion. This communication channel is effective in conveying facial expressions, and if the video screen and image is large enough, can convey gestures. Often this type of communication is not necessary if the meeting is concerned with a particular aspect of the design, since people tend to look at the drawings and models rather than at each other. However, it is useful when the meeting moves onto more social interaction. An alternative to full motion video is to provide a still image of the participants, that is either static like a photograph, or updated occasionally when needed. The hardware and software requirements for this channel of communication are high, so the use of this channel needs to be justified.

Listening = access a reproduction of what is being, or has been, said. Similar to reading, communication can come through text channels (e.g. with transcribing systems that convert voice into text and vice versa), files or reading on the screen (e.g. in a chat window or on a shared whiteboard), exchanging text in various forms, like email and similar messaging systems. This type of communication is often overlooked, but is an important aspect of a VDS.

4.5 Summary

Communication in a networked environment depends entirely on the tools that enable various types of communication. We take for granted the immediacy of communicating when the people interacting are in the same physical place. We have learned to take for granted the ease of talking to someone on the phone or leaving a written message or voice mail. We are still learning how to use computer-mediated communication effectively. The explosion of alternatives and technologies can cause us to withdraw and rely on familiar forms of communication, or to use the new technologies eagerly and without concern for their effective use.

This chapter outlines the different types of computer-mediated communication and illustrates them with specific tools. In all cases, the communication tool is described in terms of its effectiveness in collaboration and design. An effective use of computer-mediated communication requires a careful consideration of the type of communication needed, the hardware and software platforms available, the speed of network connection, and the skills of the people communicating. This does not mean that every instance of communication needs to be deliberate, but that there should be guidelines for the effective use of communication tools. This chapter presents the basics of the technologies available and outlines the considerations in their effective use.

References

Cherny, L. and Weise, E. R., Eds. (1996) *Wired Women: Gender and New Realities in Cyberspace*, Seal Press.

Condon, C. (1993) The computer won't let me: Cooperation, conflict and the ownership of information *in* S. Easterbrook *CSCW: Cooperation or Conflict?* London, Springer-Verlag: 171-185.

Jessop, L. M. and Valacich, J. S., Eds. (1993) *Group Support Systems: New Perspectives*, New York, Macmillan.

Lebie, L., Rhoades, J. and McGrath, J. (1996) Interaction process in computer-mediated and face to face groups, *CSWC* 4(2-3): 127-142.

Rheingold, H. (1995) *The Virtual Community*, Harper Perrenial, NewYork.

Sanderson, D. (1996) Cooperative and collaborative computer mediated research *in* T. M. Harrison and T. D. Stephen, *Computer, Networking and Scholarly Communication in the 21st Century University..* New York, SUNY Press, pp. 95-114.

Sudweeks, F. and Allbritton, M. (1996) Working together apart: Communication and collaboration in a networked group, *7th Australasian Conference of Information Systems (ACIS96)*, Tasmania, Department of Computer Science, University of Tasmania.

Turkle, S. (1995) Life on the Screen Identity in the Age of Internet, Simon & Schuster.

Five

Shared Representation in a VDS

Shared representation is a key component in the functioning of a virtual design studio. Design is highly information intensive, where the shared information includes passive documents such as information contained in handbooks, standards, and regulations; and dynamic documents such as information in the design requirements and brief, drawings, and subcontractor's documents. Designers use a variety of information sources to augment their knowledge and creativity in order to comprehend, elaborate and evaluate the design alternatives that emerge during the design process. We view collaborative design development in a virtual design studio as a process of collaborative construction of *individual and shared understanding* and a mapping of this understanding onto a *shared design representation*.

In a virtual design studio, there is a reflective relationship between collaborative design as a social activity that produces new information and the explicit representation of that information. The shared representation accommodates and provides a means for sharing the contribution of each participant. In order to do this effectively, consideration needs to be given to the structure and content of the representation. We suggest that the structure be based on a hypermedia model of information and the content be based on an agreed upon ontology of the domain.

5.1. The Roles of Shared Representation

Design theorist Donald Schoen has made several attempts to reveal the implicit relations between the cognitive aspects of the design process and the design representation. In his pioneering work, "The reflective practitioner: How professionals think in action", he depicts the design process as a "reflective conversation" between the designer and the design situation (Schoen, D. A. 1983) Chapter 3). Schoen describes each design step as a situation, in which the designer creates or modifies design representations, and the situation responds back to the designer, exposing the consequences of the design activities. The designer interprets these activities and their results to understand the reflection of the new situation, and then represents the corresponding changes. Representation produces understanding through interpretation. During this "reflective conversation", the design evolves through repeated cycles of representing and interpreting the design situation. Kliensuasser, as cited by (Leslie, H. G. 1996)), has a similar view of the design as a "process of commitment and response that continues until the designer's conscience is satisfied". Extrapolating these views, we can say that the *driving force in a computer-mediated design process is the dynamic interaction between the designer and the design representation*, rather than a pre-defined algorithm for finding the resultant design. This idea is illustrated in Fig. 5.1.

Such an understanding of design assigns an *active role* to the design representation, making it a "live" participant in the design process. Later, Schoen (1995) adds the idea that designers use design representations as a canvas to create a virtual "design world". Design representation, like a mirror, allows the designer to see ideas that before existed only as insights. Reflecting these visions enables new understandings of the design problem, which did not exist before constructing the representation. For these reasons, the shared representation of design in a virtual design studio must be a dynamic document, able to change in content and structure as the design project progresses.

Fig. 5.1 *The "reflective conversation" with design representation.*

In a virtual design studio, there is a strong sense of collaboration, where the various participants either actively work together on the same task, or rely on the information generated by others in order to develop their own contribution to the project. In any collaborative activity, the development of shared understanding is a necessary condition for successful completion. In the design of complex systems, this shared understanding is critical to the success of the project. When there are several tasks, each one done by a different person, there is less need for shared understanding of each task. However, there is a need to have a shared understanding of the whole design problem.

We extend the metaphor of "reflective conversation" to collaborative design to be able to accommodate both individual and collaborative activity. We consider shared representation as a *representation form capable of handling and reflecting individual and shared understandings*. The idea of shared understanding in a VDS is illustrated in Fig. 5.2: through a cycle of individual representation and interpretation of a shared representation, the collaborators develop a shared understanding. The conversation is effectively between the individual and shared representations.

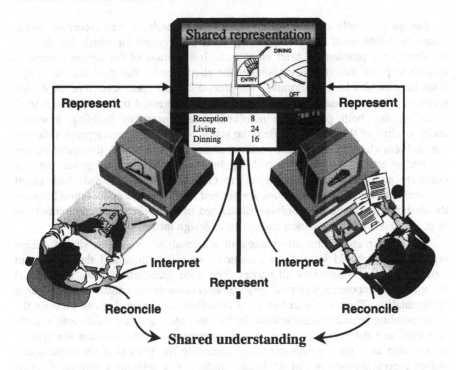

Fig. 5.2 *The role of shared representation in collaborative design.*

In the case of a lack of shared understanding each participant remains within the limits of his own interaction with the shared design representation, indicated by outer "represent/interpret" loops. Consequently, shared representation reflects a collection of individual understandings.

Shared representation is a necessary, but not sufficient condition for the development of shared understanding. The art of shared understanding requires the development of mutual understanding between the designers and the ability to compromise in the decision making. In this case the interaction follows the "interpret/reconcile/represent" path, contributing to the development of shared understanding, and shared representation reflects the development of the shared understanding.

The development of a shared representation of design information needs to address issues related to the structure and content of the design information, and, in order for sharing to occur, a special consideration for the presentation of the information to the participants. The structure of the information has to do with the way the information is organised and retrieved as a computer representation. The content of the information has to do with the aggregation of the elements of the design as an explicit representation of objects and properties as well as drawings and models.

Design is usually categorised as an ill-defined problem, i.e. according to the recursive definition of Fisher and Reeves (1992) a problem for which defining the problem is the problem. A brief view at the initial stage of the design process is enough to prove this statement. Neither the client nor the designer nor the design team have an idea how to formulate the precise or final specification of the design problem. Usually initial design requirements are expressed in terms of high level concepts, and both parties are involved in a process of building a shared understanding of the problem. Often, the act of building a shared representation of the problem changes significant portions of the problem. Thus, designers do not "derive" an artifact (for example, building, landscape, bus stop, and guitar) out of a complete and precise description of the client's problem. Instead, both client requirements and possible solutions are defined in an iterative cooperation between the designer and the client. Solving ill-defined problems requires communication of problem domain information and dynamic design information.

For these reasons, the information in a virtual design studio shared design representation should be able to accommodate information and descriptions in terms and styles adopted by all parties. The wide spectrum of tasks in a virtual design studio imposes a variety of requirements towards the construction of shared representation. There is no unified view or universal schema that can produce the corresponding shared representation. In this section, we discuss different aspects that influence the construction of shared representation. We consider the type of information associated with design and formulate the principles for constructing shared representations in virtual design studios. The principles address the two components of a shared representation: structure and content.

Table 5.1 *Considerations in constructing a shared representation.*

Dynamic information	Working on a design project, designers usually need to find and retrieve a substantial amount of information relevant to the project. Once found, the relevant information needs to be made accessible to the other participants. The shared representation should be able to expand as the project progresses and relevant external information should be linked to the reason the information was retrieved.
Active media	Traditional media and materials used by designers for constructing shared representations (for example, paper, pencil, markers and glue are the materials for the architectural designers) are passive. Though they allow us to express different aspects of the design they leave to the designer the responsibility for checking for violations of design constraints. A shared representation in the virtual design studio can incorporate related design constraints or direct connection to the electronic information source with these principles.
Common models	The development of a shared representation in virtual design studios begins with the design or selection of the underlying information model. The different design domains have different information models that approximate each domain. The key challenge in constructing shared representations is the understanding of design domain semantics. Identifying a

	common model as a starting point for a project can provide a framework for linking information and for changing the model later in the process.
Transparency	Shared representation should allow designers to concentrate on the content rather than the form in which they specify the design information. On the other hand, the information needs to follow some shared conventions in order to be understandable to all participants. Therefore, a shared representation needs to be balanced between transparency for the content of the input and opacity for the structure of the input.
Domain orientation	A shared representation should be domain oriented. Conformity to this principle allows designers to interact with the actual design domain rather than with general computer representations. The use of templates in an electronic document is a direct implementation of this principle. Communication among designers is facilitated by a shared representation that models the basic abstractions of the corresponding design domain, thereby tuning the semantics of different computer representations to the specific domain.
Consistency	The design delivery in virtual design studios, both at intermediate and final stages, is an active presentation of that part of the shared representation that is relevant to a current need of the designer. As the design evolves, the knowledge and information connected with it are increasing. Thus, a shared representation should maintain some consistency and keep track of these temporal changes.
Evolving approximations	Shared representation does not completely duplicate the designers' understanding - whether a collection of individual or shared understandings. We consider shared representations to be constantly evolving approximations of the design as a result of the changes in understanding that they inspire.
Consistent interfaces	The interface for the access to different elements of the shared representation should follow a consistent metaphor, regardless of whether the technological support of the virtual design studio is based on a unified integrated environment or on a collection of applications.

5.2. Structuring Shared Representations as Hypermedia

The first virtual design studios were developed as educational environments, where Web technology was used for information sharing and communication. At that time, the design of hypermedia representation was an artisan activity and resultant representations differed with respect to individual designer's creativity and experience with Web technology. The shared representation itself was a collection of individual representations, inheriting the positive and negative aspects of each representation.

The general idea that stands behind such a distributed shared representation is pictured in Fig. 5.3. In addition to the individual designs, the shared representation includes archived messages and a collection of related materials and links, which constitute the electronic library of the project.

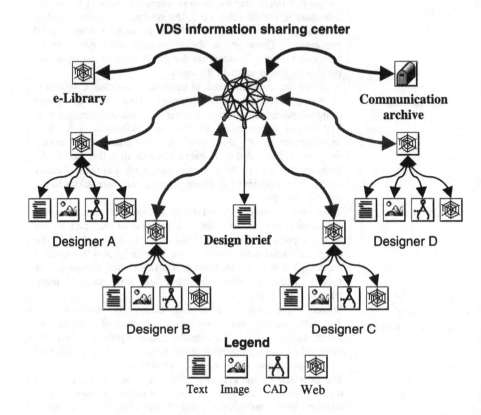

Fig. 5.3 *Hypermedia shared representation.*

The shared representation of design information used in these early studios was mainly visual, including images from photos and sketches, CAD drawings and snapshots of video conference whiteboards. The organisation of the information was adhoc, developed by individuals with little thought to the impact on shared understanding.

Fig. 5.4 shows an example of the use of images and text in a hypermedia document developed in a virtual design studio. Images are used for a variety of purposes:

- Illustrations of design precedents that designers consider relevant to the understanding of their own designs;
- Representations of sketches for the early stages of design development;
- Photographs of the site;
- Digitised plans, elevations, and perspective drawings when they were originally drawn on paper.

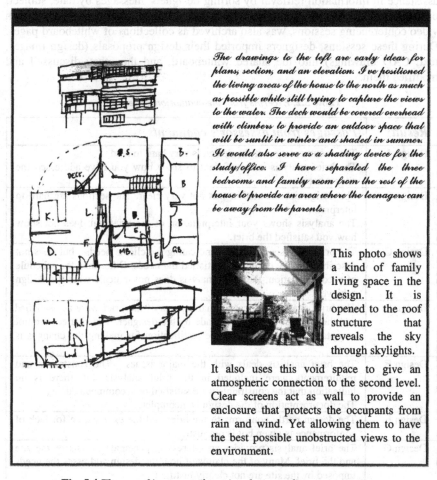

The drawings to the left are early ideas for plans, section, and an elevation. I've positioned the living areas of the house to the north as much as possible while still trying to capture the views to the water. The deck would be covered overhead with climbers to provide an outdoor space that will be sunlit in winter and shaded in summer. It would also serve as a shading device for the study/office. I have separated the three bedrooms and family room from the rest of the house to provide an area where the teenagers can be away from the parents.

This photo shows a kind of family living space in the design. It is opened to the roof structure that reveals the sky through skylights.

It also uses this void space to give an atmospheric connection to the second level. Clear screens act as wall to provide an enclosure that protects the occupants from rain and wind. Yet allowing them to have the best possible unobstructed views to the environment.

Fig. 5.4 *The use of images and text in a hypermedia representation.*

CAD drawings represented the design development. In the case of team work, designers needed group access to the CAD drawings. In the case of individual projects, even with a common brief, designers did not need to collaborate with each other to develop the design further. Therefore, they could choose to develop their designs using hand drawings or CAD drawings.

Designers who used text to give an interpretation to their images achieved better results in communicating their ideas and intents associated with their designs. Designers who put an emphasis entirely on visual perception relied on the viewers' interpretation of the design. Some comments on the documentation by the client are shown in Table 5.2.

Documented communication was also part of the shared representation. Asynchronous communication in the early Web-mediated studios was text-based, using email with an automatic archiving facility. Thus, the communication archive was accessible for all designers. Early communication archives provided limited assistance in information retrieval by sorting designers' messages by date, subject, or the person who sent the message. Synchronous communication, realised through video conferencing sessions, was also archived as collections of whiteboard pages. During these sessions, designers imported their design proposals (design images, text, CAD drawings) into the shared whiteboard, and then they discussed and modified them.

Table 5.2. *Excerpts from the evaluation of designs.*

Result	*Passages from assessor's comments*
Design A	The documentation of the design is very hard to read ... The brief analysis is insufficient to show how you have addressed the clients needs.
Design B	The design documentation was not very clear. The sections are hard to interpret... The analysis shows your interpretation of the brief but does not show how you satisfied the brief.
Design C	The brief analysis is factual - indicating the clients needs - but does not describe how the design has satisfied the needs. Other than the schedule of accommodation, the brief analysis does not indicate what the design achieves.
Design D	The brief analysis indicates what aspects of the brief were not satisfied and the changes to the brief made by the designer. The changes are not acceptable to the client and the justification for making the changes is weak.
Design E	The brief analysis deals with the major issues... The constraints and requirements were included in the brief analysis, but there is no indication that the constraints were satisfied or accommodated. The documentation of the design is incomplete.
Design F	The design partly conforms to the brief and the explanation for lack of conformance is given but is not justifiable.
Design G	The brief analysis provides an interesting personal analysis of the site and the brief. Many of the claims of how the design addresses the needs imposed by the site are not clearly justified. ... the drawings do not show dimensions so it is hard to see the size of the spaces ... the axonometric drawing is too hard to follow.

Web hypermedia representation is attractive due to the ease with which the designer can communicate a combination of text, images and CAD drawings and other design information. The impression among studio participants was that all that designers needed to do was to somehow organise this information as a collection of pages and add some clues for navigating within it. As shown in Table 5.2, this was not always sufficient for understanding the design.

What was the reason for occasional incompleteness of the representation or the various misinterpretations? In addition to difficulty in navigating the web pages, it seems that it was not easy for the client to understand whether the design satisfied the brief requirements or not.

While there is a long tradition in the creation of paper-based shared design representations, there is little experience in designing hypermedia representations.

The advantage of hypermedia - the absence of the constraint of a linear structure and flow of information - has caused difficulties in building coherent shared representations. In cognitive psychology, coherence is not regarded as an isolated feature of the representation, but as a result of a cognitive construction process. Imposing a coherent structure on a representation and conveying that structure by means of appropriate cues could substantially improve the understanding of the information that a given representation communicates.

5.2.1 Structural Consistency

The structure of a hypermedia design representation can be approached from at least two points of view: semantics and order of access of its elements. Semantic structure identifies the building blocks of the representation: the information units and the semantic relations between these units. Hierarchical structuring is a convenient way to cope with a large amount of detail in the representation.

The semantic structure of design representation does not specify the way in which the designer should access its elements. The role of the access structure is to present parts of the semantic structure, depending on the design process and the background and the level of expertise of the designer. Design as a recursive and evolutionary process requires a network access structure rather than a linear one. A meaningfully structured representation can substantially assist the "reflective conversation".

Directed acyclic graphs and tree hierarchies provide consistent ways of structuring hypermedia representations. A tree hierarchy has more rigid requirements than a graph - a page in a tree structure should have only one parent. This constraint is effective when representing small parts of a design, but it becomes a serious problem for representing overlapping hierarchical structures like aggregations of design elements, which have common parts or multiple functions. Furnas and Zacks (1994) proposed a solution to this problem by combining both techniques into a new structure, which they called multi-tree. Multi-tree structures can be interpreted as a union of trees, where the descendants of any node form a tree, but a node can have more than one parent. In other words, they are directed acyclic graphs that have identifiable substructures that are trees. In this arrangement trees have some degree of autonomy, that means that the structures could be reusable.

Structural consistency is closely related to the information segmentation - the amount of information that may be stored in each atomic node of the shared representation. This subject is very sensitive to the preservation of the contextual cues. "Over" fragmentation may result in a lack of interpretive context, when granularity can cause difficulties in following the structure. In such cases, the shared representation fails to mediate effective communication.

This distinction of semantic and access structures requires the specification of rules for creating and modifying them. Determining these rules requires a deep understanding of the domain. Shared hypermedia design representation is not a stand alone entity - its real strength is in the potential for almost online building of the design documentation and the ability to be incorporated in the studio environment as part of the electronic library (see Fig. 5.3). These aspects require consideration of the consistency of the hypermedia presentation.

Consistency in presentation is related to the metaphor we use to visualise the structure of the design representation and to the way we preserve the structural context during presentation. Both aspects are interrelated. Visualising the structure together with the content of an activated page can provide the structural context. In this case, a designer can locate the page within the shared representation with respect to the neighbouring pages and links and can relate its content to this structure. We consider that this increases coherence and supports the comprehension of semantic relations.

Research in the field of visualisation of hypermedia structures provides several visualisation techniques (see Gloor 1997, pp. 101-124). An image map, which explicitly illustrates the relations between different elements of the presentation, remains the preferable way of presenting structures. A "spiderweb" style map (Utting and Yankelovich 1989) is a straightforward reflection of the actual linking structure. Obviously, such a map becomes a meaningless mess if the structure is not hierarchical and the number of pages or links exceeds just a few.

Once the representation is structured hierarchically there are a number of techniques to display its structure. Donald Knuth, in the first volume of his "bible for programmers", described a few notations for visualising tree structures - graph tree, indention graph, and a nested set (Knuth 1973, pp. 305-313). Most visualisation approaches in hypermedia either directly implement one of these methods or use a combination. We illustrate these methods using the same underlying hierarchical representation.

The graph tree notation of the structure is illustrated in Fig. 5.5. The obvious advantage of such visualisation is that it follows the tree metaphor - explicit nodes and arcs-making it easy for perception and cognition. In addition, it can be scaled, thus displayed together with the active page. As the number of pages and hierarchy levels increases, the visibility and the expressive power of this pictorial rendition decreases.

The indentation view is similar to a table of contents in a book. This similarity means that this visualisation displays the connection between structural context and labelling convention. The method, as shown in Fig. 5.6, provides a clearer illustration of the distinction between hierarchical and other linked structures. The absence of the arcs is an advantage when dealing with large hierarchical structures. Depending on the point of view, the advantage of the method is also its disadvantage - it orders the hierarchical structure in a sequence of paths. Thus, if you want to inspect the far right branch of a tree you need to view the location near the bottom of the indention graph. Assigning particular colours to each level partially compensates for the inconvenience caused by this "linearity".

Nested sets[1] convert the tree metaphor into a two-dimensional spatial configuration, as illustrated in Fig. 5.7, where each page is nested within its parent page. This method also explicitly shows the non-hierarchical structures. Another

---

[1] More precisely this is a special case of the idea of nested sets - a collection of sets in which any pair of sets is either disjoint or one contains the other (Knuth 1973, p. 309).

advantage is that a designer can easily isolate everything related to a particular page, as it is graphed "inside" the page on the diagram.

A designer can zoom in and out of the hierarchy of the shared representation. In addition to the colour coding in Fig. 5.7, we can change the area of each "page" with respect to the weight value assigned to each page. The weight value can be estimated as a function of the page size, page completeness or any other page parameter or combination of parameters. For example, a smaller area may mean that the design issue that the page represents requires further development. Similar to the indention view, nested sets provide a way of getting the picture of the order dependency. According to Feiner (1988), the visualisation metaphor of nested sets is the most convenient one for the purpose of editing and updating tree-structured representations. The use of visualisation techniques in hypermedia shared representations provides a means to reduce the overall effect of the cognitive overhead. Additional reduction can be achieved by embedding in the representation a means to indicate the current position with respect to the overall structure of the representation, visualisation of the path which the designer is following during the session with the shared representation, and the directions for the next step. An example of a library of building designs that follows this recommendation is SAM[2], where each web page provides navigational links to information on that page and links to other pages that are part of the same building.

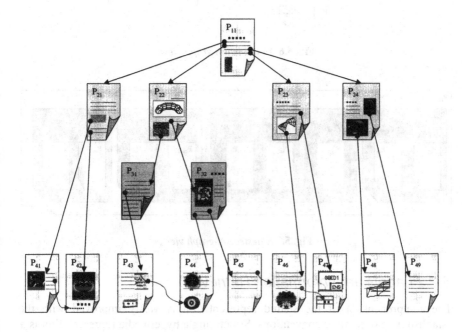

Fig. 5.5 *A graph tree view.*

---

[2] http://www.arch.usyd.edu.au/kcdc/caut.

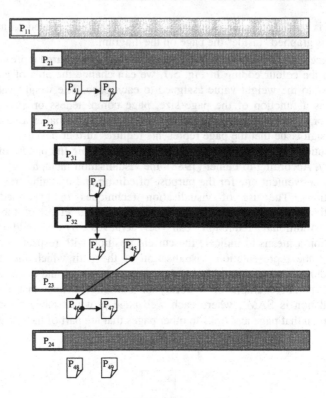

Fig. 5.6 *An indention graph view.*

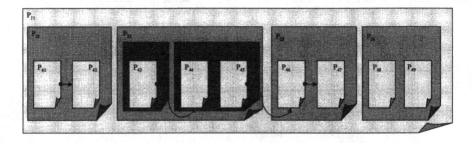

Fig. 5.7 *A nested set graph view.*

5.2.2 Labels and Information Retrieval

The comprehension of the shared representation is vastly improved with the establishment of naming conventions. Structuring a hypermedia representation is a necessary, but not sufficient, condition for consistency - it tells little about the meaning of the content. Knowledge of that kind can be encoded by introducing rules for appropriate labels of representation elements.

Naming can be viewed as an additional communication channel. By using appropriate names, a designer could improve the comprehension of the design ideas, triggering expectations about the kind of information to be found in that particular part of the representation. On a file system level, the use of names which correspond to the meaning of the information in the file reduces search efforts, bypassing the access structure. Following naming conventions at the file system level helps in updating shared representation or guessing the name of a file with particular information.

Naming conventions should include link labels. The idea is illustrated in Fig. 5.8. If the link label expresses a semantic relation between link source and link destination, then the chain of labels makes explicit the semantic structure of the design representation, helping other design collaborators to understand the reason for the connection between particular parts. However, so far, neither the design community nor researchers in hypermedia have adopted any standard conventions for naming procedures.

Sometimes a designer may have an idea about the content of the page, but may not know the path leading to that page. This effect is amplified in large-scale projects where the shared design representation may grow from a few pages to several hundred and more. This problem is addressed in content-based information retrieval methods. We consider the issues related to the keyword indexing and full-text search.

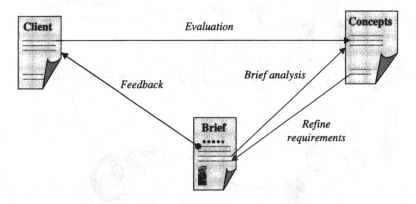

Fig. 5.8 *An example of naming conventions in a VDS.*

Both cases require the development of a set of keywords that describe each page as part of a particular shared representation. In the case of keyword indexing, each page is assigned a set of keywords and a designer's query is matched against this set. With the evolution of the design and the change of page contents, some of these sets may change in order to reflect the new content of the page. In any case of full-text search, a designer's keyword can be used to generate a set of related terms and then the text in the page is parsed against this set. Such an approach covers more semantic ground than the simple keyword match, including a variety of invisible linguistic relations, like synonymy and antonymy.

Fig. 5.9 illustrates the idea of "slicing" the shared representation. Assuming that the query expresses the designer's interest, the result of the query should be the relevant slice of the shared representation. The algorithms for automatic transformation of a query string into a set of keywords require the development of context-sensitive semantic approximations.

5.2.3 Dynamic versus Static Linking

Hypermedia representations in existing virtual design studios are based on static linked pages. Static connections and link endpoints are hardwired into the representation by their creator. Thus, the update of the links within the design representation with new alternatives or information is done manually. The advantage of staying with the static links schema is the better control designers have on the structure of the representation. However, there is no easy way to automate the updating activity. The negative effect appears when some of the information, like the design solutions that have not been accepted, is taken out of the shared representation. In this case, the manual update is not an efficient solution.

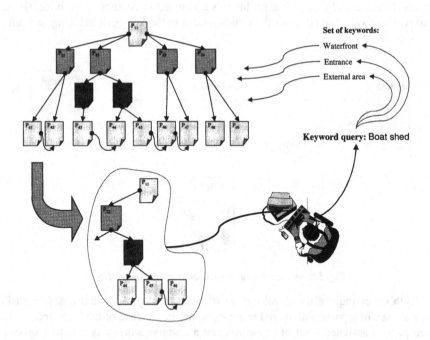

Fig. 5.9 *Context "slicing" of shared representation.*

Partially, the preference to static linking was due to the weak structure of the representations used in the first generation of virtual design studios. However, if we follow the consistency rules, the actual design information can be encoded in the form of a design database, as shown in Fig. 5.10. Again, designers communicate information through hypermedia presentation, but the links within this presentation are generated when accessing the underlying portion of the shared representation.

Dynamically linked portions do not have any fixed link end points, thus the modification and update of the shared representation in the virtual design studio becomes more convenient because newly added or deleted portions are unlinked automatically to and from the existing parts. This is a considerable advantage compared to static hypermedia.

A shift in shared representation towards a structured hypermedia encoded in database form requires semantic organisation of the design information and formal categorisation of the links.

Shared representation structured in database form

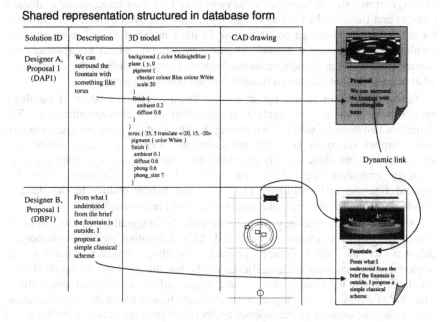

Fig. 5.10 *Shared representation structured in a database form.*

5.3 The Content of Shared Representation

In order to understand the content in the shared representation, designers need to use common *conceptualisation* of their area of interest[3]. A conceptualisation of an area of interest is an abstract and simplified view, which labels and describes the entities in that area and the relationships among those entities. Obviously, the area of interest has a dynamic nature, evolving together with the design development. When representing and communicating design information, every designer is

---

[3] We use "area of interest" instead of "domain" because the design development usually involves knowledge from several domains.

explicitly or implicitly committed to some conceptual schema. We call the explicit specification of conceptualisations an ontology.

Before we proceed further, we give a brief excursion in the etymology of the term "ontology". Ontology has originated in philosophy as a systematic account of the nature and the organisation of reality, an abstract description of the world (Neches, Fikes, Finn, et al. 1991). The etymology of the word ontology (onto - being, logia - world, discourse) refers to the existence of the world.

Through the field of mathematical linguistics, the concept of ontology entered the field of artificial intelligence as a formal system for representing domain concepts and their related linguistic realisations by means of basic elements. Researchers in artificial intelligence in design have extended the interpretation of ontology from a simple hierarchy of keywords and relevant terminology to domain theories and frameworks for knowledge representation, even a conceptual structure for sharing ideas in design collaboration. In the context of shared representation, ontology is viewed as a formal structure or system, which encapsulates the semantics of a design domain conceptualisation. Ontology defines the semantics of what is known about the design domain that the ontology covers.

Gruber (1993), in an attempt to narrow down the interpretation of ontology, specifies ontology as "an explicit specification of a conceptualisation". The definition had become well known among the knowledge engineering community, when Gruber (cited in Uschold and Gruninger 1996)), probably feeling that something was missing, vaguely extended the scope of ontology, stating that an ontology embodies "agreements about *shared* conceptualisations". This has sparked Uschold and Gruninger (1996) to add a new quality to the debates, viewing ontology as an "explicit account of a shared understanding".

We view design ontology as a framework for integrating various facets of shared knowledge as shown in Table 5.2. This integrating aspect of ontology is different to the ideas behind product modelling. Product modelling, as implemented in projects such as Bjork (1992), has the objective of establishing a standard format for sharing design data across different computer applications. The idea of ontology is at a higher level of abstraction of the shared representation, considering the content of the representation rather than the detail of the format of the representation.

Table 5.3. *The role of ontology in knowledge integration.*

Integration facets	The role of ontology
Theoretic-conceptual	Provides an extended information model of the area of interest. The model includes concept definitions and descriptions of the relations between these concepts.
Semantic	Provides a vocabulary of terms used in the conceptualisation and in the representation.
Information and data structures	Provides the structure of the representation schema, for instance the collection of objects and properties of those objects.
File system	Provides naming conventions.

Work on product modelling contributes to the identification of the potential difficulties in the development of shared representations for the virtual design studios. Some design domains, like electrical and mechanical engineering, have clearly defined components and products, which are modelled as assemblies of these components. However, architectural design and building construction have turned out to be difficult for information modellers. What are the entities that constitute a building? Whereas architectural design operates in terms of spaces and the elements that populate these spaces, building construction deals with entities such as walls, windows, doors and finishes. How can we unite these different design metaphors?

Current approaches in product data modelling have not provided a satisfactory answer to these questions. The major problem is in the static composition of these models. Such information models neither correspond to the evolutionary nature of the design nor can they accommodate the different views which designers have on each particular problem. For example, the models developed in RATAS (Bjork 1989 and Bjork 1992) take a relatively restricted view of buildings which fits only some types of buildings and, for instance, is not useful from a point of view of the structural engineer. COMBINE (Augenbroe 1996) concentrates on the factors which influence the energy performance of the proposed building. Despite many efforts (Bjork 1992), there is still disagreement about the capacity for expression and standardisation of building representations, not only during the many stages of design and construction, but also for the different engineering contexts.

This diversity of conceptual views and modelling strategies is the main reason for the relatively difficult "hill climbing" in design information modelling and, consequently, in the straightforward adoption of information models as shared representations. Rosenman and Gero (1996) propose to take multiple views, models and interpretations of a design object with respect to each particular design stage and viewer's background and competency. For example, a room entity may be treated variously: (i) only as a space; (ii) as a space with defining bounding surfaces; (iii) as an assembly of building elements such as walls, floor, ceiling, doors and windows or; (iv) as an assembly of a space and building elements. Dynamic combination and configuration of information models under a meta-strategy is a healthy idea, however, the structure of each model is quite complicated. This factor, together with the existing overlap between some models, hampers the ability to follow the structure of the model and limits its expressiveness - features that are crucial for the shared representations in virtual design studios.

Overall, the main purpose of the development of hypermedia representations and ontology is to make possible the integration of diverse design information in a consistent and coherent structure. The incidence of digital design media has increased the urgency of the need for an integrating knowledge model from a research objective to a practical imperative. The mere exchange of geometric data is not enough. We need to be able to map from the intuitive categories with which a hypermedia representation operates, to equivalent formal data structures. The computational success of such encoding depends on the consistency of the integration model on all levels of abstraction.

When using ontology to shape a shared representation, it is necessary to specify:

- The basic elements that constitute an ontology and the relations between them;
- The types of ontologies included in the modelling framework: and
- Some rules and functions for combining and manipulating the entities and, at a higher level, the ontologies.

What does an ontology look like? There is no standard form for describing and representing ontology. A type hierarchy, specifying classes and their subsumption relationships, is a very simple example. Relational database schemata also serve as an ontology by specifying the relations that can exist in some shared databases and the integrity constraints that must hold for them.

Specifying an ontology will include the development of a thesaurus – terms, synonyms, and antonyms (Uschold and Gruninger 1996); consider the degree of formality by which a vocabulary is created and meaning is specified. In specifications that are more formal, the sense of a word is defined as a particular combination of synonyms that distinguish it from other words in the language. The whole set of values of all features automatically composes the thesaurus. Linguistic databases, like WordNet (Miller, Beckworth, Felbaum, et al. 1993), are examples of such ontological vocabularies. Vocabularies in more informal specifications are closer to the traditional dictionaries that we use. In the knowledge-sharing context, ontologies are specified in the form of definitions of representational vocabulary.

Following from the different approaches to organising the concepts in building design, we present two different approaches to ontology definition in virtual design studios. The first is the Activity/Space ontology, as presented in Maher, Simoff and Mitchell (1997), where the concepts of activity and space provide the focus for reasoning about the design. The activity elements consider the intended use and function of the building, and the space elements consider the requirements and provisions for creating and bounding the space in the building. The second is the Function/Behaviour/Structure ontology, as presented in Gero (1990), where function specifies the purpose of a design element, behaviour specifies its response to its environment, and structure specifies the geometric and material properties of a design element. The two ontologies complement each other in focussing on either the spaces created by an architectural design or the physical entities that are constructed to form the design.

5.3.1 Activity/Space Ontology

We present the "Activity/Space" ontology as an example of an ontology for architectural design, which we have used as the basis for the shared hypermedia representation in architectural design studios. The Activity/Space (A/S) ontology specifically focuses on architectural design, the design of space bounded by physical objects, in contrast to other types of design, such as the design of engines or computer chips where the solid parts of the design are the focus. The A/S ontology delineates the categories of building design knowledge as "activity" and "space", as shown in Fig. 5.13. Activity is related to the functionality of the design, or the activities that can take place in a given space. This knowledge model addresses the need to represent *requirements* corresponding to both the functionality of the spaces in the building and the geometric or physical description of the building. It makes explicit the representation of activities, spaces, and their relationships.

Each node in the hierarchy presented in Fig. 5.13 can be considered an object, in the object-oriented programming sense. In its simplest form, an object has a name and slots. The content of the slots may vary for each particular instance. Virtually any type of information can be attached to a slot, including another object. In our case, the object "Building Design" includes two slots: "Activity" and "Space". Each of the slots may point to another object: the set of slots that describe activities and spaces, respectively.

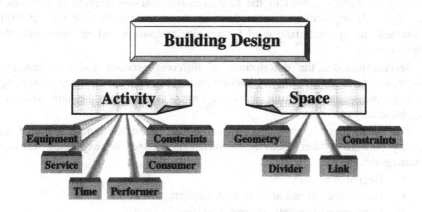

Fig. 5.11 *Activity/Space design ontology.*

The work on the Activity/Space design ontology started after the evaluation of the student projects in the 1995 international virtual design studio. The client for the project was an Australian architect who specialised in the design of health care facilities. The brief and the design needed to have a common representation due to the complexity of the requirements. The A/S ontology was used as a structured representation to organise the hypermedia design presentation. The ontology gives us categories that we can use to describe the design development and the structure, and provides a means to access the information relevant to each category.

We consider the basic categories of the A/S design ontology: activity and space. Each of them is represented in the form of an hierarchical ontology, identifying the categories of knowledge that specify an activity and a space. For more detail on the A/S ontology, see Maher et al (1997).

An activity is defined as a purposeful action, whose performance requires a particular amount of space, time and an object that performs this activity. Spatial need, time and performer are the notions of the activity ontology which are *always relevant*, e.g. there is no activity which can be defined without spatial and time requirements and without the object that performs this activity. The other notions of the activity ontology are relevant in a particular design context or design stage. The spatial need is defined by a relationship between activity and space.

Time is a quantitative category represented by an interval value which corresponds to a time period. We use the time category to be able to present the necessary knowledge to arrange activities with respect to the time coordinate. For consistency, we call this interval a *time envelope*.

The performer category denotes the object that carries out the activity. The consumer category denotes the object over which the activity is executed. In the design of a building, performer and consumer could be a person, organisation, department, or other subdivision. In some cases performer and consumer can coincide.

Equipment includes the description of the instrumentation and furniture necessary for activity realisation. Ontologies for description of instrumentation used by an activity consist of the characteristics that are relevant to performed activity, including occupied space (part of the space required by the activity), consumed energy, materials, used for activity realisation and relations with the environment.

Service includes the descriptions of different services and environmental resources which support activity performance. This includes heating, ventilating, lighting and water tempering. In some cases, services can be interpreted as supplementary activities.

The constraints category contains knowledge about the requirements of the activity towards other activities. Such knowledge is expressed through subcategories like:

- Degree of privacy;
- Interference of one activity with another;
- Interdependence between two activities.

This specifies the knowledge necessary for the preliminary analysis of activity layout.

The spatial needs of an activity are defined by the spatial needs of the action itself and the activity configuration. In general, the spatial need could have a very complicated form. Initially, the spatial needs of an activity are formulated in a rather vague form, usually without any metric. For instance, an activity can be performed in an open space (e.g. "jogging in the park") or within a facility or a building (e.g. "searching for a book"). The simple example shown in Fig. 5.12 illustrates the idea of the spatial need. The figure illustrates the activity "searching for a book". The spatial need of this activity is defined by the spatial needs of:

- The performer, who needs to be able to access every level of the bookshelf;
- The equipment, in this case the bookshelf.

In this sense, building reusable containers of activity configuration knowledge could be a useful source for the evaluation of the spatial needs. Spatial needs are the bridge between the activities and spaces in the A/S ontology.

We define a *region of space* to be the coalescence of all activity components necessary to perform that activity. This general definition is suitable for handling many types of spaces because it neither distinguishes between open and closed regions, nor considers the mathematical notions of point, line or surface. Further, we use the notion of a *spatial envelope* to refer to the geometric description of the space. Spatial envelope *s* is a three dimensional hypothetically bounded region of space that enables the realisation of activity **a**. The spatial envelope approximates and visualises the spatial need of the activity. The spatial envelope is the first step towards the building of the space. Replacing activity with a spatial envelope means introducing an explicit geometry and metric.

Fig. 5.12 *The spatial needs of an activity.*

In the context of spaces, geometry is the category of knowledge that identifies conventions for representing 2D or 3D space. The description can be based on the combination of geometrical primitives and the values of their parameters, e.g. length, width, and radius of curvature. These geometrical primitives correspond to the spatial envelopes of respective activities.

Dividers are the real physical bounds of the space. Adding the appropriate dividers transfers a spatial envelope into a physical room, level or building, which encompasses these activities. Dividers inherit the characteristics of the materials used to implement them. Brick walls, concrete slabs, and glass separators are examples of dividers.

Including dividers in our ontology means that we need to include a link category, which describes the connections between separated spaces, and the accessibility and suitability of different spaces within the designed facility. Knowledge of the links implies the necessity to represent the path to each space. Doors, windows, and stairways are examples of links.

Like the category for activity, the knowledge associated with a space includes constraints. These constraints can express the rules imposed by building codes for maximum and minimum sizes of different types of space, or constraints specific to a particular design firm reflecting their own specifications of the type of buildings they design.

In addition to the categories of knowledge that represent concepts, the Activity/Space ontology includes relations that define the explicit connection between entities, or the realisation of the concepts. We identify two types of relations:

- Relations between entities of the same kind, for example, only between spaces or only between time intervals;
- Relations between entities of different kind, for example, between activities and spaces.

An example of a relation between entities of the same kind is *overlap*. This is a high level kernel relation which operates over regions of space, time intervals or activities.

The Activity/Space ontology provides the categories of knowledge for the dynamic development of a design. The design begins with a hierarchy of required activities, specified in the brief and represented using the slots associated with knowledge about activities. When the lowest level of activities has been identified (this depends on the required detail of the design), the space associated with each activity is designed. The spaces are aggregated into larger functional spaces until they come together to form the whole spatial design. Fig. 5.13 illustrates the expansion of activities, mapping activities to spaces, and the aggregation of spaces.

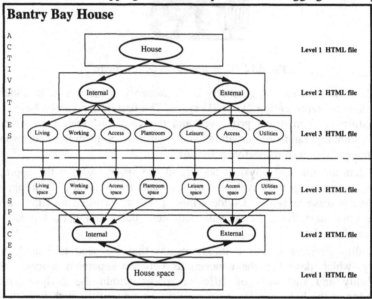

Fig. 5.13 *A Web-based shared representation based on the Activity/Space ontology.*

This dynamic representation of the design can be mapped into a hypermedia structure. At each level, the description of the corresponding set is stored in an HTML file. These descriptions compose a set of active linked tables that formalises the organisation of the brief. The links follow the decomposition of activities into particular subactivities. In addition to each activity, a link is attached to the corresponding space that has to be designed and documented. The top page of the document includes a navigation tree. Each page of the document has information about current and upper levels, and an "emergency" link to the navigation tree. The document[4] is discussed in more detail in Maher, Simoff, and Cicognani (1997).

5.3.2 Function/Behaviour/Structure Ontology

The Activity/Space ontology is only one of the possible bases for constructing design representations. This ontology reflects mainly the spaces and accommodated activities. However, it does not connect the properties of the structures defining and supporting these spaces with the functions/activities of the spaces. To represent such information we can use an ontology based on the Function/Behaviour/Structure (FBS) view of design. This ontology is effective in capturing the design information associated with the physical components of a design. Our presentation of the FBS ontology is based on our interpretation of the idea of design prototypes, as introduced by Gero (1990).

The major components of the FBS ontology are the concepts of function, behaviour, and structure, as illustrated in Fig. 5.14. Each physical component of the design is described in terms of its function, behaviour, and structure. The function of a design component is the intended purpose of the component. The behaviour of a design component is the response of the component to its environment. The structure of a design component is the description of its geometry and physical characteristics.

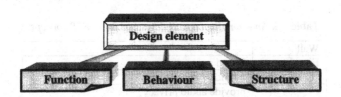

Fig. 5.14 *The Function/Behaviour/Structure ontology.*

An example of the FBS ontology for the structural design of a building is shown in Fig. 5.15. The second level of the hierarchy refers to the major functional systems of the building, that is, the vertical load system, the lateral load system, and the foundation system. The third level refers to the structural systems that contribute to the functional systems, such as the arch, the diagrid, and the core. Each node of the ontology has slots related to the function, behaviour, and structure of the structural system.

The FBS ontology can be used at any level of abstraction of the design. Identifying the levels of abstraction and the properties that make up the function, behaviour, and structure of the design components requires a formalisation of the design knowledge in a particular domain. This is best clarified with an example. Table 5.4 shows the representation of a wall using an FBS conceptual organisation.

When using the FBS ontology for organising the information about a design project, it is possible to analyse the design process in terms of the development of

---

[4] http://www.arch.usyd.edu.au/kcdc/vds96/elective/brief.html.

the function, behaviour, and structure information. Usually, designing is considered the act of producing a description of a design solution. Most of the tools that assist in the development of a description of a design emphasise the specification of what we are calling the "structure" of the design. By using the FBS ontology, other aspects of specifying information about the design become apparent.

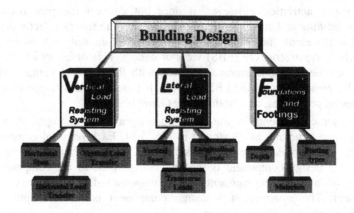

Fig. 5.15 *An example of the FBS ontology for the structural design of a building.*

Table 5.4. *An example of a wall described as an FBS concept.*

Wall	
Function	bound a space
	provide visual privacy
	provide audio privacy
	provide protection from the environment
	provide structural load resistance
Behaviour	transparency
	sound transmission factor
	thermal insulation factor
	compressive stress
	overturing moment
Structure	3D model
	material
	thickness
	compression loads
	transverse loads

In order to clarify the use of the prototype representation, we present an overview of the design process as it relates to the relationships between the concepts of function, behaviour, and structure. This analysis is based on a similar analysis done by Gero (1990).

The initial stages of designing are related to the development of an understanding of the purpose of the design. This purpose is conceptually equivalent to function in our ontology. Since there is not a direct mapping between the purpose of a design and its ultimate form, a transformation directly from function to structure is not always possible. When we are designing, we may think that this transformation is direct, but it is usually based on our experience of designing in a particular domain.

The first transformation that can be modelled explicitly is the mapping from the function of the design to the expected behaviours:

$$F \to B_e$$

During this stage of the design, we consider the intended functions and their implication on the behaviour of the design.

Using the Wall example, providing privacy is directly related to the transparency of the wall. If privacy is an intended function of the wall, then the amount of transparency allowed is pre-determined.

The next transformation that can be modelled explicitly is the identification of alternative structures and their actual behaviours:

$$S \to B_a$$

During this stage of design, several alternatives may be considered, and their consideration is expressed in the same terms as the expected behaviours. In the Wall example, different wall types may be considered in terms of their transparency, audio privacy, and structural characteristics.

Once the intended functions and alternative structures are considered, an analytical part of the design process determines the feasibility of the design. This process compares the expected and actual behaviours of the current design alternative:

$$B_e \longleftrightarrow B_a$$

When the comparison indicates a satisfactory solution, the design of this particular component is finalised. Further iterations on the design may add to, or change, intended functions, causing the design component to be reconsidered in terms of its function behaviour and structure.

The use of the FBS ontology has a relatively large overhead in identifying the relevant levels of abstraction and the FBS representation of design components and aggregations. However, it has the benefit of making explicit many of the considerations in the development of the design, something that current models based on CAD tools lack.

5.4 Shared Representation - Ontology and Hypermedia

We have seen that sharing content through ontological integration is at a deeper level than sharing the structure through representational integration. Ontological integration concerns the heterogeneity among different conceptualisations.

A Web-based shared representation offers an information organisational structure for the construction of electronic documentation. The regularity of this structure allows the implementation of algorithms for automatically generating and linking node templates.

Fig. 5.16 illustrates the dimensions of content and structure according to their degree of structure and formality. The identification of ontology for a specific design project can be specified in a highly formal manner as a set of concepts with a common vocabulary, or informally as an agreed organisation of content. The selection of a hypermedia structure can also be specified along a range from an informal layout of web pages to a highly specified set of templates for defining information as web pages. The degree of structure and formality is a choice that designers must make before beginning a virtual design studio.

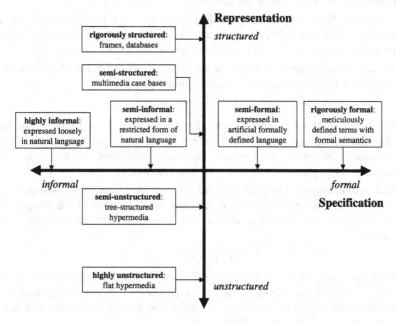

Fig. 5.16 *Dimensions of content and representation.*

References

Augenbroe, G. (1996), COMBINE Project: The broad perspective, *International Construction Information Technology Conference, InCIT*, Sydney.

Bjork, B.-C. (1989), Basic structure of a proposed building product model, *CAD* **21**(2): 71-77.

Bjork, B.-C. (1992), A conceptual model of spaces, space boundaries and enclosing structures, *Automation in Construction* **1**: 193-214.

Feiner, S. (1988), Seeing the forest for the tree: Hierarchical display of hypertext structure, *Proceedings ACM Conference on Office Information Systems*, Palo Alto, CA, pp. 205-212.

Fischer, G. and Reeves, B. N. (1992), Beyond intelligent interfaces: Exploring, analyzing and creating successful models of cooperative problem solving in E.

Rich and D. Wroblewski (eds.), *Applied Intelligence, Special Issue Intelligent Interfaces*, Kluwer Academic Publishers, 1992, pp. 311-332.

Furnas, G. W. and Zacks, J. (1994), Multitrees: Enriching and reusing hierarchical structure, *Human Factors in Computer Systems, CHI'94*, Boston, MA.

Gero, J. S. (1990), Design prototypes: A knowledge representation schema for design, *AI Magazine*, **11**(4): 26-36.

Gloor, P. (1997), *Elements of Hypermedia: Techniques for Navigation and Visualisation of Cyberspace*, Boston, MA, Birkhauser.

Gruber, T. R. (1993), A translation approach to portable ontology specifications, *Knowledge Acquisition*, **5**(2): 199-220.

Knuth, D. E. (1973), *The Art of Computer Programming*, Addison-Wesley Pub. Co, Reading, Massachusetts.

Leslie, H. G. (1996), Strategy for information in the AEC industry, *International Construction Information Technology Conference, InCIT96*, Australia, The Institution of Engineers, Australia.

Maher, M. L., Simoff, S. J. and Cicogniani A. (1997), Potentials and limitations of Virtual Design Studio, *Interactive Construction On-line*.

Maher, M . L., Simoff, S. and Mitchell, J. (1997), Formalising building requirements using and activity/space model, *Automation in Construction*, **6**(1997): 77-95.

Miller, G. A., Beckworth, R., Felbaum, C., Gross, D. and Miller, K. (1993), *Five Papers on Wordnet*, Cognitive Science Laboratory, Princeton University, CSL Report 43.

Neches, R., Fikes, R., Finn, T., Gruber, T., Patil, R., Senator, T., et al. (1991), Enabling technology for knowledge sharing, *AI Magazine* **12**(3): 37-56.

Rosenman, M. A. and Gero, J. S. (1996), Modelling multiple views of design objects in a collaborative CAD environment, *Proceedings International Construction Information Technology Conference InCIT96*, The Institution of Engineers, Australia.

Schoen, D. A. (1983), *The Reflective Practitioner: How Professionals Think in Action*, New York, Basic Books.

Schoen, D. A. (1995), *Reflective Practitioner: How Professionals Think in Action*. Arena, Aldershot, England.

Uschold, M. and Gruninger, M. (1996), Ontologies: Principles, methods and applications, *Knowledge Engineering Review* **11**(2).

Utting, K. and Yankelovich, N. (1989), Context and orientation in hypermedia networks, *ACM Transactions on Office Information Systems*, **7**(1): 58-84.

Part Three

The Shared Environment

Six

The Distributed Design Studio

Design studios, now equipped with extensive computing facilities, are places where designers interact and discuss design projects, organise and structure the project data, transfer and share design representations, and develop and publish design documentation. In all of these activities, information can be handled in electronic form. Following the traditional office paradigm, large amounts of project data files (such as drawings, documents, spreadsheets, databases, manuals, forms, communications, schedules and discussions) move around the studio from one computer workplace to another, where they are processed on the individual "desktop". The use of file server technology is usually reduced to the most rudimentary operations of moving files from one shared disk to another. Sometimes the same information is unnecessarily duplicated, sometimes important files remain either locked on the personal computer or lost somewhere on a barely navigable list of shared directories on a file server.

We use the term "VDS environment" to label the set of software tools installed on the networked studio computers to support VDS activities. Usually the arrangement of a personal computer "desktop" depends on the person who is using that computer and reflects his/her cognitive schemes for organising information. In computer labs within organisations, computers have a typical set-up. Because the design project is a communication-intensive task, it is critical to understand that the VDS environment is more than just a collection of tools and personal computer "desktops". For facilitating computer-mediated design, project development and presentation, the *virtual design studio environment* unites isolated "VDS desktops" in a technological scenario. Various communication and information sharing and processing technologies are amalgamated in a transparent way for participants to collaborate. A specified metaphor of desktop integration is an added advantage throughout the design collaboration. Neglecting this integration can lead to a devastating misuse and waste of technology. As a result, instead of taking advantage of powerful network computing, designers can "bounce" off the VDS, having no idea how to organise and operate the environment, how to design and monitor others' design work, or collaborate with other participants.

Therefore, once it has been decided to have a virtual design studio, it is necessary to spend time and effort in designing it, and, possibly, making this design common for each participant in the studio. Here, we take a comprehensive view of the environment, combining many of the issues from more focused VDS environments (see, for example, Tan and Teh 1995).

The set-up of a virtual design studio environment comprises the following key issues:

- Metaphor(s) and models;
  - For communication and collaboration;
  - For organising, structuring, sharing, discussing and electronically publishing design representations, supporting documentation and other related information (such as documents, manuals, drawings, spreadsheets, forms, correspondence, plans and proposals);
  - For structuring, managing and sharing the information within the environment.
- An agreement about design support, information archiving and documentation sharing, including;
  - A central location for accessing the latest documentation of the design project;
  - A set of file formats for exchanging documents within the studio;
  - A set of tools that model, draw, document, and describe the design using approved formats.
- A selection of communication tools, including;
  - Meeting tools and meeting server;
  - Point-to-point collaboration tools;
  - A forum for posting notices;
  - A set of email addresses for sending messages;
  - A broadcasting system for contacting all participants in a group.

Some of these issues have been addressed in the groupware research and development (see, for example, Marca and Bock 1992). Groupware is a new category[1] in computing, focussed on blending an integrated electronic support of communication, coordination and collaboration of groups of professionals. Such support aims to help the carrying out of tasks and to combine users' efforts on project development, from wherever any member of the group happens to be. Each category of software support, discussed earlier in this book, is an intrinsic part of a groupware environment. Therefore, groupware concepts and environments can provide powerful underlying technology for the distributed VDS environments.

To participate in a virtual design studio, a person needs to comply with the agreements on underlying technology and accepted studio formats, and understand the corresponding knowledge. Here, we discuss the alternatives for putting together the components in the categories listed above to produce an effective VDS environment.

A design project can be distributed in a network structure. Each participant in the project occupies a particular node in this structure. The organisation and design of the environment for each node depends on the available hardware and software. The possibilities for virtual design studio environments can be described in terms

---

[1] There is more or less an agreement that this software category appeared when, in 1989, Lotus, now a part of IBM, delivered The Lotus Notes. It took a few years for the world, including Lotus developers, to truly comprehend the significance and potential of the groupware paradigm.

of the integration of the tools in each node with other nodes. The ideas of integration and autonomy are illustrated in Fig. 6.1.

Integration deals with:

- The compatibility of the hardware platforms, operating systems and networks that are incorporated in the VDS environment;
- The common applications which can run, communicate and exchange information in such an environment;
- The interface metaphor that can integrate the access to the applications in the distributed VDS environment.

In the case of international studios, the compatibility of information coding standards also needs to be taken into consideration.

Autonomy describes the level of independence of each node from the others required to perform all tasks related to a design project. For example, a node in a distributed VDS environment can include anything from a portable personal computer up to a local network. Some nodes are only equipped with software to access, view, and transport design documents; others can instead create a whole range of multimedia applications, which can be shared within the network.

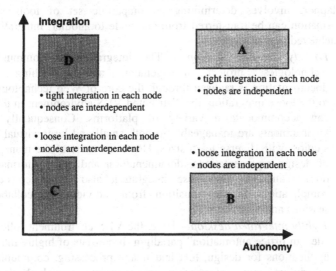

Fig. 6.1 *The dimensions of distributed virtual design studio environments.*

The "position" and "size" of each node, represented by rectangles in Fig. 6.1, depend on the variety of machines, networks, operating systems and applications. Rectangle A represents a VDS whose nodes are built on a single computer platform, for example, PC-compatible machines. Machines in this node run compatible operating systems, for example, Windows 9x/NT. The VDS software support, in the case of a single-platform environment, is easier for integration and maintenance. In the case represented by rectangle B, the studio includes several platforms, for example, Sun SPARC stations, Silicon Graphics machines and Macintoshes, which run different operating systems. By utilising existing resources, multi-platform environments are more flexible to use. However, the whole environment may result in being less reliable.

A and B in Fig. 6.1 correspond to different high autonomous hardware and software configurations. Each of these configurations provides sufficient support to complete a design project. C and D represent scenarios based primarily on single and multiple platforms, respectively. The supported software, however, is not sufficient to complete a project through all design stages. For example, one of the nodes can specialise in high quality drafting and publishing, while another node specialises in modelling and analysis. An advantage of a scenario described by C and D is the relatively low expenditures for software licensing over the whole studio.

Less autonomy in the nodes does not necessarily mean less efficiency of the virtual design studio. The studio will need to be organised according to the mapping of distributed tasks.

According to these dimensions the VDS environments could be largely classified in the following categories:

- A *distributed environment* – Each node in the network has a set of tools that runs entirely within the node. Integration, which follows the desktop metaphor, involves determining a compatible set of tools so that information can be transferred from one node to another. Integration can be achieved in two ways:

  - *Loosely coupled desktop* - The integration of communication technologies, project management, and publishing design documentation is realised through the core of Web technology. Due to the loose integration, the distributed VDS environment in this case can accommodate a variety of platforms. Consequently, these environments are manageable in both small and large virtual design studios, with diverse team sizes. However, most of the management of design representations, documentation and other information is done manually. The loose integration also brings considerable complications in the transition from individual to collaborative sessions and vice versa.

  - *Tightly integrated desktop* – Here, the VDS environment follows the "design office automation" paradigm. It consists of highly integrated applications for design, text and image processing, communication, scheduling, and information management. The high level of compatibility between objects and corresponding applications in these environments sensibly increases the automation of collaborative information management. The underlying technology is usually platform dependent, which can cause considerable difficulties when trying to integrate existing structures and functionalities. This problem can be neutralised by careful selection and arrangement of components, which run on at least a few existing platforms.

- A *centralised environment* – Each node in the network has a set of tools that runs in coordination with a central server, supporting the data and communication needs of all nodes. This type of environment is driven by the client/server paradigm and it is platform independent. The functionality of these emerging environments is limited by the internet protocols and environment metaphors, sometimes additionally restricted by the Web metaphor. The underlying technology supports the development of highly customisable and adaptive distributed VDS environments. A centralised environment can be provided in two ways: following the desktop metaphor, including a common set of tools similar to the distributed environment, and following the place metaphor of virtual worlds.

- *Desktop metaphor* – The desktop metaphor assumes that all nodes have the same integrated package of client applications for communication and collaborative work, and that one of the nodes acts as a server for these applications. These environments have the advantage of a similar, thus consistent, interface to all tools and easy access to information on the central server. The disadvantage in this approach is the relative immaturity of the integrated packages and the resulting frustration when certain features are not yet implemented.

- *Place metaphor* – The virtual world provides a place where the VDS activities are fully supported. A virtual world integrates communication and interaction through the design and use of a place. This place has many of the physical studio functions. Participants can set up a virtual organisation in a similar fashion as they would set up a physical office space. The technology supporting virtual worlds is, however, still in its infancy, although research and interest in this field is growing fast.

Scenarios of real virtual design studios can be based on a combination of paradigms and strategies from these categories. This chapter presents the distributed design studio in more detail, emphasising asynchronous collaboration and project information management. Chapter 7 looks more closely at the centralised virtual design studio, emphasising the synchronous collaboration and project development. We present these environments in the form of possible scenarios, alternatives for the selection of tools and technologies, and ways of combining and integrating them in the scenario.

6.1 Loosely Coupled Desktop

In this case, the distributed design studio is spread across a variety of platforms, operating systems and their configurations, as shown in Fig. 6.2. This scenario is suitable for organisations with an established information technology infrastructure. The virtual design studio can be constructed on top of the existing hardware and software systems. Each node of the project can include personal computers and heterogeneous networks of workstations and servers. This approach relies on software for communicating and sharing design information that supports cross-platform formats and protocols. Its major attraction is that the participants do not have to adopt a completely new working environment for collaboration.

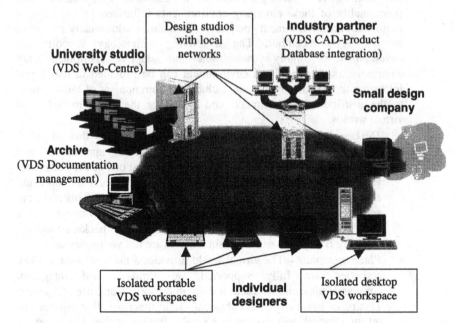

Fig. 6.2 *The underlying structure of a multi-platform distributed VDS environment.*

6.1.1 Integration Agreements and Interface Design

The next step in the studio set-up is the agreement on the metaphors and models that will be used in the studio environments. Table 6.1 shows such a list for a loosely coupled VDS. These agreements implicitly specify the structure and functionality of environment components, and the scope of the terminology which participants have to know to be able to operate their interface.

A convenient way to integrate the various components is to select from the beginning the file formats that will be used within the studio and their Web support, as shown in the example of file specification in Table 6.2. Some formats are supported internally by the Web browser, others require additional plug-ins, or external (to the browser) applications. In any case, the Web environment in every node has to be completed with the appropriate tools to read selected file formats.

The next step is preparing a detailed list of the groups of tools and the corresponding software. Examples of the selection of software for each tool category are shown in Table 6.3. Each selection can be from different software developers and, therefore, may use incompatible file formats, and may possibly run on only one hardware platform. Hence, one of the functions provided by the Web technology is joining the various formats used in the VDS. The file formats not agreed between participants (in our example - not explicitly listed in Table 6.2) have to be supported by at least one of the applications listed in Table 6.3. These decisions will ensure that design representations can be transferred and decoded among all nodes.

Table 6.1 *Functional categories and their elements in a loosely coupled VDS in terms of the metaphors and models they followed.*

Functional categories and elements	Metaphors and models
Management	
VDS nodes	The "network" metaphor
Schedule	The "calendar" metaphor
Designer's database	Relational data model
Team manager	The metaphor of a "switchboard"
VDS evaluation	The metaphor of "structured interview"
Communication	
Meeting point	The metaphor of a "place"
Forum	The metaphor of a "bulletin board"
Email cast	The "mass mailer" metaphor
Individual email service	The "address book" metaphor
Logbook submission	The "journal" metaphor
Project (in architecture)	
Brief and documentation	Activity/Space ontology
Site description	The "multimedia handbook" metaphor
Assessment scenario	Distributed jury model
Online standards	The "multimedia handbook" metaphor
Tool tutorials	The "multimedia handbook" metaphor
External library catalogues	The "link centre" metaphor

Table 6.2 *Specification of kernel file formats and browser support for a loosely coupled VDS.*

File formats	Web support (Netscape Communicator)
Text documents	
HTML, Plain ASCII	Internal
PostScript	External application (Ghost view)
PDF	Plug-in (Adobe[2] Acrobat Reader)
Images	
GIF, JPEG	Internal
CAD Drawings	
DWF	Java viewer (Arnona[3] CADViewer Lite)
3D Models	
VRML	Plug-in (Cosmo Player[4])
Archives	
ZIP	External application (platform dependent)

Fig. 6.3 illustrates the information organisation of a front page for a loosely coupled VDS, based on the list defined in Table 6.1. Once the metaphors and the information models are agreed and the overall outline of the studio is designed,

---

[2] Adobe Systems Incorporated. http://www.adobe.com.
[3] Arnona Internet Software Inc., http://www.cadviewer.com/.
[4] Cosmo Software Inc., http://cosmosoftware.com/.

VDS developers have to fill the structure with the corresponding tools and link all components. Below, we present examples of information design and implementation of the major functional features of a loosely coupled VDS.

Table 6.3 *Specification of tool categories and corresponding software for a loosely coupled VDS.*

Tool category	Software (number of supported platforms)
Text processing	
Word processing	Microsoft Word (2)
Spreadsheet	Microsoft Excel (2)
Database management	Filemaker Pro (2)
Image processing	
Static	Adobe Photoshop (3)
Dynamic	GIF animating tools (platform specific)
Graphics, CAD & 3D modeling	
Graphics software	Microsoft PowerPoint (2)
CAD drawings	AutoCAD (2), ArchiCAD (2)
3D modeling	AutoCAD (2), FormZ (2), POV-Ray (2)
Hypermedia design	
Web site design	AOL Press (2), Dreamweaver (2)
Web publishing	Microsoft Word (2)
Design presentation	Microsoft PowerPoint (2)
Multimedia portfolio production	Macromedia Director (2)
Communication tools	Netscape Communicator Suite (3)
Forum for notices	Bulletin board (CGI script, running at the university server - see Figure 6.2)
Mail-cast	Netscape Messenger (3), operating over a list of participants email addresses
Email	Netscape Messenger (3), supplied with the individual address.
Meeting tools	Netscape Communicator (3) for access to the meeting point
Meeting point (server)	Virtual campus - University of Sydney
Point-to-Point collaboration tools	Netscape Conference (3); Platform dependent video conferencing software (InPerson for SGI, CUSeeMe for Macintoshes and PCs)
Utilities	
Remote access	Telnet (platform specific)
File transfer	FTP (platform specific)
Task automation and customisation	Platform dependent languages
Archiving utilities	Zip/Gzip - platform dependent utilities

6.1.2 Management and Collaboration

Computer-mediated management of design projects includes sophisticated time coordination of numerous design activities. Adding a map, as shown in Fig. 6.4, with the indication of the geographical position of each node and the time shift with respect to the GMT time zone, will assist designers when planning their collaborative activities.

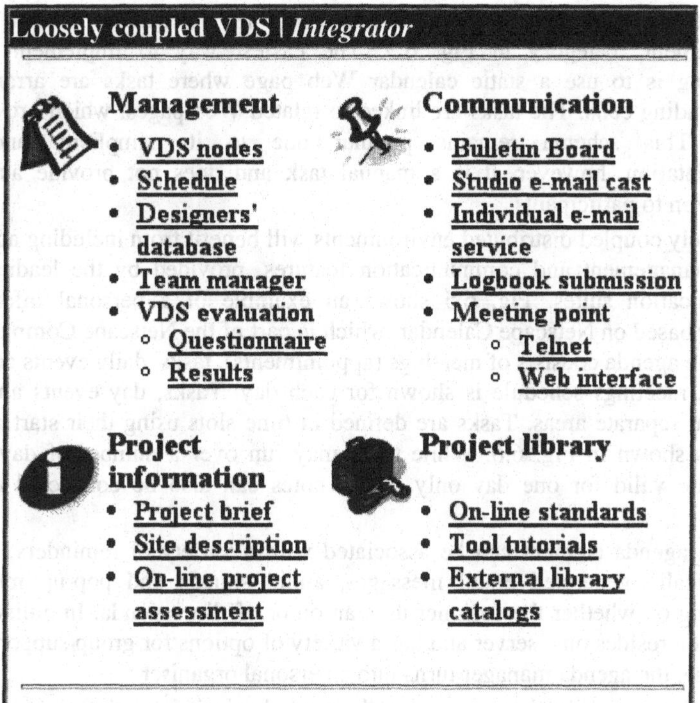

Loosely coupled VDS | *Integrator*

Management
- VDS nodes
- Schedule
- Designers' database
- Team manager
- VDS evaluation
  - Questionnaire
  - Results

Communication
- Bulletin Board
- Studio e-mail cast
- Individual e-mail service
- Logbook submission
- Meeting point
  - Telnet
  - Web interface

Project information
- Project brief
- Site description
- On-line project assessment

Project library
- On-line standards
- Tool tutorials
- External library catalogs

Fig. 6.3 *A front page that integrates a loosely coupled VDS environment.*

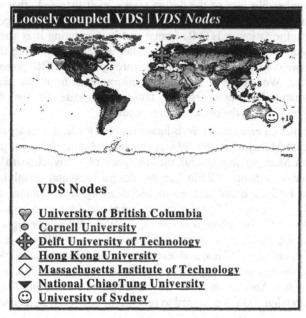

Loosely coupled VDS | *VDS Nodes*

VDS Nodes
- University of British Columbia
- Cornell University
- Delft University of Technology
- Hong Kong University
- Massachusetts Institute of Technology
- National ChiaoTung University
- University of Sydney

Fig. 6.4 *An example of an access page to the VDS main nodes.*

There are a variety of ways to implement the "Schedule" section in the "Management" category in Fig. 6.3. The easiest way to implement project scheduling is to use a static calendar Web page where tasks are arranged in corresponding cells. The tasks are linked to related Web pages, which provide the details. This schema remains popular due to its simplicity and easy implementation, however, it is a manual task and does not provide automatic notification to participants.

Loosely coupled distributed environments will benefit from including advanced group management and communication features, provided by the leading Web communication suites. Fig. 6.5 shows an example of a personal information manager based on Netscape Calendar, which is part of the Netscape Communicator suite. The agenda consists of meetings (appointments), tasks, daily events and daily notes. A meetings schedule is shown for each day. Tasks, day events and notes appear in separate areas. Tasks are defined in time slots using their start and due dates, as shown in Fig. 6.6. While tasks may run over a number of days, daily events are valid for one day only. Daily notes can also be connected to daily events.

Each agenda element can be associated with a variety of reminders, such as automatically generated email messages, audio signals and pop-up messages, depending on whether the designer uses an on or off line agenda. In online mode, the agenda resides on a server and has a variety of options for group support. In off line mode, the agenda manager turns into a personal organiser.

The designers' database provides the underlying information for the group management support. This can be a classical relational database. From that database, through different SQL queries, the VDS manager can generate and update the membership lists of the design teams, mail lists and other information related to designers. The easiest access to the database is the manual generation of the necessary information in HTML format and incorporating it as static pages in the loosely coupled studio. The automated alternative is connecting the database with a Web-based front-end (for example, through the ODBC protocol) which means that the Web page(s) presenting information from the database are generated dynamically upon request, thus any update of the database is automatically reflected in the presented information.

Fig. 6.7 shows an example of Web-based support for team management, linked under the "Team Manager" in the "Management" section of the front page in Fig. 6.3. The Team Manager implements the metaphor of a "switchboard", providing structured access to team bulletin boards, design logs and email broadcasting facilities. The bulletin board and email broadcasting are examples of standard communication techniques. The design log takes the idea of a paper-based log book and makes the information available on the Web. A designer logbook has two parts: the time log recording how much time was spent of different tasks, and the design log, a record of individual and team design ideas and sketches. When a team is no longer involved in the studio these facilities can be disabled, as shown for Team 4 in Fig. 6.7. Apart from the password protected access, this Team Manager for a loosely coupled VDS is designed to rely on the core of Web technology.

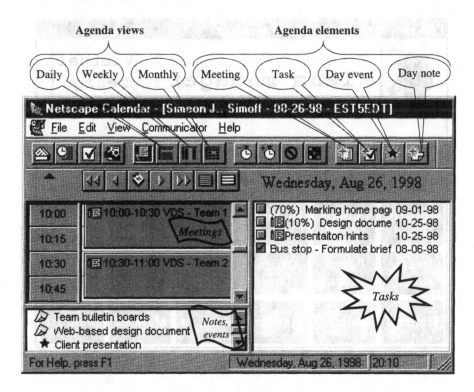

Fig. 6.5 *Personal information management in distributed VDS environments.*

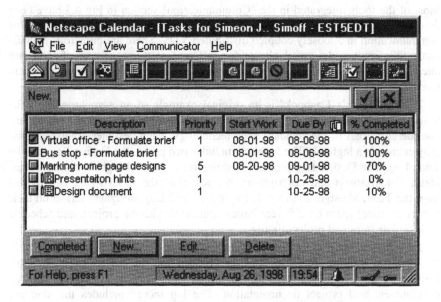

Fig. 6.6 *Task arrangement – tasks are quantified in days.*

Fig. 6.7 *A web-based Team Manager for a distributed VDS.*

6.1.3 Communication and Collaboration

Most of the tools integrated in the "Communication" section in Fig 6.3 have been described in Chapter 4. Asynchronous tools seem to be the best choice for communication in a loosely coupled distributed VDS. There are numerous MIME-compatible multimedia email clients for different platforms. Some of them are integrated in the Web communication suites (e.g. in Netscape Communicator and Internet Explorer).

The "Designer's Logbook" is an original example of an asynchronous Web-based design collaboration tool, implemented using CGI scripts, which are considered as part of the standard Web technology. Each designer involved in the project creates a logbook. The logbook includes two parts - the Design Log and the Time Log. The Design Log provides a structure in which designers organise their ideas, visualisations and descriptions. An access to the Design Log is provided from the Team Manager in Fig. 6.7. Using the Time Log, designers reflect on their efforts (as time) spent on different issues connected with the project, and schedule their further steps and project timing.

Fig 6.8 shows part of the Time Log implemented as a Web submission form. In this example, activities in the logbook are grouped in 6 categories: communication, learning (skills development), conventional and Internet research, design development and project documentation. The log record includes the standard "tag" - name of the designer, time and date of submission and submission number for that designer, the time intervals spent on each category of activities and the subject. The "Subject" section includes the same topics in which designers place their work when submitting the Design Log. The aim is to establish a connection between the time allocated to each category of activities in the Time Log, and the actual content described in the Design Log, whose records contain ideas, pictures, drawings, excerpts from discussions and other shared information.

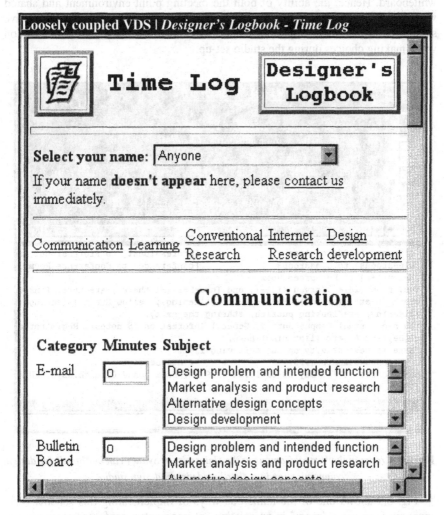

Fig. 6.8 *The Web-based Designer's Logbook.*

The logbook in this example provides a starting template for creating a logbook in a virtual design studio. Logbook records can be used to document the design process, by recalling key points, solutions, research results and other relevant work done on the project. If the virtual design studio is established for educational purposes, then the logbook can become part of the learning and monitoring stages.

Synchronous communication in a loosely coupled studio depends on the variety of platforms used within the studio. In a heterogeneous environment, combining a Web-accessible meeting point for online communication (at least, text-based) with a cross-platform shared whiteboard will serve this purpose. The advantage of this schema is the similarity of the interface on each platform. An important point when working under this schema is to cross reference the discussion and the page on the whiteboard. Hence, the ability of both the meeting point environment and shared whiteboard to document the information exchanged during the collaborative session is an extremely important feature that has to be taken into consideration when making choices during the studio set-up.

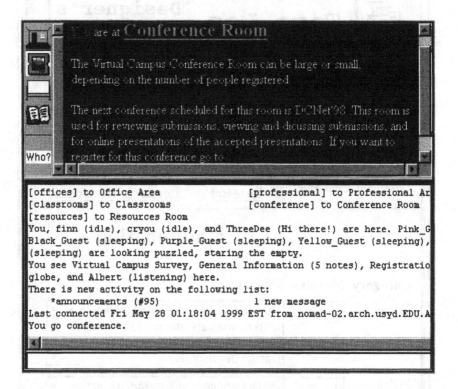

Fig. 6.9 *A room in the Virtual Campus at the University of Sydney can be "hired" for design communication in a distributed virtual design studio.*

Fig. 6.9 shows one of the numerous ways of implementing this schema. This approach is to use a "room" in an existing environment: a conference room in the Virtual Campus at the University of Sydney. An important issue is the ability of the environment to document the discussion for analysis and use during revisions of design decisions. A recording device in each room provides the facility for documenting design meetings. The collaboration tools, represented by the icons to the left of the room frame, provide facilities to enhance the design meeting. For example, the slide projector tool allows the group to view Web pages as slides, where a selection of a new slide updates the view for each person in the room. The example of the use of a virtual conference room at an existing facility is becoming more common. As more of these collaborative places are created, their availability to people that do not have an in house virtual conference facility improves.

Netscape Conference whiteboards can be used for cross-platform collaboration. Fig. 6.10 shows a moment from a collaborative design session on such a cross-platform shared whiteboard. An image or a 3D model can be inserted on the whiteboard, and the collaborators can mark up the images while discussing design issues. In practice, the shared whiteboards are not very popular when used across long distances on the Internet. One reason is the strain of synchronous communication over relatively low bandwidth, another is the restricted functionality offered by the popular shared whiteboard applications.

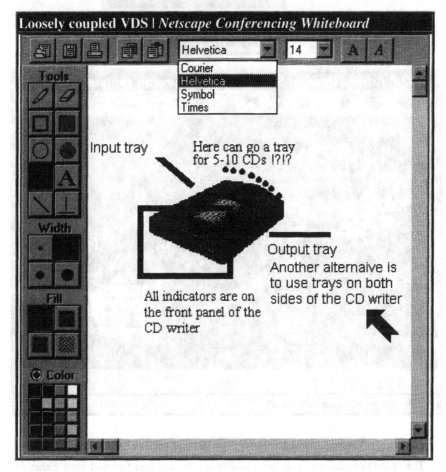

Fig. 6.10 *A cross-platform whiteboard shared by three participants during conceptual design.*

Going beyond shared whiteboards is the option of shared CAD drawings. An example of such a scenario is shown in Fig 6.11. In addition to the CAD viewer functionality, shown in the horizontal toolbar at the top of Fig. 6.11 (e.g. viewing individual layers), the CAD viewer is combined with whiteboard capabilities - the toolbar to the left, for adding comments, encircling elements of the drawing and other red-lining of CAD drawings.

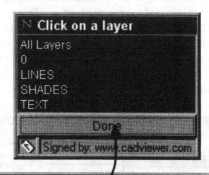

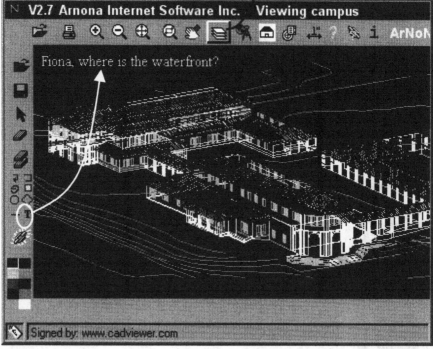

Fig. 6.11 *Sharing CAD drawings in a loosely coupled VDS.*

The "CAD comments" can be stored in a separate text file and kept either on one of the servers in the VDS, preferably in the "Archive" node following defined naming conventions, or on a local machine. If stored on the server, the red-lines are accessible to any participant and can be loaded, together with the drawing, so each designer can see others' comments. If stored locally, then participants can pass them via email and open them in a similar manner to the CAD drawing. This approach utilises the power of established design tools (CAD systems in our example) and the convenience of Web technologies for immediate publishing, accessing, viewing and managing design data. Note that in this case designers do not need to convert their drawings into bitmaps - they are shared as files originated by the CAD software, preserving its advantages in the visualisation, e.g. zooming and panning.

6.1.4 Handling Project Information, Library Support and Documentation

The electronic representation of the brief allows online assessment of design solutions. In a loosely coupled VDS, the assessment can be implemented in a manner similar to the "Designer's Logbook". The "Project Library" integrates available hypermedia tutorials, references to online standards and connections to accessible electronic catalogues of related libraries. They can be allocated either on one of the VDS servers or linked to available resources on the Internet. For example, the "Archive" server can be used to share between studio participants standards supplied on CDs. The alternatives and considerations for representing project information are the subject of Chapter 5.

6.1.5 Diversity and Discontinuity in Loosely Coupled VDS

Designers working in a distributed VDS, organised under the paradigm of "loosely coupled desktop", may experience discontinuity between working in the VDS environment and on a personal desktop. This discontinuity can be described in the following terms:

Technological inconsistency: Designers are forced to switch between conventional desktop software and Web-based tools and interfaces. Individual applications, which are part of the conventional desktop, are usually employed in asynchronous cooperative design development, as files are passed from one desktop to another. Collaboration systems like shared whiteboards usually have limited functionality and they are rarely used in non-collaborative sessions. Designers have to learn how to use new tools, and interfaces, in order to achieve collaboration tasks.

Platform heterogeneity. Sometimes, in one node, designers may need to operate on different computer platforms, operating systems and desktop environments, and take manual care of project information management. On the interface level, desktop environments differ in the terminology used to label objects with the same functionality. Even the default icons, which in a desktop environment are supposed to be the equivalent of road signs, differ considerably. Fig. 6.12 shows the current diversity for one of the most common objects in the desktop environment: the "container" for deleted files.

These differences can become even more dramatic when naming files. Fig. 6.13 shows an example of a reference to "index.html" (small caps) within an HTML document to another file, named "INDEX.HTML". Such inaccuracy does not cause problems when tested within a DOS/Windows or MacOS environment, but

the link will not work when transferred to an UNIX server, due to the case
sensitivity of the UNIX command processor.

Mac   **PC**   **Sun**   **SGI**

Trash   Recycle   Waste   Dumpster
         Bin

Fig. 6.12 *Even a standard element of the desktop metaphor differs across different
platforms.*

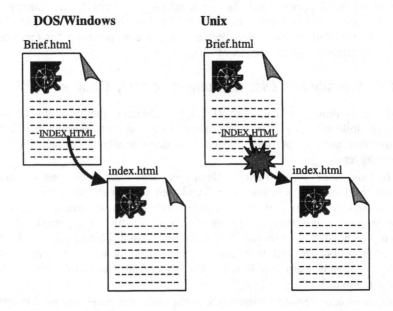

Fig. 6.13 *Sometimes what works in one system does not work in another.*

The availability of different software on different platforms introduces
discontinuity. Fig. 6.14 shows a selection of video conferencing tools for a
distributed VDS environment based on three platforms: PC-Windows, MacOS and
SGI Irix. The first two platforms are supported by CUSeeMe. When working on
the SGIs, designers have to use InPerson. The two systems do not communicate
with each other. Transferring work developed during a collaborative session on one
of the systems can be done mainly through manipulating image files, converting
them to appropriate formats.

Individual versus shared design. Due to limited functionality of collaborative
tools, designers may experience some discomfort switching from individual mode

to collaboration. Moving files from the "personal" part of the workspace to the shared area could cause some difficulties. For example, moving a CAD drawing to a shared whiteboard may require taking a snapshot of it, then either pasting it or saving it in a particular format which can be imported in the whiteboard.

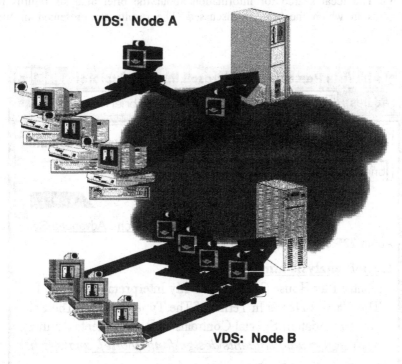

Fig. 6.14 *In a multi-platform VDS with different video conferencing tools designers need to shift between platforms and between video conferencing tools for performing similar design tasks.*

Orientation in individual sessions. During individual sessions designers, can operate with a small number of applications, even one application, at a time, keeping the desktop relatively "clean and ordered". During collaborative sessions, due to the relatively loose integration, the desktop is usually quickly overloaded with open windows linked to different collaborative tools (web browser, chat channel, video windows, etc.), which can create complications with event synchronisation, and orientation within the information stream.

The loose integration in this scenario makes information management and retrieval almost a manual task. Hence, when organising the individual VDS desktop, designers can introduce additional tools for information organisation and retrieval. Such tools are usually platform dependent and present information in terms of the metaphors used by that platform. A designer retrieves information from the "outside" by using Web searches. Information from the "inside" – that is, contained within the VDS archives – is usually indexed by whoever maintains the environment.

The use of the Web format for all information can be turned into an advantage when searching for information. Finding information from within a potentially very large Web site can be supported by a local customised Web style search engine. Fig. 6.15 shows AltaVista Personal search engine in action on a local desktop. The local search for information about the brief analysis returns the documents in which the brief is discussed. The results are presented in Web format.

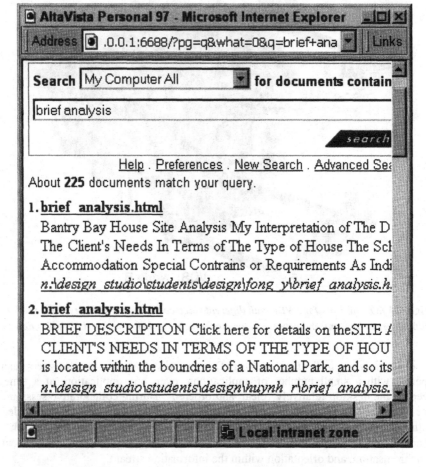

Fig. 6.15 *Local search facilities based on Web technology.*

The loosely coupled desktop metaphor is the straightforward way of setting up a virtual design studio in the case of an existing infrastructure, characterised by a diversity of existing hardware and software. However, the major compromises in this approach include the large amount of manual work involved in information management and the extended technological knowledge required from designers to work in such a studio. A significant effort is required to make the technology integration effective. This can change if the design of a virtual design studio starts from scratch, that is, the selection of hardware and software is specified and purchased for the needs of the virtual design studio.

6.2 The Tightly Integrated VDS Desktop

The initiation of a new virtual design studio may coincide with the establishment of a new company, research centre, or a new joint venture between a group of universities, companies and/or individual designers. Such an event is an excellent reason for creating a joint global strategy for the utilisation of information technology. The strategy can include an agreement for a common platform (for example, Intel-based), operating system (or compatible operating systems), kernel set of applications and common interface design. The basic studio components do not change, as shown in Fig. 6.16. Nevertheless, platform commonality offers several considerable advantages in the arrangement of a distributed VDS.

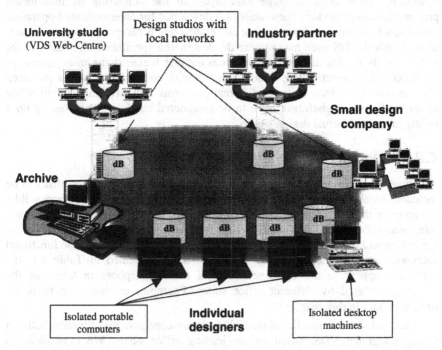

Fig. 6.16 *Highly-integrated VDS environments are based on a common platform.*

The VDS is organised by following the office automation paradigm, which structures the environment in each node around an *integrating database*. To stress this difference, the database symbol has been shown explicitly in each node in Fig. 6.16, except for the "Archive", which in both cases should have a backend database. Utilising the potential of the operating system for which they are designed, office automation suites add another layer, which brings new qualities to the environment, in particular:

- Tighter integration between applications supporting studio activities, such as drafting, word processing, spreadsheet computing, multimedia presentation and reporting, database management and project scheduling;
- A structured message system and message manager for communication and collaboration within the suite and synchronisation of studio activities.

Commercial environments which support the highly integrated desktop scenario are known as "heavy weight" groupware, with Microsoft Office, Lotus SmartSuite and Corel Office Professional suite as flagships. Their word-, spreadsheet- database- and graphics/image-processing applications constitute an already highly integrated environment. The applications, which comprise these suites, have an integration of Internet access functionality, i.e. they incorporate references to objects on the Internet in the files that they produce.

Each of these environments is supported by backend databases and servers,[5] which automate group and individual access to document repositories, project scheduling, multimedia message exchange and the delivering of multimedia presentations over the net. These suites are developed for object-oriented operating systems, which support object linking and embedding paradigm. However, the set-up of a typical VDS node may require the design of a specific configuration of the suite - usually the default configuration does not match exactly the arrangements of the VDS environment. These issues, together with compatibility issues (between the versions of an office suite for different platforms and between different office suites for the same platform), have to be considered carefully when setting up a tightly integrated virtual design studio.

6.2.1 Integration Agreements and Interface Design

This time the studio set-up starts with an agreement about the platforms that will be included. Ideally, a single platform arrangement is preferable, but, if impossible, the strategy then is to combine only platforms for which there exists a common integrated office suite. The studio set-up starts again with the agreement on the metaphors and models that will be used in the studio environments. The functional categories and the metaphors are similar to those presented in Table 6.1, the variations appear in the implementation of these metaphors in terms of the metaphors offered by different office suites. Examples of these variations are presented later in this chapter.

Table 6.4 shows a parallel of possible software configurations for constituting a tightly integrated VDS, based on the leading office suites. We have included common tools for those categories that currently are not supported by both suites (the lists of tools assume that the studio is based on a single platform - PCs running Windows OS). The tools listed in square brackets are the solutions that work for two platforms - Macintoshes and PCs.

In this scenario, the agreement about the file formats in the studio (similar to the one presented in Table 6.2) incorporates the file formats compatible with the selected office suite. This scenario also assumes that some tools cannot be included

---

[5] For example, Domino Server for Lotus SmartSuite and Microsoft Exchange Server for Microsoft Office.

in the integrated environment, for example, a CAD application is not part of an office suite and therefore does not produce a file format recognised by the office suite.

Table 6.4 *Tool categories and corresponding software for a tightly integrated VDS.*

Tool category	Software	
Text processing	Microsoft Office	Lotus SmartSuite
Word processing	Microsoft Word	Lotus Word Pro
Spreadsheet	Microsoft Excel	Lotus 1-2-3
Database management	Microsoft Access [FileMaker Pro]	Lotus Approach
Image processing		
Static	Adobe Photoshop	
Dynamic	GIF animating tools	
Graphics, CAD & 3D modelling		
Graphics software	Microsoft PowerPoint	Lotus Freelance Graphics
CAD drawings	AutoCAD [ArchiCAD]	
3D modelling	AutoCAD, [FormZ], [POV-Ray]	
Hypermedia design		
Web site design	Microsoft FrontPage [Dreamweaver, AOL Press]	Lotus Notes Designer
Web publishing	All Microsoft Office applications	All Lotus SmartSuite applications
Design presentation	Microsoft PowerPoint	Lotus Freelance Graphics
Multimedia production	Macromedia Director	
Communication tools		
Forum for notices	Bulletin board (based on Microsoft Outlook) [CGI script]	Bulletin board (from Lotus Learning Space)
Mail-cast	Microsoft Outlook [Eudora]	Use external client [Eudora]
Email	Microsoft Outlook [Eudora]	Use external client [Eudora]
Meeting tools	Microsoft Netmeeting [CUSeeMe]	
Meeting point (server)	Netmeeting server [CUSeeMe MeetingPoint]	
Point-to-Point collaboration tools	Netmeeting [CUSeeMe]	
Utilities		
Remote access	Telnet (platform specific)	
File transfer	FTP (platform specific)	
Task automation and customisation	Visual Basic Macros	LotusScript
Archiving utilities	Zip/Gzip - platform dependent utilities	
Docking utilities	Newton Utilities	

The interface design, in the case of tightly integrated studios, deviates from the Web page oriented paradigm. On the one hand, the high level of integration sets high demands on the design of the VDS desktop. The information in the VDS workspace can be structured in terms of the content produced during the design process, or according to the applications available to designers. These strategies complement each other rather than compete. On the other hand, the interface design has to exploit the advantages of the metaphors and means for interface design implemented in the office suites. We reflect these tendencies in the design of the VDS studio interface.

With some extra effort during the design stage, it is possible to achieve considerable integration in distributed desktop environments that incorporate different platforms, in particular, Windows PCs and Macintoshes. "Considerable" integration means that it goes beyond the file exchange level to the level of application functionality and interface consistency across platforms. The design of the environment requires careful selection of the combining metaphor and underlying software support, to create the perception of an almost single-platform environment.

In general, the arrangement of the desktop might not necessarily be the optimal for each of the platforms and their desktop metaphors. In other words, designers familiar with one of the platforms may find parts of the interface alien to that environment. However, this is the cost of the interface consistency, which makes the transition between platforms transparent for the designer.

We demonstrate a cross-platform integration, taking an application-oriented approach. A popular metaphor for organising the access to selected applications is the "toolbar". It consists of groups of buttons, arranged according to some selection criteria. Each button can be associated to any alias, thus, we can compose both application and document oriented toolbars. In this example, we limit the discussion to application toolbars, where buttons are associated only with applications. Fig. 6.17 shows an organisation of the access to a VDS environment on a Macintosh platform under MacOS, based on toolbars with buttons which invoke corresponding applications. In general, this is not the usual metaphor for the Macintosh desktop, which is document-oriented.

In this example, toolbars are designed, managed and executed by a separate application invoked during the start up of the VDS environment. The application-oriented toolbars provide more structured access to relevant applications than the aliases placed on the "desktop".

Fig. 6.18 shows similar desktop interface arrangements for the PC-based section (under Windows 95/NT) of the VDS environment. The implementation of the toolbars on the PC is based on the Microsoft Office Toolbar manager. Although there are visual differences on the surface, the logical organisation of button groups is similar, thus the designer can easily orient himself. Even the Windows toolbar has been moved to the top of the screen. To a certain extent, this approach minimises the difference in the control and operation of different parts of the distributed VDS environment, although they run different operating systems.

Taking into account that for each platform there are both common and different applications in each category, it is reasonable to arrange each toolbar so that buttons which correspond to the applications, common for both platforms, are on top. In Fig. 6.17 and 6.18 these are the first five buttons. The others are buttons that correspond to specific applications. If we want to impose tighter constraints, we can restrict the selection of tools in each category (with the exception of the "Utilities" category) to systems which run on both platforms. This approach is extremely useful in "large" VDS nodes, which include both platforms. VDS designers will not be confused when working on different machines - they will follow the same cognitive map for orientation in the VDS environment.

In addition to the toolbar approach, the desktop environment in Fig. 6.17 and 6.18 includes direct access to the commonly used asynchronous communication means: the incoming (the "VDS Inbox" icon), outgoing (the "VDS Outbox" icon) and broadcast mail (the "VDS Mailcast" icon) using the associated email client on each platform.

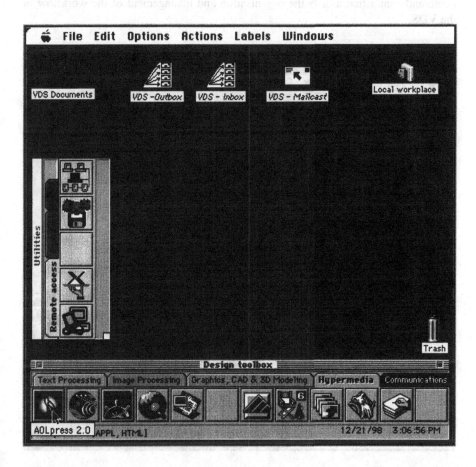

Fig. 6.17 *Application-oriented toolbars for the Macintosh desktops in a distributed VDS environment.*

Earlier we have mentioned that for tighter integration it is preferable to build the distributed VDS environment on a common platform. In this case, designers of VDS environments can use to a maximum extent the means offered by the support for the selected platform. We discuss this scenario in terms of Windows PCs, although a similar capability is offered by any consistent use of a hardware and software platform.

The integrated interface and desktop organisation of the virtual design studio employs the metaphors built-in in the office "integrators". Fig. 6.19 demonstrates interface and information design based on the metaphor of a flexible "file cabinet". The software support for this metaphor is implemented in Lotus SmartCenter[6]. Each drawer consists of folders. The content of each folder can be associated with a file, Web page, address book, project calendar, active reminder notebook, even with a specialised dictionary or thesaurus. The file cabinet drawers form a command center that assists the organisation and management of the workflow in the VDS.

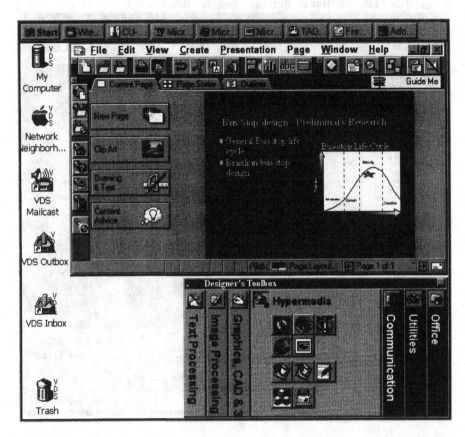

Fig. 6.18 *Application-oriented toolbars for PC desktops in a distributed VDS environment.*

The drawers presented in this figure are only part of the file cabinet of a VDS environment. The logical arrangement for the VDS desktop includes a Web drawer, "VDS Nodes", which has similar purpose and functionality to the "VDS Nodes" page from Fig. 6.4 in the loosely coupled environment. The second drawer in Fig. 6.19 is a document-oriented information container. In this drawer, designers keep various electronic documents used during the project development:

---

[6] We refer to Lotus SmartCenter 97, which is part of the Lotus SmartSuite.

dictionaries, thesauri, CAD and other vector drawings, images, texts, spreadsheets and other design documents and design information.

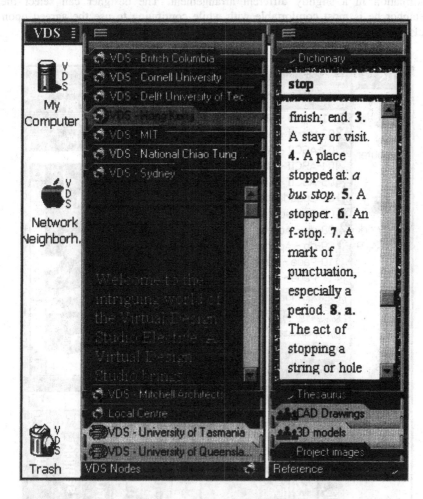

Fig. 6.19 *"VDS nodes" and project information (labelled as "Reference") in a tightly integrated VDS desktop, organised using Lotus SmartSuite.*

When making crucial decisions about the selection of an underlying interface and information management metaphor, it is necessary to take into account the familiarity of designers with the interfaces in consideration. In addition to the common interface selected for the studio machines, it is advisable to provide alternative ways to operate within the VDS environment. The extra effort spent in consistent data structuring and environment configuration will pay off when running the studio.

For example, including alternative interfaces in a tightly integrated VDS environment can make it easier to extend the studio or include an additional platform. Fig. 6.20 shows the "Designer's Toolbox" accessible both from the filecabinet and toolbar interfaces. These different interfaces present the same information in a slightly different arrangement. The designer can select the metaphor he is most comfortable with while continuing to use the agreed upon tools and formats.

Fig. 6.20 *Different interface metaphors used simultaneously in a distributed VDS environment.*

Largely speaking, the implementation of a toolbar of controls in object-oriented operating systems is merely an arrangement of folders (directories) and shortcuts (aliases). The underlying common directory structure for the files and applications shown in Fig. 6.20 is shown in Fig. 6.21. When viewed from the application environment interface, these structures usually remain transparent to the user. Similar structures could be implemented for sorting and accessing design representations, documents, communication transcripts and other related design information.

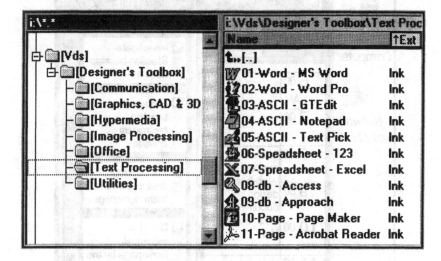

Fig. 6.21 *The underlying directory structure for the example in Fig. 6.20.*

The intuitive interface elements provided by the office integration metaphor (in our example - the file cabinet) provide a rich means for the design and arrangement of the desktop interface for access to distributed VDS environments. The drag/drop rearrangement of these elements, the convenient access to local information and active folder content, and remote Web documents, influences the management and collaboration in such environments.

6.2.2 Management and Collaboration

Powerful project, personal and team information managers are integrated parts of the groupware "giants". Although manager functionality varies across different products, the kernel components - calendar, task planner and logistic manager, contact book and active notepad, are implemented in almost every desktop manager to automate task prioritisation and scheduling, meeting appointments, long-term events, the organisation of work information and contacts.

This support can be integrated within the main metaphor used to organise the information on the desktop and within specialised applications. Fig. 6.22 illustrates the idea of incorporating project calendar and active notepad ("VDS Calendar" and "VDS Reminders" drawers, respectively) through the file cabinet metaphor. The project logistics and design planning in this example reflect the concurrent development of two projects: a virtual design office and a bus stop. Participants

can be notified of the coming events and can keep track of completed tasks by
"ticking" boxes as shown in Fig. 6.22.

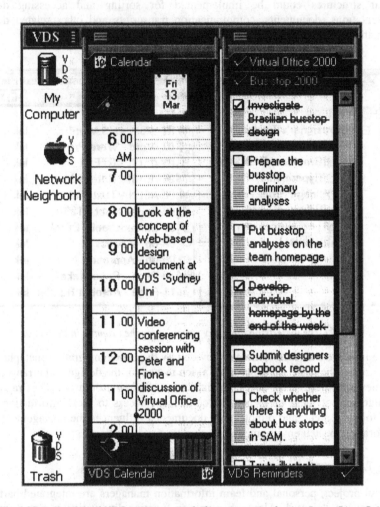

Fig. 6.22 *A distributed VDS environment desktop, organised using Lotus SmartSuite.*

When selecting the personal information manager the following issues have to be
taken into consideration:

- The integration of the tool, and file and message formats with the rest of
  the VDS environment;
- The ability of the tool to exchange information with portable computing
  devices;
- The compatibility of the interface metaphor with the rest of the
  environment.

Personal information managers can be used away from the VDS network and
later the changes can be incorporated and synchronised with other information in

the VDS environment. The scheduling software can assist a designer in handling most aspects of the management of meetings and appointments - creating, automatic scheduling and rescheduling, changing and categorising them. Project coordinators can create repeating appointments, for example, scheduling weekly meetings. The automatic set-up of reminding email may include an attachment of drawings, images, spreadsheets or other design materials relevant to the meeting, or may print these files before the meeting. Designers can manage different threads in their work by linking meetings from the same thread. When the schedule is becoming overwhelmingly busy an interactive time line eases the resolution of time conflicts.

The components of personal information managers are highly integrated with each other and with the other components of the groupware suite. Fig. 6.23 presents an implementation of designer's logbook using a "planner" page. The categories in this case are labelled by different colours. The groups of categories are indicated by the letters: "C" - Communication, "L" - Learning, "R" - Research and "D" - Design development.

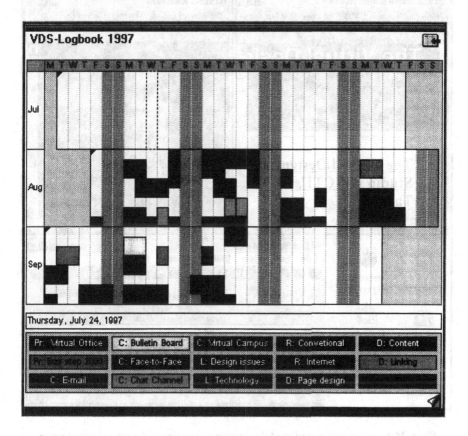

Fig. 6.23 *A designer's personal time log, based on a customised "planner" page in Lotus Organiser.*

During the development of the design project some tasks usually require more computing resources and sophisticated data structures whereas other tasks require more planning and research. The arrangement of the tasks and their distribution among participants in the virtual design studio provide the guidelines for additional tuning and customisation of individual desktop environments. Sometimes such a need may occur as a result of the metaphor selected for the organisation of the VDS environment. For instance, if the command centre of the VDS environment desktop is based on the application-oriented approach, the functionality of the desktop of the studio coordinator may need additional document- and site-oriented support. The coordinating role requires frequent access to a number of studio Web pages and sites, including individual and team homepages, design documentation pages and design group discussions. Fig. 6.24 illustrates the idea of using additional specialised software support – in this case the MultiWeb Viewer[7], for structured and simultaneous retrieval and caching of groups of pages.

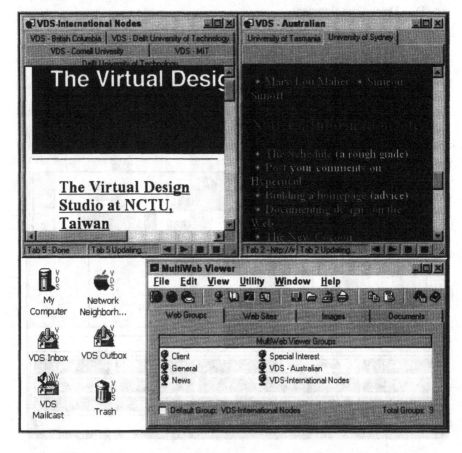

Fig. 6.24 *A specialised extension of the desktop environment of a project coordinator.*

---

[7] http://www.multisource.com/indexmultiweb.htm.

The access to the team manager in Fig. 6.25 shows the advantages of the combination of an integrated desktop with existing Web-based studio components, in this example, the Web-based VDS manager from the loosely coupled scenario. The configuration of the file cabinet in this case elegantly replaces a Web page which links the VDS nodes and VDS document repository.

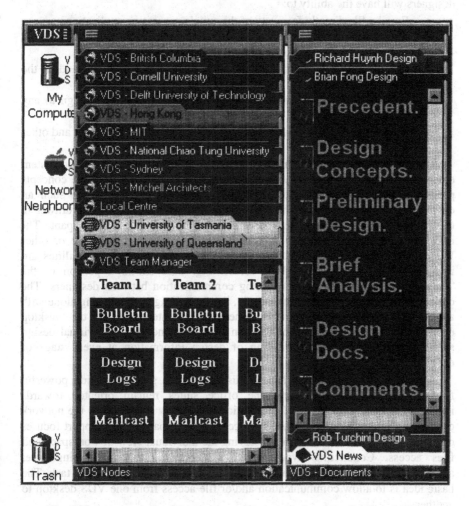

Fig. 6.25 *An arrangement of project coordinator's desktop in a distributed VDS.*

6.2.3 Communication and Collaboration

The tight integration offers new dimensions to the communication and collaboration in the VDS environment. Due to identical installation and configuration of the suite in every VDS node, designers should be able to communicate information between nodes with minimum additional conversions and manual information management.

Communication and collaboration in a VDS environment, based on "heavy weight" groupware, will be significantly smoother if a dedicated specialist in information technology performs the set-up and support. Competent set-up, both of the configuration of client suites and communication server will provide participants with the complete power of such integrated suites. In particular, designers will have the ability to:

- Email a file directly from any of the suite's processing applications;
- Automate the synchronisation, updating and control procedures of document reviewing, collaborative editing and publishing;
- Secure design documents stored across the VDS workspace and in the VDS archive;
- Deliver slide presentations during the development of the design to any VDS node;
- Transfer and exchange data between the applications of the suite and other applications used in the design process.

The use of a common integrating metaphor creates a cohesive and consistent environment, with low cognitive overhead, due to the familiarity of the concepts presented. When kept within the metaphor, designers can operate in such an environment having less technical knowledge. For example, a separate drawer in the file cabinet can contain the contact data for each studio participant. The information from the "drawer" is passed directly to email, fax, phone or other Internet synchronous communication clients. These communication utilities are invoked directly from the address folder. Fig. 6.26 shows a portion of the "drawers" environment activated during communication between designers. The collaboration is occurring asynchronously, that is, a designer is working alone with access to the other designers' documents. The integration of the desktop environment allows access to information from other nodes in the virtual design studio, enhancing the communication of design information at every stage of development.

Although the applications that we discuss in this section provide powerful features for collaborative work, the office suites remain oriented towards individual desktop computing. Collaboration is typically supported by the network capabilities in sending files, email, and access to Web pages. This support focuses on asynchronous communication, preserving the individual view of workspace and files access. Conducting synchronous collaborative work with single-user applications in a VDS spatially and temporally distributed is not a trivial task. The basic idea is to allow communication and/or file access from one VDS desktop to another.

Synchronous communication is possible in desktop computing by using a specific tool for talking or collaboratively editing a document. Talking to another designer is possible using a chat window or a video conference. The style of communication is very different in each: a chat window enables talking through typing messages and a video conference allows talking through an audio connection. This leads to different communication styles in synchronous communication. For example, typing skills become essential for successful text-based collaboration.

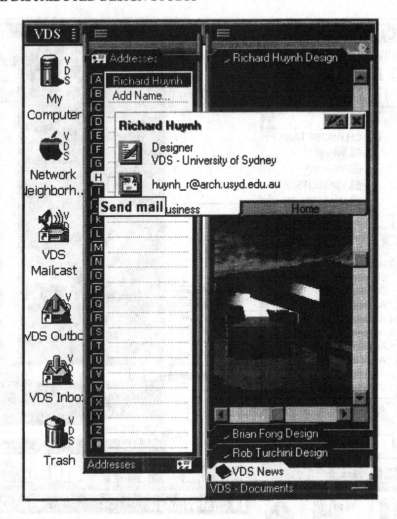

Fig. 6.26 *Asynchronous information communication in a distributed VDS environment.*

Fig. 6.27 depicts a moment from design collaboration. In this scenario, designers are talking to each other in a chat window while referring to the same portion of the project - the water tank for the designed house. The chat window provides for synchronous communication, both participants are present while the messages are sent. This figure also illustrates the use of another drawer - "VDS documents" - for examining the design concepts of another team member. Folders in this drawer contain web design documents developed by individual team members. This folder provides for access and possibly for editing shared documents. However, it does not necessarily provide for collaborative, synchronous modification of the shared documents. Collaboratively editing a shared document is equivalent to a chat tool for talking, except the focus is on the document being developed rather than the conversation.

Fig. 6.27 *Collaborative work in a distributed VDS.*

An alternative to a chat tool is NetMeeting. NetMeeting, as it can be guessed from the name, uses the metaphor of "meeting". Meetings are held via dedicated servers. In the NetMeeting environment, in addition to the common audio, video and chat communication channels and the whiteboard collaboration tool, participants can collaborate at each other's desktops. This type of collaboration is illustrated in Fig. 6.28.

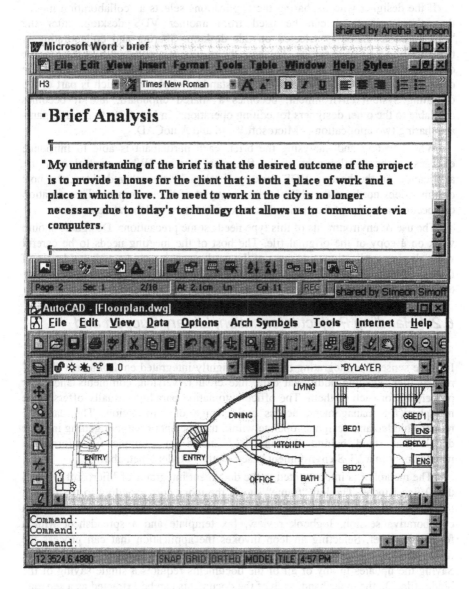

Fig. 6.28 *Sharing a single-user application in a collaborative session on a VDS desktop.*

There are several ways of collaborating, depending on the level of interference allowed to various parties. When working, designers can select one or more applications running on the desktop and announce them as "shared". When sharing an application, other designers will be able to see the actual work going on in these applications, but will not be able to interact with it. This mode can be used for demonstration or training sessions, for showing the dynamic development of some ideas and to consult with others.

If the designer who is sharing the applications selects a "collaboration mode" then the applications can be used from another VDS desktop, after the "collaboration" mode is selected on this desktop. Sharing and collaborating is realistic for a pair of desktops. To share the results of a collaborative session, the designer who has been the host of the meeting should email the final file(s) to the other participant. During the meeting, the standard clipboard, which is part of the operating system environment, becomes a shared clipboard, and it becomes available to the other designers for editing operations. In Fig. 6.28, two participants are sharing two applications - Microsoft Word and AutoCAD.

When reading and analysing the brief, each participant is able to introduce changes in the development of the floorplan drawing. When control over the application on the hosting VDS desktop is taken by the other desktop, the host designer does not have the ability to use any part of the workspace. This situation can become a source of frustration in cases of intensive collaborative sessions.

The use of environments of this type needs some precautions. Designers should work on a copy of the original file. The host of the meeting needs to be careful when sharing applications and parts of the workspace, to avoid accidental losses of files, or sharing private files and applications. The information handling issues are the subject of the next section.

6.2.4 Handling Project Information, Library Support and Documentation

In some sense, the integrating database in tightly integrated environments "binds" related files, keeping additional data, like creator, version, comments and other properties, for each of them. The office automation paradigm usually offers some metaphor for management, access and change of information. The database remains hidden and designers operate within this metaphor without getting into the details that stand behind it. Fig. 6.29 shows an example of information management in a VDS environment based on the "binder" metaphor.

The metaphor is implemented in the document integrator of Microsoft Office - the Office Binder. The left "frame" shows the icons corresponding to the files in the binder, in this case a project task diagram, communication transcript from a collaborative session, logbook review, fax template and a spreadsheet with a formalised brief. Selecting an icon invokes the application that can process the information of the corresponding type - in this example this is Lotus WordPro. Saving the updates in any or all of the documents requires a single saving of the binder file. On the other hand, each of the documents can be extracted as a separate file in the corresponding format, or, in terms of the metaphor - released from the binder.

The use of different metaphors in organising and accessing the VDS workspace can bring some confusion about the physical allocation of the data files. Applications, which are part of a suite, usually use specific default directories to store their data or document files. Other applications, which are not part of the suite, but are integrated in the VDS environment, may use another directory for the same purpose. Thus, when setting up a highly integrated studio environment, the default data file directories for studio work should be explicitly defined.

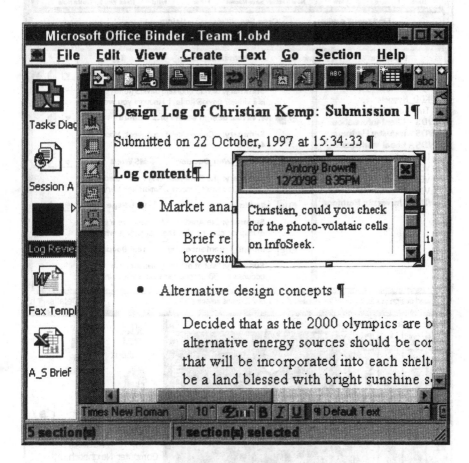

Fig. 6.29 *Using the "binder" metaphor to organise and manage a variety of information chunks in a distributed VDS environment (based on Microsoft Office Binder).*

The VDS desktop can include advanced information management tools with automatic classifying functions, which index and cross-reference information in the local workspace, including word, spreadsheet and database files, email messages, even bookmarks of Web sites. In Fig. 6.30, the information about related topics or subjects is kept together in a single active reference, the "tracker".

The tracker not only keeps the already classified information, but also updates its content (the list of files associated with that tracker), putting the new data together with related information. In a sense, one can think of a system of trackers as an active binder, which automatically selects what is to be attached to the already existing batch of files.

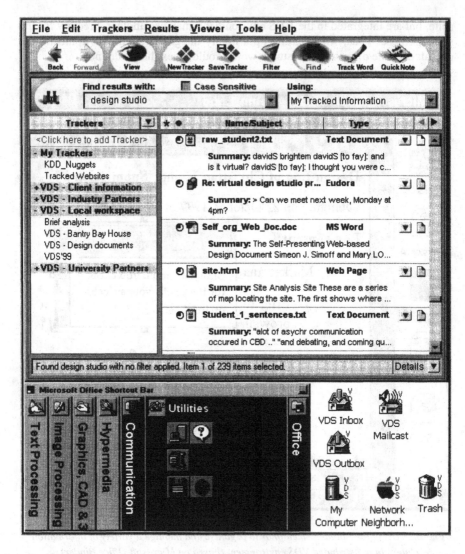

Fig. 6.30 *Advanced information management in a distributed VDS environment.*

Tracker Pro, in particular, scans a variety of data sources, including several hundred data file formats. The designer does not need to remember the file names, types and locations or email folders and bookmark files to find the information related to the subject. Studio participants may shift between a virtual design studio project, courses in design computing and consultant work for a real-estate agency.

Recalling a tracker brings up the information organised under the subject in consideration. Usually, the topics of interest include keywords associated with them. Thus, a keyword search is another way to recall a tracker. The example in Fig. 6.30 shows the use of the words "design studio" to recall text files, MS Word documents, web pages, email messages and other related files from the trackers under the "VDS - Local workspace". Retrieved items are described by automatically generated summaries. A designer can also add "cover notes"[8], as shown in Fig. 6.31.

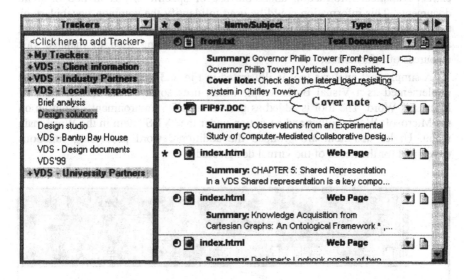

Fig. 6.31 *Cover notes contain additional information added by designers.*

6.2.5 Customisation and Further Automation in a Tightly Integrated VDS

Further integration and automation of the workflow within the virtual design studio can be achieved by customising the suite, adding functionality written in the scripting language of the selected integrating suite. For example, a macro can accompany a particular set of data files, defining the order to process them and passing the right file to the right application. Some typical tasks in a virtual design studio, like formalisation of the brief according to a particular information integration model, file conversions, and report generation, can be semi or fully automated in this fashion. For example, if the VDS environment is built using the Microsoft Office suite, then a relatively simple script in Visual Basic can generate database structures for handling the data from a design brief. Fig. 3.28 (Chapter 3) shows the visual representation of a created structure in Microsoft Access.

Using the scripting language, the designers of the studio environment can add some specific functionality to the VDS environment, for example, linking elements from CAD drawings to spreadsheet tables, an addition of text analysis functionality to the word processing tools, or automated notification about document updates. "Heavy weight" groupware environments provide a wide range of customisation opportunities: from simple application menu customisation to powerful object-

---

[8] Cover notes are similar to the "Comments" in a Macintosh MacOS file system.

oriented scripting languages for different task automation and even building of specialised applications.

An example of a specialised application is a text analyser. A text analyser can extract statistical information about the use of specific words in one or more documents. This information could be used to identify the common vocabulary of the designers or to provide information in order to improve readability. Text analysis is a relatively new addition to the tools being used to manage vast resources of information.

A simple text analysis tool is illustrated in Fig. 6.32. The text analysis tool is implemented as a Visual Basic script, which uses some of the functionality of Microsoft Word. The tool is added as part of the VDS environment - a button on the Microsoft Word toolbar and an option under the "VDS" item in the Word main menu. Under this item are grouped the additional word processing functions developed for the needs of the virtual design studio.

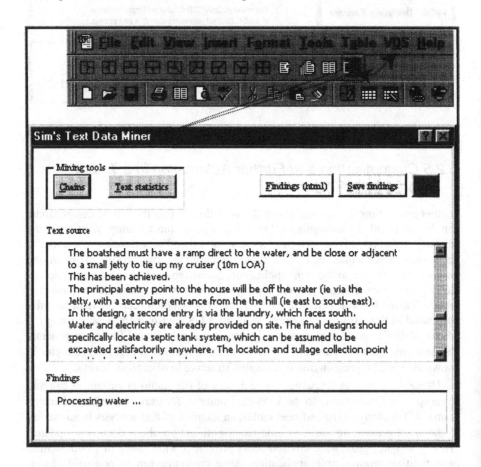

Fig. 6.32 *A simple text analysis assistant added to the VDS environment.*

6.3 Recapitulation

The distributed VDS environments discussed are not mutually exclusive categories. Each scenario has its strong and weak sides, and they complement each other. Although collaborative technologies promise fundamental change in collaboration over the Internet, they still remain a complementary part of the single-user environments. On the other hand, although the hypertext metaphor of the Web provides great potential, it has a number of metaphorical and technical constraints, such as the development of Web languages (HTML, Java, CGI), and the continuous modifications to its standards.

The distributed VDS workspace is designed to provide a rich set of tools to support various design and collaboration activities. The metaphors used to organise these tools usually come from real-life environments. These metaphors are used to organise and support the tools for design and communication. Designers are then called to select and customise the appropriate tools to satisfy their needs.

References

Marca, D. and Bock, G. (eds) (1992) *Groupware: Software for Computer-Supported Cooperative Work*, IEEE Computer Society Press, California.

Tan, M. and Teh, M. (eds) (1995) *The Global Design Studio*, Centre for Advanced Studies in Architecture, National University of Singapore, Singapore.

Seven

A Centralised VDS Environment

The previous chapter looked at various tools and techniques for implementing distributed VDS environments. Nodes were integrated in a single environment by agreeing on a specific set of standards and tools. This kind of integration is essential in any VDS.

In this chapter, we consider a centralised VDS in which a single server handles all the tools and specifications to achieve transactions between nodes. The centralised VDS approach minimises the discrepancies between working individually and collaboratively, and unifies the environment shared by nodes. The idea of a common environment for both individual and collaborative activities is supported by the research in CSCW. Some of this research suggests that when working, the individual adopts at least two roles: *personal manager* and *worker*. As *personal manager*, the individual plans, coordinates and schedules the activities in the future. As *worker*, the individual performs various tasks in order to achieve the goals set during the personal management phase. The idea of *cross-platform Internet groupware*, seems to best integrate this double aspect of being a manager and a worker in a multi-platform VDS.

The progress in the development of cross-platform groupware systems has a strong influence on the design of centralised VDS environments. Groupware systems offer means of customisation, according to tasks and user's needs. Currently, research efforts are focussed on using Java-based groupware, which allows the development and performance of platform independent software.

Centralised VDS environments follow a client/server model, where single users access the central server. The central server contains all the tools and information needed, and it controls all the input/output flow to the clients. In a sequential process, the client's input is transmitted to the central server, which processes it and returns the result before processing the next input. In this way, clients and central server are easily synchronised, although a high number of transactions between clients and server slows down the whole environment.

The strengths of a central VDS can be found in:

- A fully integrated set of tools, which can exchange information with simple operations;
- An easy accessibility to the environment;
- An intuitive integrated interface, working with natural language and icons;

- A reduced load of set-up times and problems (for example, installing software);
- Interchangeability between platforms (Unix, Macintosh, DOS/Windows based).

The major weakness of a central VDS is the difficulty in replacing a familiar tool with the central server tool once the environment has been established. Most of the applications used in these environments are specifically designed, and they require programming experience to be modified. However, this apparent inflexibility can be reduced by using standard protocols, such as HTTP, in order to give users maximum choice.

In this chapter, we present two different approaches to running a centralised VDS, based on two concepts: the desktop and the place. We will use these two concepts as *metaphors of reference*, that is, conceptual frameworks which represent, by comparison with the physical world, a way of managing the VDS.

The *desktop* metaphor consists of a set of tools – for communication and collaboration – running on the shared environment, which provides the complete set used in the VDS. This set of tools is centrally served.

The *place* metaphor, instead, represents a single place, where users *go* to communicate and collaborate. Tools are embedded in that place's supporting software. A VDS that runs as a *place* should be thought of as a physical office, where designers find all the tools and information needed to complete various tasks, which sometimes may not be strictly related to the design process.

7.1 The Desktop Metaphor

The desktop metaphor refers to the use of VDS tools as if they were lying on a working desk of a physical office. On the desktop, and nearby, a designer finds tools for drawing (e.g. pencils and rulers), communicating (e.g. telephone), archiving (e.g. folders or filing cabinets), organising (e.g. diary), finding information (e.g. catalogues or archives), and so on. In general, he has access to all the office resources needed to perform the design task. On the electronic desktop – which is based on a metaphor of the physical one - all the functions are collected on the same interface, in this case, visible on the computer screen.

In this section, we illustrate two technologies that can be used to build a VDS based on the metaphor of the desktop: NCSA Habanero, which uses the TCP/IP standards and Java programming language, and TeamWave, which uses proprietary protocols. Written entirely in Java, Habanero includes the networking facilities, routing, arbitration and synchronisation mechanisms necessary for sharing data and key events. TeamWave, based on the research results of the GroupLab project team at the Department of Computer Science, University of Calgary, is a proprietary protocol used to implement shared applications.

7.1.1 Habanero

Habanero[1] is an example of a collaborative framework, based on Java applets. The applications or tools that work in the Habanero framework were programmed in an ad hoc manner. The environment can be easily adapted to perform various tasks: synchronous interaction and messaging, real time visualisation and modification of objects, exchange of documents and drawing files. Fig 7.1 shows an environment which includes various clients, all connected via the Internet to a node selected as a central server.

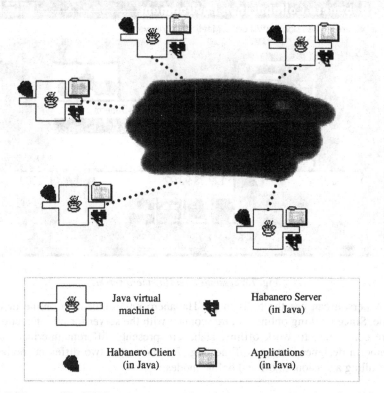

Fig. 7.1 *A centralised VDS environment, with a single server running, based on NCSA Habanero.*

VDS environments based on Habanero can act as clients only, or clients and servers at the same time. As a server, a node can host a number of sessions, accepting connections from other clients. A single designer can interact with other nodes, running various applications in real time. However, running multi-user applications might slow down the network connections quite considerably, and it would be preferable, when setting up the environment, to dedicate special attention to the quality of the applets and the number of users who are going to use them.

---

[1] http://www.ncsa.uich.edu.

A session in Habanero is defined by a session name, the names of people connected, and server information. To join a collaborative session, a participant selects the host and the session name. In the configuration shown in Fig. 7.2, a session called "Virtual Design Studio" runs on the host called "fay.arch.usyd.edu.au" at the port 2000. Multiple sessions can run at the same time on the same host as shown in Fig. 7.2. Where it is impossible to attend two physical meetings at the same time, it is possible to attend two virtual meetings.

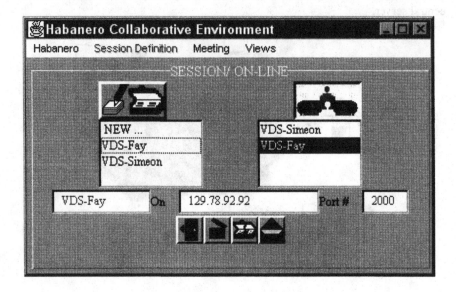

Fig. 7.2 *Sessions on a Habanero server.*

A person can use the tools in the Habanero environment in online or offline mode. Since working online requires contact with the server for all interaction, it is more convenient to work offline. Habanero presents different interface controls whether a designer is on or offline. Fig. 7.3 shows the two different toolbars for controlling a session, in off and online modes.

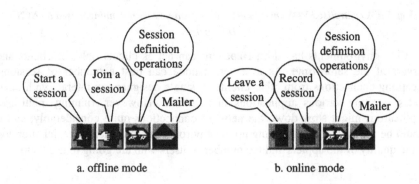

Fig. 7.3 *Basic environment controls in off and online modes of the VDS environment.*

We have configured an arrangement of the desktop in Habanero for the VDS, as shown in Fig. 7.4.

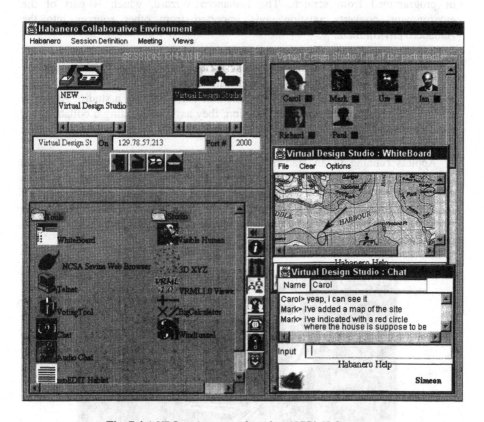

Fig. 7.4 *A VDS environment, based on NCSA Habanero.*

The upper left of the window shows the sessions that are active, with the session control panel indicating that the person is working online. The upper right side of the window shows the participants in the studio project. This view shows the first name and a picture of each person. Additional information about the person's connection to the environment is available. The lower left side of the window shows the tools available in the Habanero environment. The tools shown include: a whiteboard, a web browser, telnet, a voting tool, a chat tool, an audio chat tool, a collaborative editing tool, a 3D modeller, a VRML viewer, a calculator, and a wind tunnel. These are a subset of applications available in Habanero, we have selected those we thought relevant to a design studio.

The right side of the window shows two applications being shared in the current session: a whiteboard and a chat room. The whiteboard is a shared drawing tool, in this case, showing a map. The chat tool is the application in which the participants in the session can talk to one another.

Habanero technology offers a basis for hosting cross platform applications, preserving the consistency of the VDS environment at all levels. These applications, also called Hablets, are then shared among the participants in the studio. Hablets can be derived from a variety of Java sources: applets, applications or programmed from scratch. The Habanero Wizard, which is part of the environment, converts existing code imported from other sources into the Habanero environment.

In addition to the traditional communication tools like "chat" and "whiteboard", an environment like Habanero can include applications like the "VRML viewer", and versions of other Internet-based applications like a web browser, or a telnet interface. These tools can become fundamental when running a studio. Although not directly related to design representation, they assist in creating a collaborative environment by providing access to other participants in the studio and other computers on the network.

Applets running in an Habanero environment look and perform the same, independently of the number of users and their platforms. The environment takes care of the synchronisation, queuing and visualisation of the document. Every participant shares the same kind of control with others, that is, s/he can modify the file in the same way others can. The working file can be saved individually, on the participants' machines.

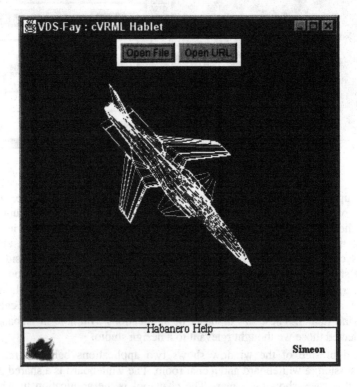

Fig. 7.5 *The Habanero VRML viewer.*

A VRML viewer allows participants to see and manipulate a 3D VRML object. In Fig. 7.5, the aircraft is viewed and manipulated by all the participants in the session. Being able to view models in 3D is becoming a necessary component of a VDS. Advanced viewing systems can include semi and full immersive systems, where participants wear stereo glasses or helmets that give a realistic view of objects and places.

Collaboratively viewing a VRML file is an extension of the ability to view a VRML file on the Web. When using a conventional Web browser to view a VRML file, the person does not know who else is looking at the file at that time. Collaboratively viewing a VRML file is similar to two people sharing the same computer (except they do not need to be in the same location), the participants in the session can discuss what they are seeing as the 3D model is being manipulated. By incorporating the VRML viewer in the Habanero environment, the other communication tools (such as a chat or video conference tool) enhance the ability to collaborate.

Another example of the enhanced features for collaborative work in this environment is the collaborative Web browser. Fig. 7.6 shows a session of discussion on a design brief, using NCSA Savina collaborative Web browser[2]. This is what "Paul" sees on his desktop; other designers will see a similar interface on theirs. If any one of the designers decides to move to another Web page, everyone participating in the session will get the new document.

A collaborative Web browser can be effectively used to broadcast information to every participant and obtain a real time response. Being able to browse the Web collaboratively, that is, seeing what others are seeing and being able to comment, is an interesting way of consulting an archive. This can be compared to going to a library with other designers, taking books off the shelves, looking at pictures, and commenting on them.

Other applications useful in a VDS are collaborative text-editing, shown in Fig. 7.7, and shared boards for the simultaneous display of pictures and data. Collaborative text editing allows text files to be shared and edited simultaneously by more than one person. Complementary to text editing, shared boards allow simultaneous editing of digital images, including facilities for adding and changing drawings, text, and imported bitmap images.

The ability to extend the Habanero environment to make use of existing single-user applications familiar to designers is a considerable advantage and should not be overlooked by the developers of VDS environments. Moreover, developers should become familiar with both the architecture of the environment and the Java programming language, in order to take the maximum advantage of the Habanero technology. The diffusion and popularity of Java is a factor to consider when choosing Habanero based environments. Also, the versatility of this programming language and its cross-platform characteristics, make Habanero an interesting alternative for setting up a virtual design studio.

Fig. 7.8 shows a Java single-user application for conceptual room design. Following Habanero technology, this application can be converted to a multi-user, shared application and incorporated in a VDS environment, enhancing

---

[2] NSCA Savina Collaborative Web Browser for Habanero is a hablet version of Hot Java Web browser.

environment functionality. Not only can the participants view the file in the design application at the same time, they can each make changes to the design.

Fig. 7.6 *Collaborative web browsing in a brief analysis session.*

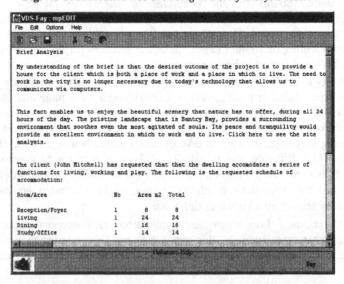

Fig. 7.7 *Collaborative editing in one of the studio sessions.*

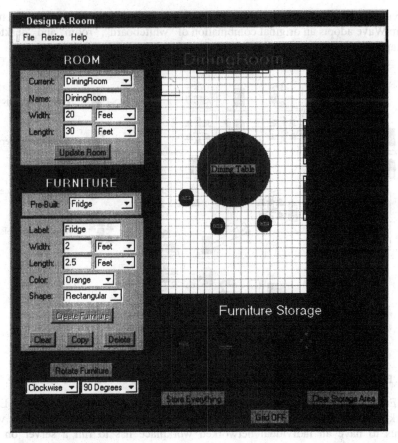

Fig. 7.8 *A conceptual design tool, written in Java, is a potential part of a Habanero-based VDS.*

7.1.2 TeamWave

TeamWave, another example of the desktop metaphor for a VDS using proprietary software and protocols, is developed as a customised shared *place*. Although the participant continues to work on the desktop, the various tools and windows make references to rooms and offices creating a place. The owner of the place decides access and permission for each individual user. Again, this environment is platform independent, based on a specific protocol for data transmission. This means that each user must run a client able to connect to a server, like in the case of Habanero, but the client will use a proprietary protocol. In this section, we will introduce the TeamWave WorkPlace software, now in version 4[3], as an example of proprietary protocol.

In TeamWave, similar to Habanero, the full configuration of a desktop workspace includes a server and a client, as illustrated in Fig. 7.9. While Habanero

---

[3] http://www.teamwave.com.

provides a set of tools (Java applets) which are based on the shared architecture, TeamWave adopts an original combination of "whiteboard", "room" and "desktop" metaphors to organise the interactions and information in the VDS.

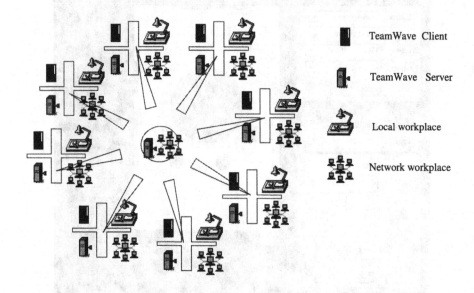

Fig. 7.9 *The configuration of a VDS environment, based on TeamWave groupware.*

Each server handles a collection of rooms which form a workplace. Each workplace corresponds to a separate copy of the same server. A designer who wants to have an individual networked workplace has to run a server on his machine.

Each individual workplace can be accessed in both local and network mode. In local mode, the place is accessible only from the machine on which the server runs. This mode is effective for local development of ideas, prototypes and similar individual tasks. The local environment is isolated from the rest of the network. In network mode, many participants can join the same server, and share the same "place".

When all the participants are connected to the network, they may experience delays if running bandwidth demanding applications. It may be more useful to run those applications in local mode, and connect to the network only when needed.

The environment conditions the way in which participants can collaborate. Each user may decide, for example, to allow public access to their own applications. When visiting a user's space, other users may bring their own objects (applications, documents, and so on) to be shared in the environment. This metaphor is similar to what happens in a physical office, where a meeting is set among participants who come with their own equipment. While this metaphor is quite intuitive and easy to embrace, it may become restrictive and slow down the whole environment if, for example, the same document or tool is replicated a number of times.

A better way to exploit the advantages of the place metaphor is to allow individuals to run their own workplaces locally, and to collaborate through a central workplace, served by a central machine. The number of central workplaces depends on the project characteristics. If participants in the studio are united in one team and work on one common project, then one central workplace should be sufficient. If several participants work competitively on a common project, and use a single "central" workplace, they might have to be organised in teams. A team may set "privileges" to isolate and protect its workspace. Privileges for each room can also be set separately, as shown in Fig. 7.10.

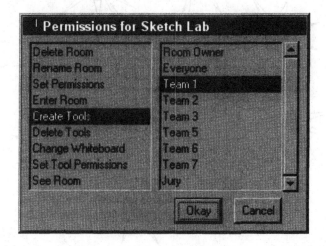

Fig. 7.10 *The organisation of permissions for the various teams.*

Several rooms can be set up in order for the same team to access various stages of a project, as shown in Fig. 7.11. Each team will then have permission to access only a certain number of them.

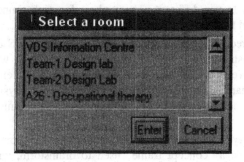

Fig. 7.11 *A selection of rooms in a shared workspace.*

Each team can run its own workplace, that is a separate TeamWave server, and they all connect to a central TeamWave server. This approach is illustrated in Fig. 7.12. Common documents and tools (tutorials, briefs, handbooks, instructions, and similar) can be placed on this central server, so that they will not need to be replicated on each team's server.

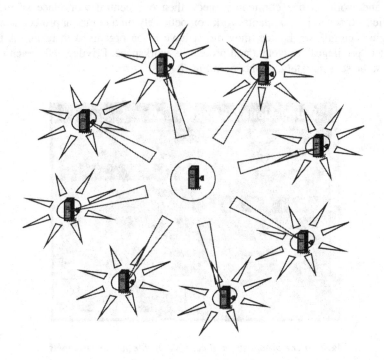

Fig. 7.12 *Competitive teams can use separate workplaces, running their own TeamWave server, and connect to a central one.*

If, for administrative reasons, it is better to have all teams on the same server, then it is necessary to use different port numbers for each connection. The same solution can be used for a team working on a large scale project.

We have prepared a sample interface of the integrated VDS desktop based on TeamWave, as illustrated in Fig. 7.13. Each room contains a whiteboard, which can be used by everyone in the room. Designing a VDS environment using TeamWave is in many ways equivalent to the design of a physical environment, where various tools and repositories of information can be organised to simulate an office space.

For example, Fay's office in Fig. 7.13 contains several tutorials; a whiteboard used for annotations; a "concept frame" used to brainstorm, with tools like the "link types" window; and other information about participants, their idling time, and location.

On the top of the room view, there is information about the whole virtual place. On the left-hand side there is information about a user's current position in the workplace, other designers who are in the same room and a comprehensive list of rooms. On the right-hand side, there is information about all connected users and their positions.

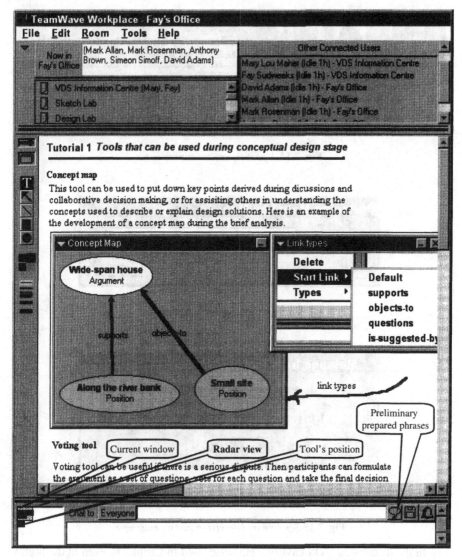

Fig. 7.13 *A view of the VDS desktop interface implemented in TeamWave.*

More information about any of the designers currently in the workplace can be found by selecting a user from that list. A business card for that user is then displayed, as shown in Fig. 7.14. The crossed icon before the "Design Lab" indicates that "Fay" cannot currently access that room.

By selecting the word "page", on the bottom right of the window, it is possible to send an instant message to another user. Fig. 7.15 shows the message composed and sent from Fay, in the "Sketch Lab", to Mary, in her office.

Fig. 7.14 *A participant's business card.*

Fig. 7.15a:

Paging Mary Lou Maher...

Message: Can you add a brief introduction to SAM?

Page   Cancel

a. Sending a message to a person

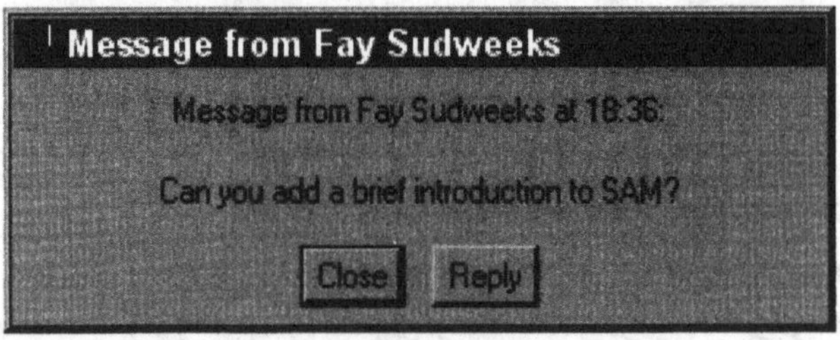

Fig. 7.15b:

Message from Fay Sudweeks

Message from Fay Sudweeks at 18:36:

Can you add a brief introduction to SAM?

Close   Reply

b. This is how the person receives the message on the desktop

Fig. 7.15 *Sending and receiving instant messages.*

In the distributed VDS environments discussed in Chapter 6, even in the highly integrated ones, designers needed to establish connections between different tools and communication channels, and to transfer files from the shared desktop to their individual workspace. In the TeamWave environment, a room is both connector and container. It connects designers as soon as they are "in" and it contains their work.

An important component of VDS environments is the integration of the local set of tools and documents with the networked collaborative environment. Documents must be able to be easily transferred and used collaboratively. This integration can be resolved in different ways. One of them is to decrease the size of the windows used, so they all fit within the user's screen. TeamWave approaches this problem in two ways: by using the room metaphor, and by providing a set of tools appropriate for that specific room. Resizing the desktop will also resize the windows contained in it, and the quality of the information produced.

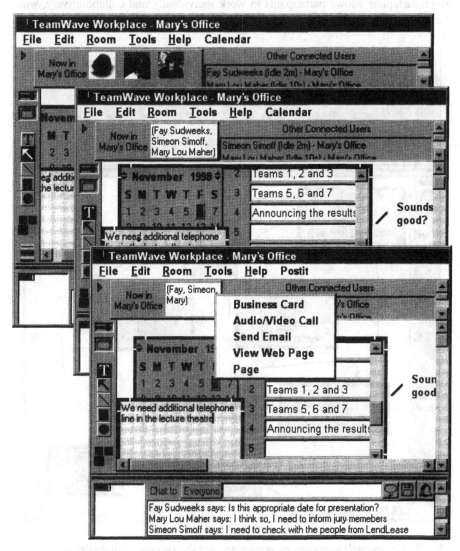

Fig. 7.16 *A moment of collaborative decision making in a VDS.*

For example, in the three windows in Fig. 7.16, participants are displayed in three different ways: full names and pictures, full names, and first names only. All the technical possibilities - for example, business cards, access to other rooms, opening tools - remain available. Fig. 7.16 also illustrates the relative freedom that each participant has during a collaborative session. Participants can be in different parts of the room, or using a different tool, without affecting the general view of the whole environment. Fig. 7.16 represents a moment of negotiation and scheduling of a final team presentation in Mary's office. In this case, the advantage of the room metaphor is clear: although on separate desktops, team members are present at the same time in the same room, and engage in synchronous work. The room metaphor allows participants to work individually and collaboratively, with minimal effort.

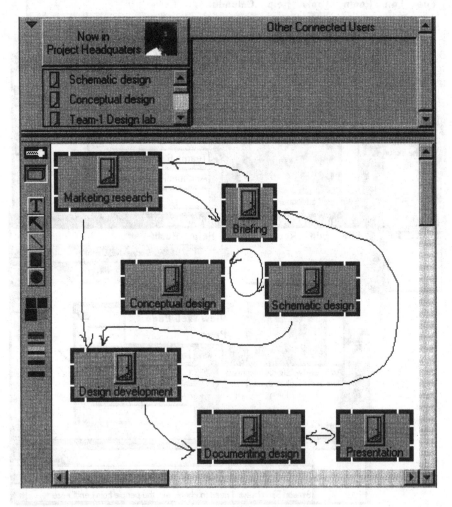

Fig. 7.17 *An example of organising environment topology according to the design process.*

Fig. 7.17 illustrates a different topology of the designed environment. Using the "pencil" annotation on the whiteboard and the "Doorway" tool, rooms are configured to support the iterative nature of the design process. The contents of each room could be transferred to the design description and documentation at a different time, and used in the design presentation.

A "doorway" is a way of linking two rooms, that is, two areas of the workspace containing different tools and different documents. The links in the model are implemented through the doorways, which also represent the developed hierarchy of the design. For example, designing a specific area of a building can be accomplished by entering the door with the same name, to find reference tools and documents related to that area design.

The TeamWave environment can be customised to meet the needs of a specific task. 3D modelling tools and special brainstorming boards can be designed and placed in the environment, creating a series of plug-ins on all TeamWave clients. The TeamWave protocols and programming language, however, makes the customisation a more complex task compared, for example, to Habanero which is Java-based. Using TeamWave has the advantage of creating an environment which has an already defined architecture, that is, a ready-to-use studio can be set up in a considerably short period of time.

7.2 The Place Metaphor

When adopting the place metaphor, preparing a central design studio is much like designing a physical studio. The studio is set up to facilitate and support design activities. A virtual design studio differs from the physical design studio in a significant way: the virtual studio can react to the people's use and presence, and it changes and responds automatically; a physical studio is passive and it reacts only when people physically stimulate it - for example, by moving furniture. Using the place metaphor, it is possible to design and develop tools which refer to a physical space, but without limiting them to activities that emulate the physical world. For example, to move from one area to another in a virtual environment we can "teleport," that is, recall the area where we want to go by a command (e.g. "teleport office") which will transfer us there. It would be unlikely, in a physical building, to be able to "jump" from one section to another without passing through contiguous rooms.

There are several approaches to developing VDSs based on the place metaphor. Computer games were possibly the first collaborative virtual places, and Smith (1998) indicates in "Habitat", developed by Lucas Film Games, the first recognisable networked virtual world.

We distinguish two major kinds of place metaphors, although this distinction is not always clearly definable: virtual realities and virtual worlds. The first kind, virtual realities, can be described as those environments where the simulation of a physical place has priority, and the sense of place needs to be recreated to simulate a physical set of sensations - mostly visual and tactile[4]. Typically, users are invited to design their own house and interact socially with other users by means of communication tools and community activities. Usually, these worlds are graphics

---

[4] See also (Rheingold 1991).

based – like, for example, Colony City, ActiveWorlds, and CAVE, described further. The representation of the environment is fundamental for the development of the community. This approach may sometimes require special equipment to fully experience the virtual space – like in the case of CAVE. Immersive graphical virtual realities use interfaces and references similar to an architectural walkthrough.

The second kind, virtual worlds, are those environments which create a *sense of place* for users to go and collaborate. Here, participants have a personal space, sharing tools and information, as part of the meta-designed environment. Their workstations are integrated in the environment. Multimedia documents can be easily shared among the participants.

These two approaches provide a similar approach to creating a VDS environment, although the mode of interaction is different. They do not exhaust all the possibilities of creating a sense of place, neither do they represent the whole range of metaphors that can be used in computer based systems. However, they give a good general description of some environments that can be used to build a VDS.

7.2.2 Virtual Realities

Although a graphical representation of the studio is not strictly necessary for its use, some environments depend on a 3D model for navigation purposes. Virtual Realities simulate physical places in order to create a sense of being in a place. Graphics become important in these environments and a good connection is required to fully participate. Virtual realities often require special equipment to be viewed, although some low-end technologies are being used to simulate physical-like activities.

Colony City

Colony City is an example of low-end virtual reality easily accessible using an Internet connection and a Web browser. In Fig. 7.18 and 7.19, we can observe two views of the virtual environment 3D model. Navigation in this environment is achieved by pointing the mouse left, right, and onward. Some objects in the environment are active, that is can be "clicked", and they provide more information, or lead to other areas of the environment.

One of the advantages of 3D representations is the ease of orientation and navigation. The interface to the virtual reality allows a direct representation of a space. This space has architectural details and simulates a physical environment. In Fig. 7.18 and 7.19, for example, it is clear that the observer is standing on the floor and what is represented is what stands in front of her. She does not need to "imagine" the space, as happens in non-graphical virtual realities.

The point of view can be changed in order to have a bird's eye view, or a plan. Activities in the virtual reality can then be achieved by using the represented objects, when active, and the interface, designed on purpose for that specific view.

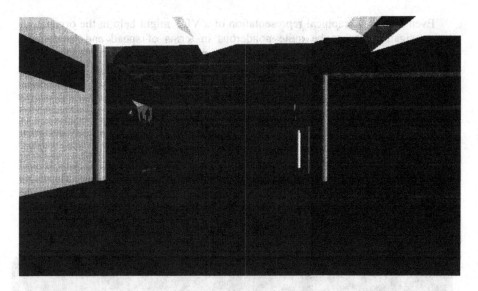

Fig. 7.18 *The inside of a building in Colony City.*

Fig. 7.19 *An external view of an area in Colony City.*

In Fig. 7.20, the 3D representation of the virtual world, in this case the "sci-fi community", occupies most of the interface. The bottom part of the window contains information about users connected to that part of the world, and the chat window, visible only to other users in the same area. On the top and right hand side are tools for navigation, messaging, and further information. These can be reorganised for various parts of the virtual reality.

Even though a graphical representation of a VDS might help in the orientation and navigation, it can be quite ponderous in terms of speed and bandwidth. Graphical items, such as the ones above, are not suitable for low speed network access: they become difficult to walk through, as they regenerate in real time according to the user's moves. In particular, Colony City is an environment developed for social reasons, and it relies on very rich graphics to give a real life-like feeling to its users.

Colony City, as other graphics-based virtual realities, is only partially designed by users. They have the freedom to choose where to live, that is selecting a place for their home, the kind of house they own (paid with a special form of credit), and they can visit public areas to participate in common activities. Generally, these virtual realities do not have specific tools that can be used in a VDS environment, but they might become relevant as they provide interesting configurations where a designed space is also represented, and it can be experienced and modified.

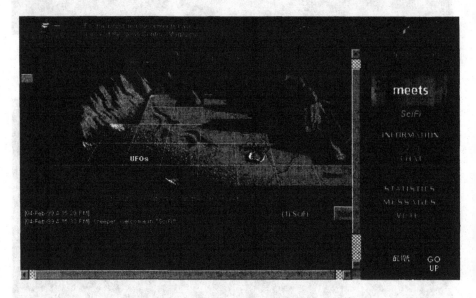

Fig. 7.20 *The Colony City interface.*

ActiveWorlds

Another graphics-based virtual reality, which combines tools for communication and collaboration, is the group of scenarios based on the ActiveWorlds interface. ActiveWorlds[5] provides an Internet based browser that allows users to navigate through the built environments of various virtual places. Accessed either as a visitor, or as a registered citizen, ActiveWorlds invites everyone to contribute to its construction by adding new buildings, special features – for example, teleporting tools – and objects. It is then possible to change the shape, colour, texture, location

---

[5] http://www.activeworlds.com.

and dimension of a specific object by using a building interface. New areas, which can be compared to new cities, can be defined by users, and then inhabited by whoever chooses to do so.

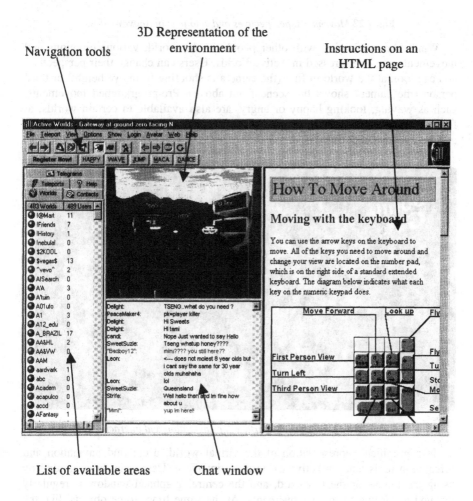

3D Representation of the environment

Navigation tools

Instructions on an HTML page

List of available areas   Chat window

Fig. 7.21 *ActiveWorlds' interface.*

Fig. 7.21 shows a snapshot of the ActiveWorlds' browser interface. A user opens the interface on his desktop, and from there s/he connects to the central server of ActiveWorlds. On the left hand side of the browser, a list of possible worlds is shown. The column next to it indicates how many users are currently visiting that particular world. To visit a world, it is sufficient to double click on the desired location, and the software will move the user automatically. Other utilities which facilitate a presence in the world and interaction with others figure on the same interface.

Fig. 7.22 *Movements, perspectives and emotions in ActiveWorlds.*

While communicating with other people in the world, various emotions and movements can be expressed in ActiveWorlds. Users can change their perspective, and can look at the world in first (the camera is shooting from eye height) or third person (the camera shows the scene from above). Pre-programmed movements, such as waving, looking happy or angry, are also available to certain worlds, as Fig. 7.22 shows. To activate them, it is sufficient to click on the desired emotion, and the avatar will perform it.

Fig. 7.23 *The graphical interface for navigation and interaction.*

In a graphical representation of the virtual world, users find navigation and orientation tools, and an active exploratory interface. Users can move around by using the mouse or the keyboard, and the central graphical window is regularly updated according to these movements. At the same time, some objects, like the "South Gate" illustrated in Fig. 7.23, perform specific actions. In this case, the "South Gate" portal will move the user to another area of the same world. In the graphical interface other users are also visible, and instructive signs can be placed as reminders.

Replicas of real places can be designed in ActiveWorlds. For example, in Fig. 7.24, a characteristic part of Australia has been inserted as a background for the world named after the country.

As new objects are added to the environment, they become immediately available to all users. Thus, for example, placing a sign with a warning in a public square is an immediate way of reaching whoever visits that place. In addition, special pop up windows can be displayed to users when needed.

Fig. 7.24 *The world "Australia" in ActiveWorlds.*

Environments like ActiveWorlds can be used in a VDS to collaboratively work on a design, which is immediately represented and available to all users. They also represent a centralised way of running the studio, since all the needed tools for the design and its refinement can be contained in the interface.

Summarising, environments like ActiveWorlds can:

- Provide a place for multiple users;
- Incorporate all necessary tools to implement a design, such as:
  - building;
  - modifying;
  - viewing;
- Allow the creation of new areas, in order to create a complexity similar to a physical environment;
- Allow the integration of various protocols under the same interface allow the integration of various protocols under the same interface;
  - Web pages;
  - Email;
  - chat;
  - 3D graphic representation;
- Distribute access to various places making them;
  - public;
  - private;
  - restricted/public;
- Represent both real places and meta-designed ones, allowing a direct control of the developing design.

Smith (1998) presents a case of ActiveWorlds used to develop a Collaborative Virtual Design Studio (CVDS). In this case, designers are called to design two kinds of environments: *virtual real places* - models of real places, translated into computer generated graphical representations, and *real virtual places* - models unrelated to any real (physical) location. Comments on the produced designs are collected during and after the design sessions in order to provide feedback to the designers. Smith's approach to constructing a designed virtual place falls in the category of virtual realities used to design a place, which is then criticised and modified collaboratively.

The CAVE Environment

The CAVE (Cave Automated Virtual Environment) is a full scale immersive virtual reality environment. The CAVE allows a person to view a 3D model in full scale, experiencing the actual size and visualising the model from the inside. Such environments can be used to experience the model and/or to create or edit a model. The idea of full scale modelling, and ultimately collaboration within full scale models, has only recently become technically feasible. Full scale modelling is still very expensive and is limited to a few sites that can provide the facilities. Here we talk about the capabilities of full scale modelling and their potential as a VDS environment.

The CAVE is originally designed for the virtual reality simulation of a 3D model, however, the CAVE also offers the option of connecting various CAVEs to a network. This allows multiple users to inhabit a simulated virtual world generated by several CAVE environments, enhancing its ability to be a VDS environment.

The CAVE is situated in a square room - 10ft each side - built with screens, with dedicated hardware and software applications. Stereo images are rear projected, and users, wearing stereo glasses, are able to inhabit the 3D fully immersive virtual environment. The screens are distributed on three walls, and a head-mounted projector shows images on the floor. Users wear stereo shutter glasses and navigate throughout the environment using a wand (literally a 3D mouse with buttons). Audio devices complete the sensory experience. The CAVE environment is a sophisticated and expensive one, and should not be considered as accessible and easy to program as other virtual realities seen in the previous sections. Fig. 7.25 shows a rendered image of a built CAVE environment.

Fig. 7.26 shows a schematic illustration of the components of a CAVE environment. The central cube, missing one side, is where users stand. Devices are connected to a central computer which does the real-time rendering and provides the images projected on the screens. Projection equipment and screens present the 3D model at a scale such that the person is fully immersed.

Specific projects related to design evaluation and collaboration are currently being implemented with CAVE systems. For example the Caterpillar Inc. Distributed Virtual Reality (DVR) Project aims "to establish an interactive, real-time ATM network connection between two Virtual Reality Visualisation Systems across the North Atlantic and to evaluate the capabilities, practicality, performance and cost of Distributed Virtual Reality Technology for performing collaborative product or process design review on industrial show case applications".[6]

---

[6] http://www.ncsa.uiuc.edu/VEG/DVR.

Fig. 7.25 *The CAVE environment[7].*

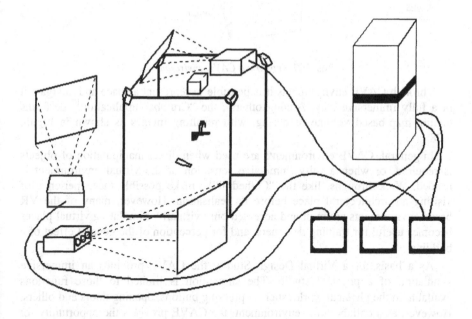

Fig. 7.26 *Diagram of the CAVE.*

Collaborative CAVE environments can be created by connecting several CAVEs through a network. A collaborative CAVE environment is organised as in Fig. 7.27. Each environment is connected to the "central CAVE," through a

---

[7] Fig. 7.25 and 7.26 © Copyright National Center for Supercomputing Applications, University of Illinois at Urbana Champaign, 1998.

specific entry port (in the figure, the port is generically indicated with "####"). All the CAVEs in the network must share the same network address and port.[8]

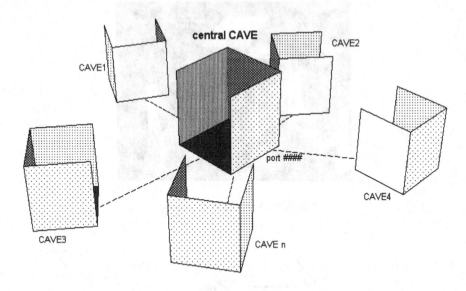

Fig. 7.27 *Networked CAVE environments.*

Through CAVE environments it is possible to represent a space and navigate it in a fully immersive way. Among others[9], the "Crumbs" application[10] performs texture map-based volume rendering, with resulting images as shown in Figure 7.28.

In general, CAVE environments are used when direct manipulation of objects is required, or when a fully immersive sensation of the virtual environment is needed. Walk-throughs, like the "Cathedral"[11], make possible the experience of visiting an architectural place before its realisation. However, many of the VR based environments are built and accessed only virtually. Simulating virtual places becomes useful for training designers, and for perception of the general effect of a building.

As a basis for a Virtual Design Studio, the CAVE provides an immersive simulation of a physical studio. The simulation is limited to those functions available in the physical world, such as pressing buttons, opening doors and others. However, as a collaborative environment, the CAVE provides the opportunity for the studio participants to collaboratively take part in a simulation of the design model. This difference between this and desktop collaborative virtual realities is

---

[8] For further specifications on the CAVE networking facility see
http://www.evl.uic.edu/pape/CAVE/prog/CAVEGuide.html#programming.networking.
[9] http://www.ncsa.uiuc.edu/VR/cavernus.
[10] http://www.ncsa.uiuc.edu/VR/cavernus/CRUMBS/Crumbs.html.
[11] http://www.ncsa.uiuc.edu/VR/cavernus/CATHEDRAL/Cathedral.html.

the immersion in a full scale model rather than viewing the 3D model on a computer screen with a keyboard.

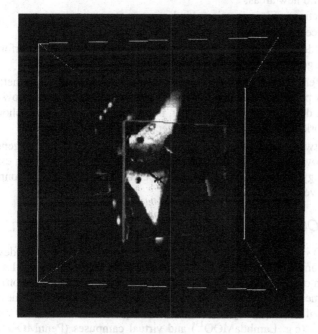

Fig. 7.28 *A rendering obtained with the "Crumbs" application[12].*

7.2.3 Virtual Worlds

Virtual worlds are complex environments, designed to support other activities, beyond building, navigating, and communicating. Although the difference is subtle and subjective, we claim that the main difference between virtual worlds and virtual realities is the content focus. Virtual worlds focus on multipurpose activities, virtual realities focus on rendering and simulation.

Collaborating is one of the key issues in developing multi-purpose virtual worlds. Education, training, and learning tasks are also a priority in these environments. For these reasons, we believe that multi-purpose virtual worlds are better suited for building VDSs than immersive graphical virtual realities.

In a VDS built as a virtual world, users can perform the following, non exclusive, activities:

- Communicate both synchronously and asynchronously, this includes having meetings, with or without videoconferencing facilities, giving lectures, and similar communicative tasks;
- Obtain a record of past conversations and activities;

---

[12] Image courtesy and © Copyright of CAVERNUS, NCSA, 1998, at - http://www.ncsa.uiuc.edu/VR/cavernus.

- Navigate;
- Brainstorm;
- Build new areas;
- Exchange files of various kinds;
- Access information from the Web.

This list does not exhaust all the possible activities that can be performed, but it represents a good start for implementing a VDS.

The preferred medium for the access to these worlds is the Internet: the whole spectrum of protocols contained in the TCP/IP suite can be used. Low bandwidth connections do not disadvantage a user, although the central server should be on a faster network, in order to keep the connection speed reasonably fast.

The software used to create a multi-purpose virtual place is generally very flexible, allowing a variety of functionalities. However, often a more expert use of the technology involved is required, compared to "ready made" environments, such as TeamWave.

StudioMOO

StudioMOO is an example of a multi-purpose virtual world that we developed for our educational virtual design studio. StudioMOO is based on the LambdaMOO software, an object-oriented MUD (Multi User Dungeon or Dimension). This class of environments started as role playing games, and soon it became one of the preferred software packages for the development of virtual worlds. Virtual communities (e.g. LambdaMOO[13]) and virtual campuses (PennMOO[14], Diversity University[15]) have been implemented starting from the basic LambdaMOO software.

StudioMOO is an object-oriented environment that gives participants the impression and the functionality of being in a room, much like a physical studio. The metaphor of the physical studio is very strong, allowing participants to anticipate the use of the various objects in the studio. StudioMOO is both text-based for those that do not have access to a high speed broad band connection to the Internet.

The Web integrated interface of StudioMOO is shown in Fig. 7.29. More accurately, Studio MOO has a Web aware interface, that is continuously updated. The Web interface includes images, text, and 3D models in VRML, that represent the contents of the virtual world. The contents of the virtual world are stored as objects in the database. The contents of the world change through interaction with the world. The Web part of the studio, written in HTML, is automatically generated by the underlying software that supports the central studio, and it is updated each time a change occurs.

The Web interface is integrated with the text interface. The Web portion is on the top of the screen and the text interface is on the bottom of the screen. The Web

---

[13] lambda.moo.mud.org:8888.

[14] http://www.english.upenn.edu/PennMOO/.

[15] http://moo.du.org:8000.

interface includes a series of icons on the left hand side that change the view of the right hand side, or provide access to other applications linked to the studio. Links in the Web view of the virtual world present more information about an object, or lead to other areas of the virtual world. Background and colours can be customised for each room.

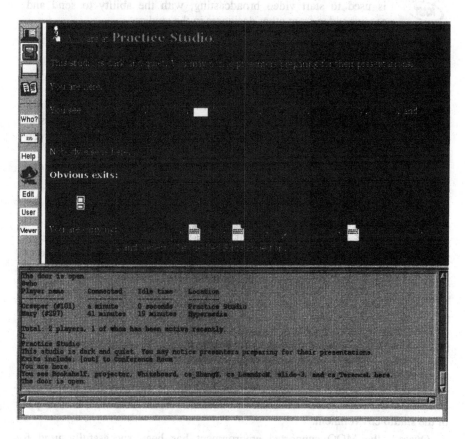

Fig. 7.29 *The StudioMOO interface.*

From StudioMOO, we have developed the Central Design Studio interface, which presents all the activities useful for a VDS concentrated in a single frame. This Central Studio Interface is illustrated in Fig 7.30. Users can access tools by selecting them on the screen. Output is displayed in windows that come up accordingly. Whenever possible, application outputs are integrated in the studio interface (as in the case of a video conference).

StudioMOO is based on the idea of users joining a common environment, and being able to share not only the environment tools, but also documents, files, slides, and information in all the forms allowed by the TCP/IP set of protocols. Equally important, each person that enters the VDS can see who else is there, much like a physical studio.

The various tools in the studio are available as icons. These icons can be defined when the studio environment is designed. Custom tools can also be added by each user, in order to adapt the environment to their needs. The function of the icons shown in Fig. 7.30 are given below:

 is used to start video broadcasting, with the ability to send and receive video from other designers in the studio;

 a telephone-like tool, which allows a user to talk privately with a person in his office;

 gives the view of the room that the user is visiting;

 gives a view of the slide projector, which can be used to show slides based on the HTTP protocol (for example, HTML pages, images in various formats, or text) to everyone else looking at the same "screen projector";

 gives a view of a whiteboard-like tool, used to write text, which can be seen by everyone in the same room;

 this tool gives access to a Web site of information related to the studio;

 gives a view of a VRML representation and allows navigation through the space, and it also gives the ability to select active objects in the environment.

 gives access to an email system.

Each user is defined as an object, as are all things in the environment. A user can customise his object definition to create an identity. The user's identity can be seen by others through an icon or picture, a selection of gender, a description, and the specification of messages as the user moves around the virtual world. The creation of identity and place is one of the strengths of this approach to the VDS. In StudioMOO each person has his own office as well as access to the other parts of the studio environment.

Overall, the MOO supported environment has been successfully used for educational and training purposes, after its origin as a game playing environment. Its use as a professional design environment is not yet tested. The strength of this environment lies in:

- Flexibility in the construction of the interface;
- Relative ease in adding new tools;
- Facilitated access and navigation, using the Web interface;
- Stability of the environment;
- User-friendly look of the environment;
- Extensibility of the studio tools to the whole TCP/IP protocol suite;
- Good performance in a low bandwidth network, using the text-based environment.

On the top side of this window, a representation of the room, which includes text, icons, and graphics, is used to interact with the environment, entities, and other users.

On the bottom of the screen, a text-based interface allows participants to talk to each other, and directly issue commands to navigate, interact with entities, or launch special applications.

These icons indicate specific functions for the current tool.

In the middle of the interface, a user can see others who are currently in the same room. It is possible to exclude participants, or to resize the video windows.

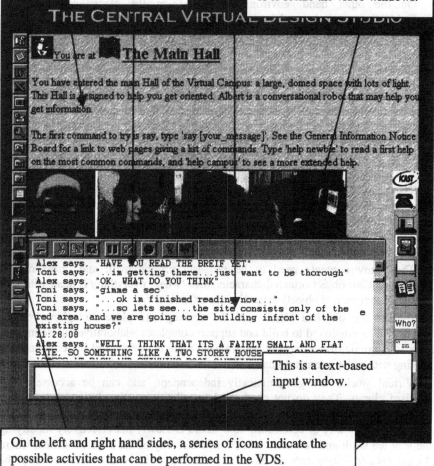

THE CENTRAL VIRTUAL DESIGN STUDIO

You are at The Main Hall

You have entered the main Hall of the Virtual Campus: a large, domed space with lots of light. This Hall is designed to help you get oriented. Albert is a conversational robot that may help you get information.

The first command to try is say, type 'say [your_message]'. See the General Information Notice Board for a link to web pages giving a list of commands. Type 'help newbie' to read a first help on the most common commands, and 'help campus' to see a more extended help.

```
Alex says, "HAVE YOU READ THE BREIF YET"
Toni says, "..im getting there...just want to be thorough"
Alex says, "OK, WHAT DO YOU THINK"
Toni says, "gimme a sec"
Toni says, "...ok im finished reading now..."
Toni says, "...so lets see...the site consists only of the
red area, and we are going to be building infront of the
existing house?"
11:28:08
Alex says, "WELL I THINK THAT ITS A FAIRLY SMALL AND FLAT
SITE, SO SOMETHING LIKE A TWO STOREY HOUSE
```

Who?

This is a text-based input window.

On the left and right hand sides, a series of icons indicate the possible activities that can be performed in the VDS.

Fig. 7.30 *The central design studio interface.*

The main problem of such an environment remains their relative scarce knowledge and diffusion, compared to the large proprietary software packages seen previously. The continuing development of this approach in universities and research organisations will determine whether their use in a professional setting is appropriate and brings advantages that the other environments don't have.

7.3 Beyond Metaphors

The desktop metaphor and the place metaphor present themselves under a number of variations. Environments which reflect the desktop metaphor are suitable for creating a workplace on the user's machine, which can be customised locally. However, users still feel that they are working in a separate, individual environment.

On the other hand, environments based on the place metaphor, like StudioMOO, are mostly used for interactions among users whose presence can be felt in the same environment. These provide a central location for all those who need to access the studio facilities. Other environments based on high-end virtual reality applications rely instead on the quality of the designed space, and its visualisation. This kind of world uses tools to construct and refine designed objects - often representing buildings and physical entities. The design of the world, more than the interactions with it, assumes priority. Features to facilitate building new objects are provided to the users. For example, a library of pre-built objects that can be directly placed to construct a house: walls, windows, roofs, and similar. Users can also choose their "avatar", the way they appear in the virtual reality, and have basic movements associated with their character.

The possibilities offered by environments based on the place metaphor are enormous. They mostly depend on the Internet protocols, capable of producing complex multimedia environments. Specific methodologies for planning virtual worlds and design interfaces have been researched in recent times [(Cicognani 1998a); (Cicognani 1998b); (Bruckman and Resnick 1995)].

These environments need to be properly programmed, and, most of all, planned, as their object-oriented characteristics (where everything is dealt with as a separate programmed object) determine their flexibility.

Beyond the physical office, and the desktop and place metaphors, virtual worlds can be employed to build and support complex collaborative environments, such as a mobile office network, where each node is never fixed but continuously moving within the Internet domain.

Virtual worlds are geographically independent, and can be accessed with standard clients. They do not need local installation on the designer's machine. They can be used from more casual places, for example Internet cafés, or mobile computers. This way of connecting to a studio is slowly but effectively modifying the way we work and communicate. From the reality of the physical office, where documents and instruments are physically stored and can be only accessed from the same geographical location, we are moving toward mobile and flexible access to a central node, repository of all the information and tools needed in a working environment.

As the networking technology becomes more and more stable, and the protocols mature into more coherent standards, the metaphor of the physical office is translated into developing multi-purpose virtual environments, which are platform and bandwidth independent. It is also important that metaphors referring to physical objects and places are used appropriately, in order to maintain coherence within the virtual environment and, ultimately, to facilitate use and access.

Working and collaborating in virtual environments are slowly moving away from the simulation of activities in the physical world. Participants are finding their own way of relating to the environment, and both developers and users are aware of the workplace changes when computer based systems are involved. Moving beyond metaphors is a natural process that involves finding a balance between technology and use, and virtual design studios can become an optimal ground for developing new technology-based strategies for work and collaboration.

References

Bruckman, A. and Resnick, M. (1995) The medioMOO project: Constructionism and professional community, *Convergence* **1**(1): 94-109.

Cicognani, A. (1998a) A linguistic characterisation of design in text-based virtual worlds, *Architecture and Design Science*, Sydney, University of Sydney.

Cicognani, A. (1998b) On the linguistic nature of cyberspace and virtual communities, *Virtual Reality: Research, Development and Application* **3**(1): 25-33.

Rheingold, H. (1991) *Virtual Reality*, New York, Simon & Schuster.

Smith, A. (1998) Metaworlds and virtual space: Towards the collaborative virtual design studio, *Conference Proceedings Online Conference: International Journal of Design Computing, DCNet 98.*
http://www.arch.usyd.edu.au/journal/vol1/dcnet/stream1/paper4

Epilogue

The virtual design studio can be understood in many ways. As a way of designing collaboratively, the virtual design studio releases some restrictions on the location of the collaborators. As a set of tools and techniques, the virtual design studio can be one of many alternative collections, each with some advantages and disadvantages. As a way of sharing documents, the virtual design studio provides a new way of thinking about shared representation and design documentation as 3D models, objects, etc.

This book starts with a concept and ends with a vision of possibilities. The concept of a virtual design studio will eventually be merged with the physical design studio and we will rarely see a design project that does not have aspects of the VDS described in this book. We have laid out the progression of understanding a VDS from the technology and tools view, to ways of putting different technologies together to provide different virtual working environments. As illustrated in Fig. E.1, there are many directions to consider when implementing a virtual design studio.

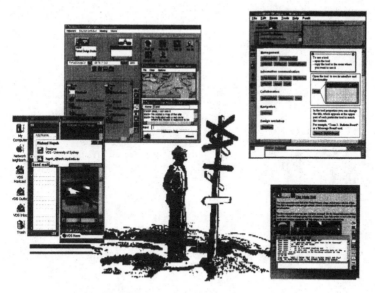

Fig. E.1 *Directions and choices.*

The tradeoffs among the alternatives are enormous and there is no clear solution for all aspects of the virtual design studio.

The use of the desktop metaphor, prevalent in individual computer workplaces, is the most common approach to setting up a groupware environment. This approach is very powerful in managing people and documents. This approach is weak in creating a community of collaborators as each member of the project interacts with a desktop instead of each other. The use of the place metaphor brings visions of games and simulation. Although not as common in the professional environment, it is extremely popular in social environments and more recently in academic research. This approach creates a sense of place and community as strong as the physical studio. The weakness of this approach is a lack of consistent and comprehensive treatment of document management.

So, it seems that the strengths and weaknesses of the various approaches complement each other. The selection of the technology for a VDS depends largely on the individuals involved and the computing environment available. Eventually, we will not be able to remember when collaboration was not a network technology issue.

Appendix: Web Resources

A.1 General Information for Virtual Design Studios

ADOBE SYSTEMS INCORPORATED

http://www.adobe.com/

This is the home page of Adobe. It includes tips and product information as well as support databases and user forums.

ARNONA INTERNET SOFTWARE INC

http://www.cadviewer.com/

This is the home page of ViewCad. They offer a free Cad sharing web account as well as product information and a free copy of CadViewer light. ArNoNa CADViewer Light is the only Java DWF viewer recommended by Autodesk.

COSMO SOFTWARE INC

http://cosmosoftware.com/

This is the home page of Cosmo Software. They offer a free download of Cosmo Player/2.1 as well as try and buy downloads of Page FX 10, Worlds 20 and Code 25. It also provides explanations in design technique and tips. There are also links to download libraries of objects, models and textures.

INSTINCTIVE TECHNOLOGY

http://www.instinctive.com/

This is the home page of Instinctive Technology, Inc. founded in 1996 to develop and market innovative Web applications for managing projects that span organisations. The company is based in Cambridge, Massachusetts. The integration of their Web collaborative product eRoom with leading office suites creates a shared project environment on the Web where invited team members can create or access Windows-based files, then review, discuss and make critical project-related decisions regarding content, tasks and objectives.

MULTIWEB VIEWER

http://www.multisource.com/indexmultiweb.htm

Multiweb viewer organises related and often used Web sites into groups, which are then retrieved automatically. The client can be preset to view the sites in a virtual design studio from any computer in the studio.

NCSA, HABANERO

http://www.ncsa.uiuc.edu/

National Center for Supercomputing Applications at the University of Illinois at Urbana-Champaign gave to the Web community the first graphical browser. Habanero is another cross-platform technology for supporting collaborative work, developed in the Center. This technology (the software environment and comprehensive documentation of how to utilise its power) is available for free at this site.

PROXICOM

http://www.proxicom.com/

The Proxicom Community Suite is one of the technologies that can be used in heterogeneous virtual design studios. It includes Java-based, threaded discussion group software, an HTML-based client interface for real-time conversation within an online community, and a content authoring and administrative tool that allows members of virtual communities to publish and maintain their own Web pages within the over-arching control of the community organiser.

SCREENPORCH

http://www.screenporch.com/

Screen Porch offers a Web-based groupware, Caucus, for teamwork, group-learning, and community activity. Caucus creates online workspaces called conferences (they follow the model of a bulletin board) which offer rich contexts for information sharing. The system uses its own server for handling such workspaces, which can be used in relatively homogeneous virtual design studios.

SOFTARC, FIRSTCLASS

http://www.softarc.com/

This is the home page of SoftArc - developer of FirstClass and other collaboration products that can be applied in a virtual design studio. FirstClass is a package which facilitates the creation of World Wide Web-based educational environments by non-technical users.

TEAMWAVE

http://www.teamwave.com/

TeamWave Workplace supports collaborative work of small groups. When deciding which way to go during the set-up of a virtual design studio, TeamWave is one of the candidates to be used. TeamWave Software has its roots in the Grouplab project at the University of Calgary. The company TeamWave Software Ltd. was founded in 1996. The company is run under the direction of Mark Roseman, the company founder and chief technical architect, and Fred Yee, the company president.

TRACKER PRO

http://www.enfish.com/products/product.html

A next generation information tracker for desktop virtual design studios. The Enfish® Tracker Pro analyses the files in the workspace, cross-references and annotates them. A large variety of file formats are supported.

WEBCT

http://www.webct.com/webct/

WebCT is a tool that facilitates the creation of World Wide Web-based educational environments by non-technical users. In virtual design studios, WebCT can be used to create effective asynchronous collaborative environments. Developed initially at the University of British Columbia, Canada, WebCT is now a new company - WebCT Educational Technologies.

XANADU

http://www.aus.xanadu.com/

This site includes a compiled list of frequently asked questions (FAQ) about project Xanadu. Project Xanadu is the name for Ted Nelson's hypertext work since 1960. This FAQ is a good starting point to learn more details about this remarkable project. The site includes papers and other documents related to the project.

A.2 Communication Resources

CHAT

http://www.worldvillage.com/wv/chat/html/chat.htm

WorldVillage is designed to support virtual communities. This URL points to the Java-based free chat system.

CU-SEEME

http://www.wpine.com/

CU-SeeMe is one of the original free software packages for video conferences. Originally developed at Cornell University, Cu-SeeMe is now distributed by White Pine. This is the latest version of White Pine CU-SeeMe video conferencing software.

EUDORA

http://www.eudora.com/
This is the site of the Eudora family of communication products by QUALCOMM Incorporated. The family includes popular email clients, scheduling and resource organisers, and other digital communication technologies.

HOTMAIL

http://www.hotmail.com/
Hotmail is a Web-based free email service with rich management, personalisation means and nice interface design.

LISTSERVE

http://www.listserv.net/listserv.stm
The home page of the LISTSERV software. LISTSERV® is a system that allows you to create, manage and control electronic mailing lists in virtual design studios. Since its inception in 1986, LISTSERV® has been continually improved and remains the predominant system in use today. The site provides comprehensive information about this communication tool, including a free lite version.

MAJORDOMO

http://www.greatcircle.com/majordomo/
Majordomo software handles email lists of users. This is a list server application package.

MBONE

http://www.mbone.com/
The site contains comprehensive information about the IP multicast technology and links to archives with the software.

MIRABILIS ICQ

http://www.mirabilis.com/

The site provides comprehensive information about the ICQ communication tools and offers the latest version of Mirabilis ICQ client.

MYMAIL

http://www.mymail.com/

This site offers a permanent "life-time" email address, but it is not free. The account can be set in several modes – Vacation, Filter and Hold modes.

NETMEETING

http://www.microsoft.com/netmeeting/

The homepage of the Microsoft Netmeeting conferencing tool. The site includes resources about Netmeeting, new versions of the software and other assisting tools.

PLACEWARE

http://www.placeware.com/

PlaceWare provides original Web conferencing solutions, which can be used in virtual design studios for Web presentations of completed projects. The site provides access to live Web seminars which demonstrates the use of the system.

WWW BULLETIN BOARD

http://www.worldwidemart.com/scripts/wwwboard.shtml

This is the place to download Matt's WWW Bulletin Board Perl script. Detailed instructions for installation, configuration and usage instructions are provided.

YAHOO

http://mail.yahoo.com/

Yahoo's Web-based free email service is similar in functionality to Hotmail.

YAHOO PAGER

http://pager.yahoo.com/pager/

This is part of the Yahoo site. It shows an example of Web implementation of pager functionality.

A.3 Virtual Worlds

ACTIVEWORLDS

http://www.activeworlds.com/

ActiveWorlds supports visual collaboration from within 3D models. From this site, there can be found links to software download areas, and demo pages of the environment.

CAVE

http://www.evl.uic.edu/pape/CAVE/prog/CAVEGuide.html
CAVE is a Virtual Reality environment for architectural design. The complete user's guide to CAVE (version 2.6) is available here. A quick scan of this document gives an overview of what CAVE is and what the advantages are of using this environment, although very expensive, over lower level virtual reality systems.

DIVERSITY UNIVERSITY

http://moo.du.org:8000
The home page of Diversity University MOO, an educational environment which assists in developing text-based virtual worlds for education.

LAMBDAMOO

lambda.moo.mud.org:8888
The first MOO, running the original MOO server LambdaMOO, developed by Pavel Curtis when still at Xerox PARC. LambdaMOO is mainly a social environment which hosts a considerable quantity of activities. It is still considered one of the best MOOs on the Internet, at least for its long history and evolution.

PENNMOO

http://www.english.upenn.edu/PennMOO/
The MOO of Pennsylvania University English Department. A virtual classroom supports interesting experiments concerning MOO-based educational environments for teaching and learning. A list of resources is also linked from this page. The MOO can be accessed by using telnet moo.sas.upenn.edu:7777.

UNIVERSITY OF SYDNEY VIRTUAL CAMPUS

http://www.arch.usyd.edu.au:7778
The Virtual Campus at the University of Sydney is an online learning environment that supports both real time interaction with others in the campus and access to learning materials. The Virtual Campus is designed to behave in a similar way to a physical campus.

Glossary

Add-in	See *Plug-in*
Anonymous FTP	Virtual design studio servers can run an *anonymous FTP* server, which lets anyone log in to that computer under the username "anonymous" and access only the public resources.
Archive	Computer server, which contains files, intended to be shared within the virtual design studio.
Archive file	A single file that contains a collection of different files and/or directories. Archive files are often used to store and transport collections of files across the Internet, since a large collection of files can be transported in a single archive file. Archives can be easily recognised by the extension. UNIX archives have the extension ".tar" (for Tape Archive) and do not have compression. Extension ".zip" indicates a popular cross-platform compatible compressed type of archive. Suffix ".arj" indicates PC compressed archives, while suffixes ".sit" are related to Macintosh "Stuffit" archives. Extensions ".sea" and ".exe" in archive files indicate self-extracting archives.
ASCII	American Standard Code for Information Interchange. This is the de facto worldwide standard for the digital representation (coding) of numbers, letters, and control codes understood by most computers.
Asynchronous	A term that refers to communication and collaboration over the network where the parties involved are not synchronised during the information exchange, for example, email.
Backup	A redundant copy of digital data made to prevent data loss in the event of hardware or software failure. Backup procedures are part of the management of computer systems in the virtual design studio, especially the studio archive. As a rule a full system backup is performed once a week.
Bandwidth	Data-carrying capacity of a communication channel. In virtual design studios this is used in two ways. When talking about underlying computer networks it denotes a measure of the amount of information that can be transmitted via a given physical transmission line in a period of time. This bandwidth is usually measured in *bits per second*. When talking about synchronous computer-mediated collaboration it denotes the richness of underlying communication channels. This

bandwidth is usually described in terms of the digital media, like text-based communication bandwidth or video conferencing bandwidth.

Bit | Binary DigIT, the smallest unit of digital data, a single digit number in base "2", in other words, either a 1 or a zero.

Bps | Bits-Per-Second, a measurement of how fast digital data is moved from one place to another. A 33.6 modem can move 33,600 bits per second.

Byte | 8 consecutive *bits*.

Browser | A client program (software) that is used to view hypermedia published on the World Wide Web, and other Internet resources. Netscape, Internet Explorer and Lynx are some examples. Browsers are able to understand Internet protocols such as HTTP, FTP, and Gopher, and interpret URLs and markup language(s). They are an integral part of virtual design studio environments.

CGI | Common Gateway Interface, the specification for how a Web server communicates with another piece of software on the same machine, and how the other piece of software (the "CGI program or script") talks to the Web server.

Compressed file | Files can be compressed in order to occupy less disk space and be moved faster.

Client | Any program used to obtain information from a server. For example, all browsers are Web clients.

CRC | Cyclic Redundancy Check, an error-checking technique used in archiving and network transmitting programs.

Database | A structured multi-user collection of information which is organised following a particular model. Databases usually support random access, multiple "views" or levels of abstraction of the underlying data.

Dial-up connection | Link that uses a modem and an ordinary telephone line to connect to a remote computer. Dial-up connections are generally slower than intranet ones.

Digital | "Digital" refers to electronic technology that generates, stores, and processes data in terms of two states: positive (represented by the number 1) and non-positive (represented by the number 0). Thus, data stored or transmitted with digital technology is expressed as a string of 0's and 1's. Prior to digital technology, electronic media was limited to analog technology, which conveys data as electronic signals of varying frequency or amplitude that are added to carrier waves of a given frequency. Broadcast, audio recording and phone transmission has conventionally used analog technology.

Domain name	The unique name that identifies an Internet site. Domain names always have 2 or more parts, separated by dots. The part on the left is the most specific, and the part on the right is the most general. A given machine may have more than one domain name but a given domain name points to only one machine. Domain name is translated by a *nameserver* into an *IP address* (*IP number*).
Download	The transfer of a file from a remote computer to a local machine.
DTD	Document Type Definition - introduced in SGML as a specific description of a markup language. DTD is written as a plain text file, usually with the filename extension *.dtd*. With the introduction of the XML standard it is anticipated that the concept will play a key role in the structuring of Web documents, including Web-based design documents.
Dynamic IP Address	A dynamic IP address is one that is chosen and assigned to a computer by the server that provides Internet access for this computer.
Email	Electronic **Mail** - messages, usually, but not limited to, text, sent from one person to another via a computer network. Email can also be sent automatically to a number of addresses (Mailing List).
File	A collection of data or information stored on a computer system. Each file has a name, which identifies it. There are many different types of files: data files, text files, program files, directory files, and so on. Different types of files have a different structure and format, and store different types of information. For example, program files store programs, whereas text files store text.
File locking	Restricting access to a file to prevent more than one person from making changes to it at the same time.
Filename	The name of a file. Different operating systems impose different restrictions on filenames. Most operating systems, for example, prohibit the use of certain characters in a filename and impose a limit on the length of a filename. In addition, many systems, including DOS and UNIX, allow a filename extension that consists of one or more characters following the proper filename. The filename extension usually indicates what type of file it is. Within a single directory, filenames must be unique. However, two files in different directories may have the same name. Some operating systems, such as MacOS, UNIX and Windows 9x/NT, allow a file to have more than one name, called an alias. (In Unix, aliases are called links or symbolic links, in Windows 9x/NT they are called shortcuts.)

FTP	File Transfer Protocol, an Internet client-server protocol for transferring files between computers.
GIF	Graphics Interchange Format, a format for image compression and storage. Especially suitable for images that contain large areas of the same color. Images stored in GIF format can have no more than 256 different colors. GIF format allows the storage of several images in one file, providing a convenient way to communicate frame-based animations over the Internet.
Gigabyte, (Gb)	1024 Megabytes.
Helper	A program launched by a browser to process files that the browser cannot handle internally. An alternative to the plug-in concept.
Heterogeneous environment	In the context of virtual design studios, this is a collection of different computer platforms, networked together. Heterogeneous environments are common in research centres. They are harder to manage and upgrade.
Homepage	The introductory page for a Web site.
HTML	Hyper Text Markup Language, the markup language used to create hypermedia documents for use on the World Wide Web. HTML files are meant to be viewed using a Web *client*.
HTTP	Hyper Text Transport Protocol is the set of rules for exchanging files (text, images, audio, video, and other multimedia files) on the World Wide Web.
Hyperlink	A connection between two pieces of information. Hyperlinks establish relations between information elements. An information element can be a word or collection of words, an image, a video fragment, a page. Hyperlinking is an essential part in the organisation of electronic design documentation in virtual design studios. Hyperlinks are what distinguishes hypermedia from multimedia and hypertext from conventional text.
Hypermedia	A method of structuring and presenting information in multimedia elements, or nodes, that are connected by hyperlinks. The World Wide Web is a form of distributed hypermedia.
Hypertext	A particular type of hypermedia, where the information includes only text.
IMT	Internet Media Types, see *MIME*
Internet (Lower case "i")	Short for "internetwork". The term is used to denote: - any 2 or more networks connected together, - any network which is using the TCP/IP protocol.
Internet (Upper case i)	Term used to refer to the largest global network of networks and computers, communicating via the *TCP/IP* protocols. Internet is not just a collection of hardware and software, it

gave birth to a "community and culture" that focuses on research and standardisation of the leading-edge communication and network technologies.

Intranet
A private network inside an organisation that uses the same underlying communication technology and software that is used on the public Internet, but that is only for internal use.

IP Address
see *IP Number*.

IP Number
Internet Protocol Number, sometimes called a dotted quad. Every machine that is on the Internet has a unique number consisting of 4 parts separated by dots, e.g. 129.78.66.1.

JPEG
Joint Photographic Experts Group, a format for image compression and storage. Preferred for images that have a variety (millions) of colours, like photos.

Kilobyte (Kb)
$1024(2^{10})$ bytes.

LAN
Local Area Network, a computer network limited to the immediate area, usually the same building or floor of a building.

Linux
Operating system, similar to UNIX, for Macintoshes and PC-compatible computers. Since PC hardware is inexpensive and Linux is essentially free, the combination of the two is a practical way of developing a reliable and inexpensive underlying structure for virtual design studios.

Listserv
The name of a software package, which has become a generic way of indicating an automated electronic *maillist*, managed by a specialised program. Listservs are an alternative to a bulletin board system.

Maillist
Mailing List - An automated email distribution program that allows people to send email to one address, whereupon their message is copied and sent to all of the other subscribers to the maillist.

Megabyte (Mb)
1024 kilobytes.

MIME
Multipurpose Internet Mail Extensions, a protocol for the exchange of multimedia email messages containing various digital media formats (e.g. enhanced character sets, PDF, digital audio and video, images, or texts). Under the new name (Internet Media Types), MIME content-types are used on the World Wide Web to specify the type of data contained in a file or being sent from an HTTP server to a client.

Modem
Modulator/DEModulator is a device that connects computers to the net via a phone line. It converts digital information from a computer to analog signals for the phone line and vice versa.

MOO
MUD Object **O**riented. A particular kind of MUD (see below) based on the LambdaMOO software.

MPEG	Motion Picture Experts Group, a popular compression method (format) used to store digital video data.
MUD	Multi User Dungeon, or Dimension, is a thematically structured text-based virtual world. MUDs existed prior to the World Wide Web, accessible via telnet to a computer that hosted the server. MUDs can be accessed through a Web site and some are perhaps better known as virtual worlds or chat worlds.
Multimedia	A mixture of different digital media – text, images, graphics and drawings, database tables, audio, and video, handled and presented as a whole by a computer.
Nameserver	A computer (and a program on that computer) that translates *domain names* into the proper numeric *IP address* (or vice versa).
ODBC	Open Database Connectivity is a standard protocol for accessing information in SQL database servers. An essential element of the virtual design studio archive for integration of different databases.
Plug-in	A (usually small) program module that adds features to a larger piece of software in which it is "plugged". Common examples are plug-ins for Web browsers and servers, image processing modules, and office suite applications.
Parameter	A variable within a procedure. An object parameter is similar to an attribute, except attributes are usually static pieces of descriptive data, while an object's parameter values are used by a procedure to generate its geometry.
Protocol	In computer networks, a protocol is an agreement for inter-computer communication.
Server	The term can refer to a program or machine: - A program that responds to requests from client programs. Usually the client and the server reside on different networked computers, but in some cases they may run on the same machine. The server and client communicate using a client-server *protocol.* - A computer, which runs a software providing a specific kind of service to client software running on other computers. A single server machine could have several different server software packages running on it, thus providing many different services to clients on the network.
Synchronous	A term that refers to communication over the network when the parties participating in the communication are present at the same time, for example, a video conference. See also *asynchronous.*

TCP/IP	Transmission Control Protocol/Internet Protocol, common name for the suite of basic communication protocols of the Internet. All application protocols, such as HTTP and FTP run on top of TCP/IP.
Telnet	A terminal emulation protocol that allows a terminal connection to other computers on the Internet. It requires a client on connecting machine and a telnet server on the remote computer.
Terabyte	1024 gigabytes.
TIFF	Tagged Image File Format, a file format that can store uncompressed and compressed images. It is supported by the largest number of digital image editing programs on the major platforms and is a good candidate for portable file format for high quality images within a virtual design studio.
Unicode	A 2-byte standard character code for international use. Internationalised HTML uses Unicode as its base character set.
URL	Uniform Resource Locator is the specification defined to allocate resources on the World Wide Web. It includes the protocol, domain name/IP address, port number, path, and resource details needed to access a resource on a particular machine.
Viewer	See *helper*.

Index

3

3D model, 148, 194
3D models, 30, 50
    Rendering, 51
    Virtual worlds, 51
    wireframe, 50

A

Activity/Space ontology, 120, 124
Asynchronous communication, 109

B

Bitmap image, 37, 42
Broadcast, 90
Bulletin board, 143
Bulletin boards, 80

C

CAD, 109, 148, 149
    graphic primitves, 50
    Object-oriented CAD, 54
    Parametric representation, 49
CAD and 3D models, 48
Centralised VDS, 177
Client/server model, 177
Coding scheme, 15
Collaboration, v, vi, vii, 3, 4, 5, 7, 13, 14,
    15, 16, 17, 30, 72, 73, 84, 93, 102, 103,
    104, 117, 133, 134, 137, 138, 140, 145,
    147, 148, 150, 151, 154, 156, 162, 166,
    167, 168, 170, 171, 176, 178, 196, 200,
    209, 212, 214, 216
Collaborative design styles, 16
Communication, 71, 144
Communication tools, 74, 134
    Asynchronous, 74
    Effective use, 100
    Synchronous, 84
Computer mediated communication, 72
Computer-mediated management, 140
Cross-platform integration, 157

D

Database, 142
Design, 105
Design database, 116
Design Log, 145
Design ontology, 118
Design semantics, 16
Design studio,
    Centralised environment, 137
    Desktop metaphor, 137, 178, 208
    Distributed environment. See
    Place metaphor, 137, 193, 208
Design studios, 133
Desktop, 133
    Loosely coupled desktop, 136
    Tightly integrated desktop, 137
Desktop metaphor, 178, 185
Digital design media, 37
Digital image, 37
Domain Name System, 17
Drawers metaphor, 159
DTD, 32
Dynamic document, 104

E

Email, 75
Experimental study, 13

F

FBS ontology, 125
File formats, 138
Filecabinet metaphor, 160
FTP, 22
Full-text search, 115
Function/Behaviour/Structure ontology,
    120, 125

G

Groupware, 164, 177

Author Information

Mary Lou Maher is the Professor of Design Computing in the Faculty of Architecture at the University of Sydney, where she also co-directs the Key Centre of Design Computing and Cognition. She is the editor of the International Journal of Design Computing, a multimedia online journal, and has published books on expert systems, cased-based reasoning in design, and computational models of creative design. Her areas of research include computer-mediated collaborative design, design and virtual architecture, and knowledge-based representation of design and designing.

Simeon J. Simoff is a Research Fellow in the Key Centre of Design Computing and Cognition, at the University of Sydney. He has published numerous papers in journals and books in data analysis and modeling, knowledge-based systems and Internet information systems. His teaching and research applies an interdisciplinary approach to design computing, combining such topics as design, mathematics, and multimedia information systems. His research areas include data mining and analysis for knowledge discovery in digital media representations, information technology, multimedia communication and flexible learning environments.

Anna Cicognani is a Postdoctoral Fellow in the Faculty of Architecture at the University of Sydney, where she received her PhD in Design of Virtual Worlds. She has published on topics such as technology and popular culture in peer journals and popular magazines for about 7 years. Her interests span from fine arts, to linguistics and philosophy, with particular consideration for the effects of technology on mass culture. She now specialises in the design of online environments, for businesses and educational institutions.